VIA FOLIOS 116

Voice of a Virtuosa and Courtesan

Selected Poems of Margherita Costa

Library of Congress Control Number: 2015948534

Printed in the United States.

Published by
BORDIGHERA PRESS
John D. Calandra Italian American Institute
25 W. 43rd Street, 17th Floor
New York, NY 10036

VIA Folios 116
ISBN 978–1–59954–093–1

Voice of a Virtuosa and Courtesan

Selected Poems of

MARGHERITA COSTA

A Bilingual Edition

Edited by

NATALIA COSTA-ZALESSOW

Translated by

JOAN E. BORRELLI

BORDIGHERA PRESS

>   *. . . wicked god,*
> *your shrieking clamor I no longer heed.*
> *Instead, I hand my fate to Time, my guide,*
>   *and Truth, who daughter is to Time, one day*
> *will make my feelings clear, and how I lived.*
>
> . . . .
>
> *Go right ahead, drown out the facts with lies*
> *to darken each bright aspect of my face.*
> *Despite you, Truth will finally succeed*
> *and make known my life's feelings, loves and deeds.*

— from *THE CABINET,* Fifth Drawer: *Beautiful Woman Laments Her Fate*

>   *. . . iniquo nume,*
> *ch'io non più curo del tuo dir le strida,*
> *ma solo al Tempo do mia sorte in guida.*
>   *La Verità, figlia del Tempo, un giorno*
> *farà chiari i miei sensi e i miei costumi.*
>
> . . . .
>
> *Sommergi pur il ver con la bugia,*
> *rendi ogni chiaro del mio volto oscuro,*
> *ch'alfin la Verità fia che ti scopra*
> *di mia vita gli affetti, i sensi e l'opra.*

— da *LO STIPO,* Quinto cassettino: *Bella Donna si duole della Fortuna*

ACKNOWLEDGMENT

My special thanks go to Joan E. Borrelli, my translator and collaborator, for rereading my Introduction and for making many stylistic suggestions. Credit goes to her also for contributing the title of our anthology.

IMAGES

The three portraits of Margherita Costa are reproduced in this book with the permission of the Biblioteca Apostolica Vaticana, all rights reserved. They derive from the copies preserved in the BAV as follows: *La chitarra* (BARB. JJJ. IX. 25), *Lettere amorose* (FERR. III. 154), and *Lo stipo* (BARB. JJJ. VIII. 47).

CONTENTS

POEMS by MARGHERITA COSTA
Selected from Seven of Her Books

INDICE GENERALE

Delle

POESIE di MARGHERITA COSTA
Scelte da sette dei suoi libri

Portrait **A** of Margherita Costa
by Stefano della Bella
with inscriptions by Alfonso de Oviedo Spinosa
From: *La chitarra* (BARB. JJJ. IX. 25) ©2015 Biblioteca Apostolica Vaticana

Portrait **B** of Margherita Costa
from Stefano della Bella's engraving, but with all inscriptions removed
From: *Lettere amorose* (FERR. III. 154) ©2015 Biblioteca Apostolica Vaticana

Portrait **C** of Margherita Costa
by an unidentified artist
From: *Lo stipo* (BARB. JJJ. VIII. 47) ©2015 Biblioteca Apostolica Vaticana

INTRODUCTION

The poet, singer, playwright, feminist, and courtesan, Margherita Costa, is the most Baroque of the seventeenth-century Italian women writers. She stands out for attempting to be original in a period when the aim of poets was to have the reader marvel at their metaphors, antitheses, hyperboles, oxymora, or complex style. She even wrote an erotic poem, "The Rape of Lilla,"[1] in competition with Giambattista Marino and dared to venture into the world of double meanings, bordering on indecency, with her comedy *Li buffoni* [The Buffoons]. As a feminist, Margherita stressed the obstacles she faced as a woman and the difficult life of women in general. She criticized men for their infidelity, and urged women to repay in kind. Some of her poems begin as lamentations, but come to humorous conclusions, thus making her one of the first Italian women poets to use humor in published works. Other poems are partially autobiographical, for they include allusions to events in Margherita's life as well as complaints about her ill fortune and lack of literary recognition — a recognition she hoped to obtain but never achieved. In her compositions, Margherita frequently remarks upon life's instability, its ups and downs, and upon people's duplicity in glorifying the powerful with the hope of gaining advantage, only to criticize in turn when the powerful fall. A great part of her work comprises encomiastic poems into which she often inserts references to herself. She was a prolific writer. She published two books of prose, six volumes of poetry, three plays, two narrative poems, and an allegorical pageantry, in verse, for knights on horseback.

Despite Margherita Costa's extensive oeuvre, the concrete facts of her personal life remain skeletal in outline. Born in Rome in the early seventeenth century into a poor family, she never mentioned the date of her birth (variously given as from 1600 to 1610), but she always stressed the fact that she was Roman and accompanied her name with the word *Romana* in all her publications, with the exception of the very last. Her father and her only brother, Paolo, were of ill repute. From letters, we find that she had several sisters. Trained as a singer, Margherita was sought after by Roman musical circles for her talent, which brought her fame but also involved her in a scandal related to the opera, *La catena d'Adone* [The Chain of Adonis], that was to be performed in Rome. (This five-act opera is considered important by musicologists for its innovative use of more arias, longer parts for the choir, ballet sections performed to singing, and a complex setting of enchanted gardens with mysterious grottoes and voices of Echo that answer to the lover's lamentation.) The work was written specifically for Costa by the composer

---

[1]See p. 99 of our anthology; henceforth only the page number will be given when referencing the text of the anthologized selections of our book.

Domenico Mazzocchi[2] (1592–1665) on Ottavio Tronsarelli's[3] libretto based on Cantos XII and XIII of Giambattista Marino's mythological poem *Adone* [Adonis]. It was originally intended as a singing competition between Margherita and her rival, Cecca (Francesca) del Padule, or, according to others, her younger sister, Anna Francesca, known as Checca. (Anna would go on to enjoy a notable operatic career, mainly from 1640 to 1654. She even staged an opera in Bologna, in winter 1652–53.[4]) At the time of the intended competition, however, Anna Francesca seems to have been too young to qualify.[5] The Roman enthusiasts had split into two groups, one favoring Margherita, who was protected by Prince Giovanni Giorgio Aldobrandini,[6] the other favoring Cecca, protected by Giandomenico Lupi. The singing contest between the two women, in the end, never took place, due to the intervention of Princess Olimpia Aldobrandini, who did not want the family name associated with a competition between two women considered immoral.[7] Mazzocchi's opera was subsequently performed seven times by castrated male singers during the carnival of 1626, in the palace of Evandro Conti, marquis of Gorga and later duke of Poli,[8] and was published that same year.[9] Although Margherita was much talked about, accused of immoral behavior, branded a courtesan[10] and even a prostitute, as a *virtuosa*, or singer, she was invited to perform for ladies of the high nobility. She was even invited to the Polish court by the future king of Poland,[11] when he visited Rome — an offer she did not accept, despite the fact that she felt mistreated in Rome. She eventually left Rome to seek a new life in Florence

---

[2]Mazzocchi was in the service of Cardinal Ippolito Aldobrandini. *La Catena d'Adone* was commissioned by the latter's brother, Giovanni Giorgio Aldobrandini. See *NGDMM* 16: 194–95.

[3]Tronsarelli's libretto, *La catena d'Adone*, described as a *Favola boschereccia* [a pastoral fable], was printed in Rome, in 1626, by four different publishers: Mascardi, Corbelli, Discepolo and Grignani. It was dedicated to Giovanni Giorgio Aldobrandini.

[4]See Megale 1992.

[5]From a letter concerning Checca, dated Dec. 28, 1652, that her sister Giovanna Vittoria Costa wrote and signed "con signora madre e sorella Vittoria Maria" (Mamone #971) ["with her mother and sister Vittoria Maria"], we learn only the names of these two other sisters of Margherita.

[6]Giovanni Giorgio Aldobrandini (1591–1637) was the son of Gian Francesco Aldobrandini and Olimpia Aldobrandini (d. in 1637) who was her husband's niece as well as that of his brother, the future Clement VIII, pope from 1592–1605. Margherita Costa, most likely, was Giovanni Giorgio's mistress for a while.

[7]A singer or instrumentalist, especially if very able, was called *virtuoso/virtuosa*, but just as actors and actresses, the performing *virtuosi* were considered immoral because of their public appearances and a less restricted lifestyle.

[8]The Palazzo Poli later became famous for its facade that serves as a background to the Fountain of Trevi.

[9]Mazzocchi's opera, *La catena d'Adone*, was published in Venice by Giacomo Vicenti, in 1626.

[10]During the Renaissance, the term *cortigiana* [courtesan] referred to a woman who through her beauty, grace, elegance, and rhetorical, literary or musical abilities, achieved the status of a professional in the business of pleasure, under the protection of male patrons. The more famous courtesans were known as *cortigiane oneste* [honest courtesans] (Russell 54–56). But with the Counter Reformation and its stricter moral code, the courtesans lost their prestige.

[11]Wladyslaw IV, Wasa, see note 79.

at the court of Ferdinand II de' Medici, where she arrived in 1628, perhaps to join other singers in the festivities organized in celebration of the marriage of the grand duke's sister, Margherita, to Odoardo Farnese of Parma. She stayed on in Florence, hoping to find protection, especially since her sister Anna Francesca later enjoyed the favors of the duke's brother, Prince Giovan Carlo.[12] Margherita's relationship with Anna Francesca was, at times, stormy. A certain rivalry existed between the two sisters, not only as singers — as is evident from a letter written by Anna Francesca to Giovan Carlo, in which she accuses Margherita of being perfidious and of having appropriated some of her dresses.[13] Margherita, on the other hand, was sometimes confused with her sister and laden with the latter's adventures.[14]

Margherita remained in Florence for some sixteen years, where she may have married Bernardino Ricci, with whom she definitely had a relationship. Ricci, an actor and *buffone* [buffoon] known as *Il Tedeschino*,[15] who also called himself *il cavaliere del piacere* [knight of pleasure], was in the service of Ferdinand II, whose court was renowned for putting on entertainments of all kinds, including fireworks, a novelty in those days. Ricci was famed not only for competing with the Spanish buffoon, Baldassarre Biguria[16] (an excellent guitar player), but also for being quarrelsome, an attitude which caused him frequent trouble and even a facial wound. Margherita seems to allude to his wounding in the poem *Tirsi trafitto* (p. 181),

---

[12] Giovan Carlo de' Medici (1611–1663) began his career in the Tuscan navy and became *generalissimo* of the Spanish navy in 1638. In 1644 he gave up his military career, having been made a cardinal. However, he resided in Florence and preferred to be called "prince" rather than "cardinal." He became a protector of the arts, particularly of the theater, and had the Teatro della Pergola built in Florence. He also supported various academies. Along with his brother Mattias, he protected singers and helped stage operas. (See *DBI* 73: 61–63.) Giovan Carlo commissioned a portrait of a very young Anna Francesca, from Cesare Dandini before 1637, which was publicly shown for the first time in 1965, in Florence (Megale 1992). A reproduction of this painting is given in Couëtoux, 104 and in Brosius, 28. Brosius ignores the preceding two contributions and thus minimizes the fact that Checca's portrait was only for the private viewing of Giovan Carlo. See Bellesi, Tavola XI, for a color reproduction of this portrait by Dandini, remarkable for its luminosity and the folds of the sitter's loosely hanging shirt that exposes the whiteness of her bare shoulders against a dark background, while the white face is complemented by very red lips and a red fluffy bow in her dark brown hair. Another portrait of Checca with a crown of flowers, also by Dandini, is given on p. 104, but unfortunately not in color.

[13] See Megale 1992, 213 and Mamone #230.

[14] Anna Francesca was also passionately involved with Corradino Orsino, a young nobleman from Pitignano, with whom she went to Naples in 1640. He fell ill and died there, provoking a scandal, since he was a married man (see Megale 1993). During her stay in Paris, Anna Francesca became the mistress of the prince of Wales, later Charles II (1630–1685) (see *NGDMM* 6: 523–24), who joined his mother in Paris in 1646 (see *EB* 5: 308–10).

[15] Ricci was born in 1588 and got his nickname as a child actor. His association with Florence started during the reign of Ferdinand I. He was frequently in Rome, where he had contact with the Ludovisi, Aldobrandini, and Barberini families and was even presented to Pope Urban VIII and Innocent X. He died on March 6, 1653 and was buried in the Church of Santa Felicita in Florence. See Megale 1995, Introduction to *Il Tedeschino* . . . 5–59.

[16] Called Baldassarriglio by Ricci. See Megale 1995, 114–15.

penned from the point of view of the shocked woman who sees her beloved return home bleeding and collapsing without recognizing his own children. We know that Margherita did have children, for she called herself "a widow with two daughters" in a letter of 1657,[17] and she is referred to as a widow in a 1645 Turin court document.[18] Nothing more of her family life is known. The name Ronaca, sometimes added to her last name by literary historians,[19] has never been explained, and simply seems to be a misreading of "*Romana*" that she attached to her name in her publications. Only her final work, the play *Gli amori della Luna* (1654), carries "Maria Margherita Costa" (without *Romana*) on its title page, as well as at the end of the dedication.

Margherita wrote most of her works while in Florence. She cultivated literary friendships with writers, from whom she obtained laudatory poems to include in her books and whom she in turn praised in her own compositions. She moreover penned many flattering encomiastic poems addressed to members of the nobility whose protection she hoped to gain. Among her friends we find Benedetto Guerrini[20] (secretary to Ferdinand II), Alessandro Adimari[21] (secretary of the *Accademia Fiorentina*), Andrea Barbazza[22] (associated with the *Accademia degli Indomiti* of Bologna), and Paganino Gaudenzi,[23] professor at the University of Pisa.

It had been speculated by critics that Margherita left Florence in 1644 because Ricci had died. This conjecture can no longer be entertained, because we now know, thanks to research by Teresa Megale, that Ricci did not die until 1653. He was in Rome in 1643, for a few months, with the Florentine ambassador Alessandro del Nero, and again in 1652. Margherita probably left Florence as her comedy *Li buffoni* [The Buffoons], published in 1641, could not have pleased the Florentine court for its allusions to actual facts (as will be discussed later), and may have caused trouble for her. At any rate, she returned to Rome in the company of the former bandit Cesare Squilletti from Catanzaro, known as Fra Paolo who, having served in the military forces of Ferdinand II, was traveling to the Eternal City as a penitent under the protection of the Barberini family. Margherita, too, considered

---

[17]Addressed to Mario Chigi on May 4, asking for assistance, see Introduction, p. 24.

[18]See Introduction, p. 23.

[19]As in *DEdLI* 2: 146.

[20]Benedetto Guerrini administered the *Camera del Granduca* from 1623 to 1657, the year of his death, first as *aiutante di camera* and then, from 1637 on, as *segretario di camera*. See Megale 1988, 74n10.

[21]Alessandro Adimari (1579–1649) became secretary of the *Accademia Fiorentina* in 1633. He published six volumes of poetry, each one consisting of 50 sonnets that are more erudite than poetic. See *DBI* 1: 277–78.

[22]Andrea Barbazza (1581/82–1656) was associated with many literary academies. He wrote a number of comedies that were not published and are now lost. See *DBI* 6: 148–49.

[23]Paganino Gaudenzi (1595–1649) was from a Protestant family. He converted to Catholicism, took minor orders, and studied Greek, Hebrew, Chaldean, and Latin. He became professor of Greek at the *Sapienza* University in Rome, but clashed with the theologian and inquisitor, Roberto Bellarmino (1542–1621), and left Rome for the University of Pisa. He was unable to obtain permission to publish his Latin epigrams and was menaced by the Inquisition. See *DBI* 5: 676–78.

herself a penitent and sought the protection of Cardinal Francesco Barberini, the pope's nephew, since her brother[24] was employed by the cardinal and might have served as an intermediary, or perhaps the intermediary was Ricci. The cardinal also helped one of Margherita's sisters (possibly a fourth one) to enter a convent as a nun: *altra del germe mio tra caste celle / hai ritolta del mondo ai ciechi inganni* [another woman of my family you removed from the world's deceits into a chaste cell] as the poet declares in the poem (p. 257) addressed to Francesco Barberini. In gratitude for his assistance, Margherita dedicated to him her *Cecilia martire: Poema sacro* [The Martyr Cecilia: A Sacred Poem]. With the death of Pope Urban VIII,[25] on July 29, 1644, however, the political situation in Rome changed and the Barberini nephews of the pope, accused of mismanaging church money, fled to France to seek the protection of prime minister Jules Mazarin.[26] Costa thus took a temporary position as a singer at the court of Duchess Christine of Savoy in Turin in early 1645. In a document addressed to the court treasurer regarding Margherita's honorarium, she is referred to as a widow.[27]

Margherita was back in Rome by August, where she must have frequented the house of the composer Luigi Rossi,[28] for in 1646 she was invited to Paris with Rossi and his group of musicians in the service of Cardinal Antonio Barberini, whose secretary, Francesco Buti,[29] made all the arrangements for their Parisian artistic engagement.[30] In Paris, Margherita sang the part of Juno in the opera *L'Orfeo* [Orpheus] by Luigi Rossi, on the libretto of Buti, while her sister, Anna Francesca, was acclaimed as Eurydice. The opera premiered on March 2, 1647 and lasted six hours. Meant to glorify the French king, it had a complicated plot (involving even some gods of the Olympus), a complex, pompous staging by Giacomo Torelli,[31] and choreography by Giovanni Battista Balbi.[32] This opera enjoyed great success and was repeatedly performed that year in Paris,[33] where Margherita obtained the protection of Mazarin, who helped her publish three of her books. One of these, *La*

---

[24]According to Margherita he became a soldier, but most likely a member of the cardinal's private militia.

[25]Maffeo Barberini, Urban VIII, was pope from 1623–1644. He promoted both of his brothers, as well his three nephews: Francesco and Antonio became cardinals at a very young age, while Taddeo was appointed prefect of Rome and general of the pontifical army. Rome reached its highest Baroque glory during his reign, especially with the works of Bernini, the pope's architect. After his death, his nephews were accused of having appropriated church money. All three fled to Paris where they were protected by Mazarin, named cardinal by Urban VIII. See Rendina 1: 82–92.

[26]French spelling of Giulio Mazzarino (1602–1661), who served as minister to Queen Anne, widow of Louis XIII (1601–1643), and to her son, young Louis XIV (1638–1715).

[27]Ademollo 1884, 38n1.

[28]On Luigi Rossi (died in 1653), see *NGDMM* 21: 723–27.

[29]On Francesco Buti (1604–1682), see *DBI* 15: 603–06.

[30]Rossi arrived in Paris in mid-1646, while the singers arrived in January 1647.

[31]Giacomo Torelli (1608–1678) was a well known architect, engineer, and stage director. See *EdS* 9: cols. 973–76.

[32]Giovanni Battista Balbi was a famous dancer and choreographer. See *DBI* 5: 367–69.

[33]Basso 2: 485–86.

tromba di Parnaso, contains poems dedicated to Queen Anne of France, to members of the royal family and of the French court, and to the artists associated with the performance of *L'Orfeo*. In one composition, Margherita mentions (p. 245) the successful, private recital for the queen by her sister, Anna Francesca, who had already been acclaimed in Paris as a singer, in February 1646, when she performed in Pietro Francesco Cavalli's opera *Egisto*,[34] staged at the Palais Royal.

Not much is known about Costa's life after 1647. She was in Venice in August 1650, as is evident from a letter by Francesco Maria Zati to Desiderio Montemagni (secretary to Giovan Carlo de' Medici) informing that he will help Margherita locally, as requested in the letter of recommendation that she had brought him.[35] From Venice, Margherita most likely travelled to Germany, for her play, *Gli amori della Luna* [The Loves of the Moon Goddess], published in 1654, alludes to a stay in Germany. In the dedication to the dukes of Brunswick-Lüneburg, the author claims that she has not written in Italian for four years while living under a foreign sky. The play was published in Venice, ostensibly on Margherita's journey back to Italy and subsequent return to Rome. The last preserved document by Margherita consists of a letter written on May 4, 1657, to Mario Chigi, commander-in-chief of the papal armies and brother to Pope Alexander VII. In this letter, Margherita implores Chigi's assistance. She describes herself as a widow with two daughters to support — one married to a Flemish captain (who is fighting on the island of Crete), the other younger and still single.[36] Margherita neither mentions her husband, nor her daughters by name. Some critics doubt that she ever married officially and assume, since the date of her death is unknown, that she died during the plague. But according to records, the first plague fatalities of 1656 occurred in Rome in June and by spring 1657 the contagion was over.[37] Margherita may likely have survived to live a few more years. A singer by the name of Mema Costa, active in Rome in 1670, could have been one of her daughters.[38]

Unfortunately, Margherita Costa attracted more interest for her private life (known more from gossip that from facts), than for her literary works. Critics dismissed her books as poorly written. They considered her an ignorant woman, capable only of a *rozzo stile* [rough style], which she herself always stressed as a bad quality of hers, in her dedications, in letters to the reader, and in many of her poems. The critics interpreted these declarations to be a boast of her ignorance rather than her way of exploiting, by exaggerating in a Baroque fashion, the tendency of Italian Renaissance women poets to minimize their ability when comparing themselves with male writers — a tradition which had become a norm in her era. Moreover, Margherita's stylistic excesses were branded as ridiculous, or outright immoral, rather than seen as Baroque peculiarities in poems often written in competition with other

---

[34]Cavalli (1602–1676) wrote some 30 operas. He was the most performed Italian composer after Monteverdi in his day. See *NGDMM* 5: 302–13.

[35]Mamone #919.

[36]Manuscript: "Lettera a Mario Chigi."

[37]Gigli 479.

[38]See Bianchi 1924, 93.

poets who had expounded similar or equal subjects. Only recently has Margherita received proper attention as an original woman writer of the Baroque period.

The first book published by Margherita Costa, *Istoria del viaggio d'Alemagna del serenissimo Gran Duca di Toscana Ferdinando Secondo* [A History of the Trip to Germany Undertaken by Ferdinand II, Grand Duke of Tuscany], is a description of young Ferdinand's trip,[39] undertaken in incognito, but secret to none — a political undertaking meant to honor Emperor Ferdinand II of Habsburg.[40] Ferdinand accomplished the journey before assuming his duties as duke upon his return to Florence on July 14, 1628, his eighteenth birthday. He first made a diplomatic detour to Rome to pay a visit to Pope Urban VIII, departing from Florence on February 23, 1627 and, traveling leisurely with his escort, reaching Rome on March 1. On March 18 he left Rome, visited a number of Italian cities, crossed the Alps, stopped in Innsbruck and Munich, and arrived in Prague to see the emperor.

The *Istoria dell'viaggio* consists of a detailed list of court gentlemen, with their names and titles, including that of Ferdinand's younger brother Giovanni Carlo (the future lover of Margherita's sister, Anna Francesca). The number of horses, mules, etc., that formed the traveling party are also given, as well as the exact dates of arrivals and departures, with names of towns stopped in, weather conditions, formalities, ceremonies, and so on. While it might seem monotonous reading, it is an excellent documentation of travel, its splendors and its hardships, as experienced by the high nobility in seventeenth-century Italy, and traces an exact itinerary not found in history books. Noteworthy is the fact that Ferdinand made courtesy calls on important ladies as well, such as the pope's sister-in-law, Costanza Magalotti Barberini; Anna Colonna, wife of the pope's nephew Taddeo Barberini, prefect of Rome; and other Roman princesses. As Margherita declares at the beginning of the book, her text is based on the notes kept by Benedetto Guerrini, who had accompanied Ferdinand on the trip and who later became his secretary.[41] This fact attests to the author's friendship with Guerrini and led to the suspicion that it was Guerrini who wrote the work but published it under Margherita's name. The book, dedicated to Giovanni de Erasso (Italian spelling), the Spanish ambassador at the Tuscan court, was published in Venice and carries no date of publication (but probably appeared in 1630). Since the prose is good — precise, short

---

[39]Ferdinand II (1610–1670), son of Cosimo II and Maria Maddalena of Habsburg, was only eleven years old when his father died. His mother and his grandmother, Christine of Lorraine, acted as regents for him until 1628, when he officially assumed all responsibilities at the age of eighteen. He married Vittoria della Rovere in 1634. He is remembered for promoting the sciences in Florence, together with his brother Leopoldo (1617–1675), who helped found and support the *Accademia del Cimento*. (See *DBI* 73: 106–12.)

[40]Ferdinand II of Habsburg (1578–1637) became emperor in 1619. He was a brother of Maria Maddalena, Ferdinand II de' Medici's mother, and thus an uncle to him.

[41]See also note 20.

sentences without needless embellishments — its author was immediately accused of not having written it herself.

In 1638, Costa published her first volume of poetry titled *La chitarra* [The Guitar],[42] which carries the false indication of having been printed in "Francfort" by "Daniel Wastch." The first few copies of the book to come off the press include an etching of the author's likeness, done by Stefano della Bella[43] — a miniature surrounded by a Latin inscription with Margherita's name, enclosed within a fancy frame, at the bottom of which appears a second Latin inscription by Don Alfonso de Oviedo Spinosa, and below which appear musical instruments and an open score book (see portrait **A**, p. 16). This etching was substituted, while the volume was still in print, with a more appealing portrait (see portrait **C**, p. 18, done by an artist still unidentified) — a likeness Margherita obviously preferred, for she included it in several of her subsequent works. Thus some of the examples of *La chitarra* carry portrait **A**, others carry **C**, causing some confusion.[44] Moreover, portrait **C** was wrongly attributed to Stefano della Bella by Charles A. Jombert.

In her dedication to Ferdinand II, Margherita explains her choice of title: the guitar, a common instrument played by the poor, is thus a worthy symbol of her lowly verse, similar to a crippled, ill-shaped dwarf. She repeats this humorous comparison in her dedicatory sonnet:

D'un nano gobbo, zoppo e mal composto,	A hunchbacked, limping and ill-formed
Serenissimo Sire, ti fo' dono,	dwarf, serene Sire, I offer to you,
che cavalca in Parnaso senza sprono,	who rides in Parnassus without being incited,
e correr senza briglia s'è disposto.	resolved to speed on without a rein.

Margherita pokes fun at herself and her style, which she describes as *rozzo* [rough]. She states in her "Letter to the Reader," that she, being Roman, is aware of exposing herself to criticism for daring to compose verses in Florence, and asks for indulgence, since her "little volume" [*piccolo volume*] is the work of a woman without any schooling. Her "little volume," however, consists of 573 pages, with compositions in various forms: *terza rima* [tercets: three-line rhyming system], *ottave* [eight-line stanzas, traditionally used in narrative poems], sonnets, and *canzonette* [poems of short lines frequently set to music]. The volume, as the reader

---

[42]Probably because Marino entitled the 1608 republication of his collection of poems *La lira* [The Lyre].

[43]Stefano della Bella (1610–1664) was active in Florence and served the Medici until 1639 when he left for Paris to return only in 1650 (see *DBI* 36: 686–90). For his portrait of Costa, see Megale 1995, 55n220, Jombert 89, #71–#72, and De Vesme 1: 53 #32 and 2: 12. Bellesi reproduces, on p. 103, not only della Bella's portrait **A**, but also his preparatory pencil drawing of Margherita that reflects Dandini's influence. Brosius, on pp. 30–31, reproduces portraits **A** and **C** and notes the resemblance between Margherita and her sister Checca.

[44]Portrait **A** is reproduced in Costa-Zalessow 2008, 113, as provided by a librarian who copied it from the Internet, not from the book in the Bancroft Library, University of California, Berkeley, which carries portrait **C**. The Vatican Library example carries portrait **A**.

will see, contains some very good poems, serious as well as humorous, of a style that is far from rough.

Preceding Costa's poems of *La chitarra* are six sonnets (two accompanied by madrigals), by the Prince of Gallicano,[45] Alessandro Adimari, Andrea Barbazza, Bernardino Biscia,[46] Alfonso de Oviedo Spinosa,[47] and Ottavio Tronsarelli, followed by three anonymous madrigals, all praising the author's beauty and literary merits.

The text of *La chitarra*, starting with the introductory *Capitolo scherzoso*, in *terza rima* [tercets] in which the author makes fun of her limping poetry, is divided into parts subtitled according to the metric form of the poems contained in each section: *Capitoli*,[48] *Sonetti, Idilli*, and *Canzonette*. These are followed by a humorous composition, consisting of ten *ottave*, by Andrea Salvadori,[49] titled *I caramogi overo gli amanti abbozzati* [Court Dwarfs or a Sketch of Lovers] to which Margherita responds with two poems (ten *ottave* each). This disputation on whether dwarfs are better lovers than are good-looking men, was inspired by the episode in Ludovico Ariosto's *Orlando Furioso*, Canto 28,[50] about the Lombard queen who took a dwarf as a lover, although she enjoyed the attentions of a loving and very handsome husband. The volume concludes with a *capitolo scherzoso* in tercets, in which Margherita justifies her verses.

The first part of *La chitarra* includes many encomiastic sonnets, beginning with the celebration of Ferdinand II's marriage to Vittoria della Rovere (in 1634), and includes the glorification of the grand duke's brothers as well as other important persons at the Medici court, along with a few in Rome. Starting with the poem addressed to Giovan Giorgio Aldobrandini, Margherita uses the technique of speaking through a *Bella donna* [beautiful woman], who is autobiographical in some cases, as in the plaint of being far away from her native city, of having changed country, fortune and love, or in deploring her bad luck and difficult past, while praising a happier present. These hints are only allusions, not descriptions of concrete facts. Her preferred theme is a lamentation, either by a man or a woman, for the lover's departure or long absence. Thematically unique is a complaint to her absent lover by a pregnant woman realistically describing her state — a description which is an absolute novelty in Italian women's poetry. The speaker is torn between an awakening motherly love and the wish that the child will die, as soon as he is born, so that he might avoid the bleak destiny of an unloved bastard (p. 59).

Another frequent topic in *La chitarra* is the grievance about her lover's infidelity and shortcomings by a woman who, subsequently, consoles herself with another

---

[45]Most likely Pompeo Colonna, who used that title. He staged and sometimes recited in comedies. See *DBI* 27: 414–16.

[46]A minor poet active around 1638. Most likely the grandson of the famed jurist of the same name. See Mazzuchelli.

[47]He also provided the Latin inscription for Costa's portrait **A**.

[48]Almost all are poems in *ottava rima*.

[49]A Tuscan writer who died in 1635, author of many works in prose and verse, including ballets on horseback, which could have influenced Margherita. See Negri 37.

[50]Canto 28 is the most erotic canto of *Orlando Furioso*.

man. Thus the tension built up in such complaints dissolves in humor. The *capitoli scherzosi* (*capitoli* used in the sense of satirical or comical compositions, most written in *ottave*) are full of humor. In the poem which she calls a "joke" (p. 61), Margherita advises women to be smart and never to love only one man at a time, unless they want to lose their liberty to possessive men. The poem draws the conclusion that it is stupid to impose laws on women if those laws are not also imposed on men. In the next poem (p. 65), about a woman killed by a scorned lover, the tragic story (told with tongue-in-cheek irony) serves to invite all women to kiss men whenever requested, unless they want to part with their lives. But beneath the humorous patina lies a criticism of men and their bullying which can lead to violence, including death. Similarly, in other poems addressed to women (pp. 83, 85, 89), the poet complains of having suffered all the tortures of love, only to realize that love is blind. She, therefore, has ceased loving and limits herself to spinning — women's true calling. Again with humor, Margherita advises women to do the same, obviously poking fun at those who believe that a woman's place is only in the home.

Among the sonnets in *La chitarra* are several that finely describe a woman's longing for the return of her beloved (p. 67), or her sadness at his departure (pp. 75, 79), poems that are masterfully rendered and merit a place among the best written in the seventeenth century on that theme so popular with musicians.

In the next to the last composition of the book, Margherita, in response to Salvadori's *I caramogi*, describes what type of men women like: not too young and not too old, not too ugly and not too narcissistic, strong and without strange peculiarities, faithful and of a noble heart — inferring that the story about the Lombard queen cannot be true. Margherita concludes her book with a *capitolo scherzoso* [humorous satire] in defense of her verses, a *capitolo* that, at the same time, glorifies women, their whims and shortcomings, because women are beautiful and well known to her, as she too is a woman.

Costa's next volume of verse, *Il violino* [The Violin],[51] comprising 168 pages, was also published in 1638 with the same false indication of printer's name and location[52] as appeared in *La chitarra*, but without the accompanying portrait. This volume, as well, is dedicated to Ferdinand II as a token of the poet's devotion, even if a small gift compared to those offered by others to the grand duke on the feast day of San Giovanni (the patron saint of Florence), as she states in an idyll (p. 93). Margherita again insists in this poem, as well as in her prose dedication and "Letter to the Reader," that her verses are rough. The volume contains only two sonnets addressed to the author, one by Ferdinando Saracinelli,[53] the other by Alessandro Adimari, both praising the poems of her *Il violino*.

---

[51]The violin is considered a nobler instrument than the guitar.

[52]A common way to avoid censure. Both books were probably printed in Florence. See note 66.

[53]A poet and librettist who served the Medici since 1606. He was involved in court entertainments from 1611–1637. He was made bailiff of Volterra in 1619 and died in Florence on Feb. 26, 1640. See *NGDMM* 22: 277.

Il violino is divided into three sections: *idilli, ottave, canzonette.* The *ottave* comprise one long encomiastic poem addressed to Margherita de' Medici, duchess of Parma.[54] The remaining poems, aside from the usual love laments on the part of a woman or of a man, strongly reflect the excesses of the Baroque style. The idyll,[55] *Violamento di Lilla* ["The Rape of Lilla," p. 99], was considered by the critic Martino Capucci as a reflection of the author's immoral life, because he failed to notice that Margherita is imitating, with a feminist twist, an erotic poem by Giambattista Marino, titled *Trastulli estivi* ["Summer Pastimes"].[56] Marino describes, in a first person voice, how a lover took advantage of his beloved Lilla on a hot summer day, claiming that she resisted only as part of the game and, at the end, he feels like a satiated conqueror. Marino adds that it is a discourtesy to let a beautiful woman depart intact. Margherita, on the other hand, titles her poem more correctly as a rape and has the guilty man describe in detail how he surprised a sleeping Lilla and forced himself on her by immobilizing her with his arms, his feet and the weight of his body. He, too, claims that Lilla's protests were faked and, now in love with her, he offers her marriage. Lilla, however, never returns, preferring another lover, which drives the rapist to despair to the point of invoking death. Margherita thus punishes the rapist by making him suffer, while she grants Lilla the liberty to choose the man she prefers. This concept is a rather modern one, for in Italy, especially in Sicily until recently, a woman who refused a man would be kidnapped (even if not raped), and thus obliged to marry her abductor as the only way to save her honor.

In another idyll (p. 109), Costa competes with the followers of Marino who sometimes selected absurd subjects in order to create antitheses and metaphors never before attempted. She describes the praise bestowed on an ugly, aged woman by her lover, who is happy with her, in spite of the fact that she has colorless, sullen and threatening blue eyes, white hair, damaged skin, black teeth, a goiter, a flat chest, deformed uneven shoulders, and rough hands. She, moreover, limps, stutters and is dirty, smelly, too tall and utterly stupid.[57] This poem, the ugliest of all the Baroque hyperboles, is not mentioned in Patrizia Bettella's book entirely dedicated to the theme of the ugly woman in Italian poetry from the Middle Ages to the Baroque.

The poem in which a desperate mother lists the difficulties her baby girl will face in life, only to see her changed into a boy, who will be loved by everyone, can only be seen as surreal (p. 117). This metamorphosis makes sense if interpreted as Margherita's protest against the restricted life of women who are deprived of a chance to succeed in a man's world. The poem is not simply a fascination with the

---

[54]Margherita de' Medici, sister to Ferdinand II, married Odoardo Farnese of Parma.

[55]An idyll is a poem having a pastoral setting.

[56]Marino 98–102.

[57]In 1637, Costa's friend Adimari published his *Tersicore,* subtitled *Scherzi e paradossi poetici sopra la beltà delle donne,* a book consisting of 50 sonnets, each describing a different woman with one shortcoming: too tall, too small, overly skinny or fat, hunchbacked, limping, deaf, mute, bald, long-nosed, goitrous, etc., but in spite of one defect, the woman is still lovable and tender, according to the poet. Margherita reacts by piling up all the defects onto one woman, creating a Baroque extravagance.

myth of Hermaphroditus[58] that had attracted the attention of Ovid,[59] and of artists and writers of the Italian Renaissance and Baroque period, as Bianchi insisted.[60]

Several compositions in *Il violino* are good examples of seriously treated themes of human emotions, such as the grief of a woman whose lover has died (p. 123), or that of a mother imploring God to restore the health and beauty of her sick little daughter (p. 125), a theme that is new for Italian women poets.[61] The *canzonette* of the volume's last section create a more cheerful tone and describe the general torments of love with verses of a musical quality (pp. 131–35).

Lo stipo [The Cabinet], dedicated to Lorenzo de' Medici,[62] was published in 1639 in Venice. It includes portrait **C** of the author (see p. 18) and prefatory verses by Juan Silvestro Gomez, Miguel de Silveira, Tronsarelli, de Oviedo Spinosa and Adimari. The title reflects Margherita's desire to be original as she groups her poems into seven different "drawers," each named after precious stones or metals: 1. "Red Carbuncles and Diamonds," 2. "Emeralds and Rubies," 3. "Gold and Pearls," 4. "Amethysts, Lapis Lazuli and Turquoises," 5. "Ambers, Corals and Sapphires," 6. "Alabaster, Bohemian Crystals and Imitations," and 7. "Peridots and Hyacinths."[63] The second "drawer" contains laudatory poems, nine addressed to different academies which, however, Margherita was never invited to join.

Noteworthy in the 308 pages of *Lo stipo* is the autobiographical poem (p. 145), written as a response to Paganino Gaudenzi's query as to how Margherita had been able to leave Rome and glorify Tuscany, her adopted country. The author declares that she was ill treated in Rome, because others were jealous of her ability to conquer hearts, but that she, Costa (the name appears in the concluding verse), is happy to have settled in Florence, where she found protection and fortune. Autobiographical hints concerning her love-life also appear. In one poem, a woman admits to loving frequently, but ascribes such weakness to the destiny imposed on her by the stars (p. 147). In another poem (p. 155), the poet acutely observes, through the eyes of a woman lamenting the loss of her beauty to the ravages of time, the unfulfilled and petty lives of women — destined to take care of house and children, they are taught to cultivate their beauty, not their intelligence, with the

---

[58]Son of Hermes and Aphrodite endowed with the beauty of both deities. He rejected the love of a nymph who prayed the gods that she be indissolubly united with him. The wish was granted and a being, having both male and female qualities, resulted.

[59]*Metamorphoses*, Book IV.

[60]Bianchi did not know that androgyny was also present in primitive cultures. See Zolla.

[61]Francesca Turini Bufalini was the first to introduce the theme of motherhood and motherly love for her sons and grandsons, but there are no poems for her daughter or her granddaughters in her *Rime* (1628). See Costa-Zalessow "Introduction," pp. 13, 18–19, and poems 49, 50, 51 in Turini Bufalini 2009.

[62]Lorenzo de' Medici (1599–1648), son of Ferdinand I and brother of Cosimo II, was an uncle to Ferdinand II and was the only adult Medici male to help the regents Christine of Lorraine and Maria Maddalena of Habsburg, while Ferdinand II was still a child. He held the title of *Generalissimo dell'Armi Toscane*, but never participated in any military action, preferring horses, dogs, and jousting. He supported the *Accademia degli Incostanti* that staged improvised comedies. See *DBI* 73: 131–34.

[63]Hyacinths: zircon gems of various colors.

result that they lead a frivolous existence, full of envy of each other. The speaker, however, has discarded all makeup, for among the poets of Parnassus a painted face carries no merit. The poem thus alludes to the author's pride in her literary achievements and, at the same time, comprises a list of beauty aids used in the seventeenth century.

The poem *Cortigiano ravveduto* [The Courtier Who Mended His Ways], too long to be included in our anthology, is a severe criticism of court life with its intrigues, self-promotion, lies, treachery, constant service, perpetual vigilance and fear of losing the lord's favor, which soon passes to a more cunning rival. The poem is a pungent satire and one wonders how Margherita found the courage to include it in her book dedicated to a Medici prince.

The bottom "drawer" contains the poem *Lagrime della Regina di Svezia* [Tears of the Queen of Sweden], not included in our anthology, a lamentation of the queen over the corpse of her husband, king Gustavus Adolphus, killed in battle in 1632. Margherita sees in this tragic event fortune's ill doings, by which a queen is crushed to death by sorrow.[64]

Lo stipo concludes with the author addressing, in *ottave*, Benedetto Guerrini (p. 165), who had advised her to burn some of her poems. Margherita, with some humor, curses the Muses, her studies, and verses, and makes a promise never to write again — a promise she obviously did not keep.

Lettere amorose [Love Letters, 1639], dedicated to Giovan Carlo de' Medici (before he became a cardinal), includes a retouched version of portrait **A** of the poet, with both inscriptions removed (see portrait **B**, p. 17), and prefatory verses by Adimari and others. In this work, Margherita tries her hand at the literary genre of letter writing, popular since the Renaissance. (Such letters could serve to illustrate the author's point of view on a particular subject, or could be the correspondence with friends and important persons, or a model for those who needed to write about the same matter.) Margherita's *Lettere amorose*, more humorous than serious, imitate earlier models and are pure literature rather than examples for practical use. However, this work enjoyed a certain popularity, as is attested by the two reprints of 1643 and 1652. Moreover, several of Margherita's letters were included in the repeatedly reprinted collection, *Scielta di lettere amorose* [Selected Love Letters, 1656, 1659, 1662, 1671, 1675, 1683, 1687], which included letters by Ferrante Pallavicino, Luca Asserino, and Girolamo Parabosco. In 1683, the book landed on the *Index of Prohibited Books* because Pallavicino's works had been condemned by the Inquisition and its author beheaded.[65]

While Margherita's *Lettere amorose* are in prose, the individual letters are usually accompanied by verses in which she skillfully manipulates the lover's poem directed to his beloved by using the same rhyming words in the beloved's answer,

---

[64]The poem evidences much poetic license. Maria Eleanora of Brandenburg (1599–1656) outlived her husband Gustavus II (1594–1632), whom she had married in 1620 (see *EB* 10: 1048–49). Their daughter, Christina, will later become queen of Sweden from 1644 to 1654, but will abdicate, convert to Catholicism, and live the rest of her life in Rome (which, of course, Margherita could not foresee).

[65]*Index* 250 and 823. On Pallavicino (1615–1644), see *DSI* 3: 162.

but with a different meaning, creating a playful stylistic technique (impossible to capture in translation).

In 1640, Margherita published three books, judging by the dates of her dedications, in the following order: *Flora feconda* [Fertile Flora], dedicated to Ferdinand II, *La selva di cipressi* [The Cypress Grove], and *La Flora feconda* [The Fertile Flora], dedicated to Vittoria della Rovere. Printed in Florence by Massi & Landi,[66] all three include Margherita's portrait **C** (see p. 18). The first is a narrative poem of the mythological type, the last is a play dealing with the same subject. Flora and Zephyr, eager to have children, undertake a trip to consult Jupiter's oracle. Upon their return, a son is born to them, but Jupiter decides to keep the baby and promises the couple other children. This mythological story is an allegory of the birth and death of the first born of Ferdinand II and his wife Vittoria della Rovere. The poem is divided into ten cantos — nine stand for the nine months of pregnancy, the tenth was added at the last moment for the death of the infant, as the author explains in her dedication addressed to the duke. A rather extravagant poem — but we must remember we are dealing with a Baroque poet trying to be original. Margherita inserts references to the oak, the emblem of the della Rovere family, into the plot, as well as a glorification of the Medici in the form of prophecies. Here, as elsewhere, Costa displays her knowledge of classical mythology, as well as her descriptive ability. The play, in five acts with eight to eleven scenes each, is an adaptation of her poem for the stage and is complex — with fancy settings, music, singing, and dancing — all of which reflect the Medici preference for grandiose entertainment based on mythological themes.

The 256-page book, *La selva di cipressi* [The Cypress Grove], subtitled *Opera lugubre* [*A Mournful Work*] and dedicated to Charles de Lorraine, duke of Guise, carries two etchings, one of a fancy cemetery surrounded by cypress trees which was done by Stefano della Bella,[67] the other the poet's portrait **C** (done by unknown artist, see p. 18). The work consists mainly of lamentations, all in *ottave*, on the death of great men such as: François de Lorraine, prince of Joinville; Francesco Maria della Rovere (the last duke of Urbino); Ferdinand I, Cosimo II and Francesco de' Medici; Vittorio Amedeo of Savoy; Prince Bernhard of Saxe-Weimar; Marquis Ambrogio Spinola; the imperial general Albrecht von Wallenstein; Bertoldo Orsini, marquis of Monte San Savino; and Ferdinando Saracinelli,[68] an acquaintance of Margherita. These lamentations are variously intoned by a relative, a mythological figure, the rivers Arno or Po, the Alps and even by a personified

---

[66]Adimari probably recommended Margherita to Massi & Landi, who had published his *Tersicore* in 1637 (see note 53). Officially they printed two of Margherita's pamphlets and four of her books. I suspect that their press also produced *La chitarra* and *Il violino*, which appeared with a false indication of printer and location. It is interesting to note that Stefano della Bella provided etchings for a number of books printed by Massi & Landi, including Adimari's (see Barroni Salvadori #10–11, 13–16, 18–19, E and F). He also provided etchings for Adimari's *La Polinnia*, printed in Florence by Cecconcelli, in 1628 (Barroni Salvadori C).

[67]See Jombert 89 #71, who wrongly concluded that the portrait must also be by della Bella #72.

[68]See note 53.

Italy, as in *Le lagrime dell'Alpe* ["Tears of the Alp"], a poem on the miserable con-
dition of her states, especially the dukedom of Savoy (p. 173). The theme of Italy,
seen as a former queen reduced to a poor, wounded servant, derives from Dante
and was used in Italian literature throughout the centuries up to the nineteenth
century and Italian unification.[69] Margherita followed this literary tradition as is
also evident in octave 46 of the lamentation for the death of Spinola, in which she
describes the personified Italy as tearing apart her dress:

Sí ch'Italia, al terror fatta tremante,	So that Italy, trembling from fear,
in abbandono di se stessa errava,	roamed aimlessly, in complete abandon,
ed ora il lagrimevole sembiante,	now lacerating her tear-drenched face,
ora la sparsa chioma lacerava.	now the loose hair of her tresses.
Della sua veste, un tempo trionfante,	From her dress, once triumphant,
le pompe a brani in cento parti dava.	she tore off all ornaments.
E consunta l'avria la Morte acerba,	Death would have consumed her,
se non che 'l Duol per maggior duol la serba.	had not Sorrow saved her for greater grief.

In the poem *Tirsi trafitto* ["Tirsi Stabbed"] (p. 181), Margherita describes the
desperation of a woman whose husband returns home wounded. Believing him
about to die, she wants to die as well, together with her children, who as orphans
would be destined for a terrible life. Fortunately Tirsi survives, saved by the duke's
doctor. This plot ostensibly refers to Ricci's wounding.[70]

In the volume's last, long composition, *Elisa infelice* ["Hapless Elisa"], a selection
of which is given on p. 189, Margherita complains about her own life and the fact
that her literary efforts are not appreciated. She therefore ascends to Parnassus to
appeal to the gods, where she is consoled by Apollo, who reminds her of the miseries
of others and points out that laurel leaves are bitter, poets must learn to suffer.

The comedy, *Li buffoni* [The Buffoons, 1641], called *ridicola* [ridiculous], is
Costa's only work with a modern edition, included in the second volume of *Com-
medie dell'Arte* (1985), edited by Siro Ferrone, as an example of a comedy in that
style, but with a written text for each character, in a time when improvisation was
the norm. Margherita dedicated her play to the actor Bernardino Ricci (*Il Tede-
schino*), who was in the service of Ferdinand II. The play was initially labeled by
critics as a potpourri of stupidities, with characters reflecting "nature's jokes" —
dwarfs, madmen, hunchbacks, and other deformed persons — within a plot based
on parody, trivialities and rough, double-meaning puns. Such distortions, together
with the exotic Moroccan setting, were taken as a Baroque extravagance, in which,
at play's end, the betrayed wife has revenge over her rival, a prostitute. The work
was also interpreted as a feminist text. However, Teresa Megale discovered docu-
ments in Florentine archives which prove that the dwarfs and deformed who ap-
pear as characters in the comedy actually lived at the court of Ferdinand II and
received regular payments under the same names as they are assigned in *Li buf-*

---

[69]See Costa-Zalessow 1968 and 1991.
[70]See Introduction, p. 21.

foni, just as Tedeschino played his own part. The work is therefore a parody of the Medici court — its lowest members playing the parts of their masters. The comedy was published in 1641, but must have been written earlier, between 1638 and 1639, because Stefano della Bella, who contributed an etching of the final scene, moved to Paris in October 1639. Moreover, *Li buffoni* was an answer to Ricci's book, *Il Tedeschino overo Difesa dell'Arte del Cavalier del Piacere,* published in Venice, without date and publisher (the modern edition by Megale includes a portrait of Tedeschino on horseback, also done by della Bella).[71]

Having returned to Rome in 1644 under the protection of Cardinal Francesco Barberini, Margherita dedicated to him her sacred narrative poem, *Cecilia martire* [The Martyr Cecilia], published in Rome by Mascardi in 1644.[72] The subject was well chosen for a cardinal of a famous Roman family. Cecilia was not only a Roman saint, but she enjoyed a renewed veneration after her sarcophagus was identified and opened in 1599, inspiring Stefano Maderno (c. 1570–1636) to chisel his masterful marble statue of her for the Church of Santa Cecilia in Rome, where it can still be viewed.[73] Margherita's poem is preceded by short explanations of the allegory of each of the four cantos entitled *Il bagno, Il martirio, Il tempio, Il sepolcro* [The Bath, The Martyrdom, The Temple, The Tomb]. The flames of the bath represent lasciviousness, the art of the devil who acts through human beings to persecute Cecilia; the saint's failed beheading, or martyrdom, is symbolic of the immortality of the soul; Cecilia's house, where she dies, is a temple (church), because the soul of a virgin is heaven's temple; while the tomb stands for eternal peace of the just. The saint's life and death are based on hagiography, while the inserted glorification of Pope Urban VIII and the Barberini family follow the traditional form of a prophecy, tied to the name of Pope Urban I, who consoles Cecilia in her last hour. The poem is definitely a Baroque work, but well composed as such. The descriptive parts are effectively elaborated. In the bath scene, the chaos created by the infernal forces comprises a Baroque bravura of infinite variety in describing heat and flames (p. 209). Touching is the eulogy of Cecilia pronounced by her husband, and contains an allusion to Maderno's statue when the saint's neck, that had been struck three times by the executioner's sword, is described as whiter than Parthian marble. The work includes the theme, dear to Baroque poets, that all must end, nothing lasts, not even for powerful men, because:

. . . *tutto è un'ombra di mortal pensiero,*	. . . everything is but a shadow of mortal thought,
un inganno, ch'ai cor danni produce.	a deception, that causes damage to the hearts.
Passa ogni sol più chiaro in dì più nero,	The brightest of suns yields to the darkest of days,
e la felicità miserie adduce . . .	and happiness leads to misery . . .

---

[71]Megale 1988, 72 and 1995, 54–55; and De Vesme 1: 55, #39 and 2: 14, #39.

[72]Sacred narrative poems were popular in the late sixteenth and seventeenth centuries. They described the lives of Christ, Mary, and the saints, or episodes from the Old Testament. A poem of five cantos called *libri,* comprising circa 280 octaves, titled *La trionfatrice Cecilia, vergine e martire romana* [The Triumphant Cecilia, Roman Virgin and Martyr], had already been published by Sebastiano Castelletti in 1594.

[73]The statue, commissioned by Cardinal Sfondrati, made Maderno famous. See *DBI* 67: 157–62.

The manuscript of *Cecilia martire*, preserved in the Vatican Library, differs from the printed text. In the manuscript, stanzas 10–38 of Canto IV are given twice — in their original version and as rewritten for publication. In the rewritten passages, Costa eliminated all references to the passion of Cecilia's husband for his wife, along with the depiction of the saint's physical beauty. These were substituted with other descriptions to maintain the same number of stanzas as those of the original manuscript.

In 1646, after performing as singer at the court of Duchess Christine of Savoy in Turin, Margherita returned to Rome and then travelled to Paris with a group of musicians at the service of Cardinal Antonio Barberini, where she obtained the protection of Mazarin, who helped her publish three books: *La selva di Diana* [Diana's Woods], *La tromba di Parnaso* [The Trumpet of Parnassus], and *Festa reale per balletto a cavallo* [Royal Pageantry, Ballet on Horseback], all printed in 1647. The last work consists of a complex allegorical pageantry with music, floats, and the appearance of gods, in which Discord yields to Peace against the background of three teams, each with ten knights on horseback, accompanied by their standard bearers. Dedicated to Mazarin in the vain hope of having it performed in Paris, the pageantry was originally intended for the Tuscan court — a manuscript version preserved in Florence bears a dedication to Ferdinand II dated January 27, 1640.[74] The work is a curious one, colorful and pompous, but difficult to perform. The text does not offer much to the modern reader, but is a good example of Baroque taste for elaborate entertainment, based on striking visual aspects rather than content.

La selva di Diana is dedicated to Duchess Christine of Savoy, who is addressed in the composition *L'Alpi* ["The Alps"]. But in praising the noble lady, Margherita inserts, at the very beginning, a reference to herself — her first name and her desperation about her unlucky star, her efforts at study and the desire to become a poet without, however, having achieved recognition with her *rozze rime* — all recurring themes throughout her oeuvre. These personal references to the author constitute the interesting parts of the poem (p. 225), the rest being a glorification of the Savoy family, written in the usual laudatory manner. More original are the encomiastic poems that follow, all dedicated to women. Margherita had been invited to sing to a group of Roman noble ladies enjoying themselves during grape-harvest time in Albano, near Rome. She also improvised laudatory poems for them,[75] finding something different to praise in each while following a ranking order, beginning with the hostess (p. 227), followed by the more important ladies (p. 229), and ending with the baby girl that was present, for a total of twelve compositions. Under the veil of praise, Margherita represents the entire span of women's lives, even if not in chronological order. She describes a baby (p. 237), a bride (p. 235), young and old married women, including an expectant mother (p. 231) and a widow (p. 233), all of whom she compliments in a different way without repeating herself.

Also included in *La selva di Diana* is a curious set of seven sonnets, corresponding to the seven days of the week, each day associated with the deity from

---

[74]Bianchi 1925, 194–95.
[75]Once published, they can no longer be considered improvised.

whom its Italian name derives and based on the original Latin: *lunedì* with Cynthia (goddess of the moon), *martedì* with Mars, *mercoledì* with Mercury, *giovedì* with Jove, and *venerdì* with Venus. Since *sabato* and *domenica* derive from the Judeo-Christian tradition, the author reverts to the original Latin:[76] *saturni dies* and *dies solis*. The purpose of these seven sonnets is to express a woman's love-torment, differing from day to day, so as to have the reader marvel at the originality of the text — the true goal of the Baroque poets (see *Lunedì*, p. 241).

Among the remaining sonnets are two that stand out. The one (p. 241) addressed to a person who had accused Margherita of not being the author of her poems, is remarkable not only for its subject, but also for its subdued response. The poet expresses no indignation against the accuser — only a calm understanding when she states that to consider a woman incapable of achievement is not unreasonable, as her contemporary world is governed by laziness and vice, while ignorance, displayed with pomp, rules over virtue. This fact, however, does not apply in her own case, Margherita states, for she loves Phoebus and is guided by him, while others lie idle in the shade. The other remarkable sonnet (p. 239) represents by far the best poem of *La selva di Diana*, for in it Margherita succeeds in creating a perfect correspondence between the gloomy, rainy day and the sorrowful feelings of a woman seeing her beloved depart — a recurring theme in her sonnets. The repeated juxtaposition of darkness with light is typical Baroque antithesis. The iterations with variations on the word *pianto* — all beginning with the sound of *p*, considered harsh — reproduce the sound of falling raindrops.

Margherita concludes *La selva di Diana* with two compositions in *ottava rima*. The first (p. 245) is a glorification of the French court and of Queen Anne. In this poem, Margherita explains that the queen favored her, and states that Paris is a city where artists are recognized and rewarded — the golden age, she claims, was reborn there. The second composition, the last and longest poem of *La selva di Diana*, is titled *Partenza da Roma dell'autrice nel 1647* ["The Author's Departure from Rome in 1647"] (p. 245). In this poem, Margherita bitterly complains that she was forced to leave her native city because she was ill-treated there, but she does not say how or why, blaming only her cruel destiny. She invites all mortals to learn from her example and to arm themselves against the blows of fortune. This autobiographical lament comprises, simultaneously, a generic complaint about life's negative side — everything is unstable, fragile, as Fortune mercilessly turns her wheel. Today's honors are tomorrow's horrors, respectfulness turns into disrespect. The higher one rises, the easier one falls to the ground. Joy leads only to sorrow. Hope only complicates life, for our existence is enclosed in a labyrinth, where serpents hide among the flowers. Margherita rightfully complains about her lot. Her difficulties were common to the lives of all artists of her period, especially singers and actors, considered immoral, and particularly artistic women

---

[76]The late Latin names were: *lunae dies, martis dies, mercuri dies*, etc., and were based on the names of the seven planets.

who, in order to promote their careers, frequently became mistresses of rich, powerful men. What set Margherita apart was her poetic calling with which she attempted to find protection. The poem *Partenza da Roma* also includes the theme of exile — not a political but a personal exile, in which the longing for a return to the native city is strongly felt. At the same time, the composition gives voice to a woman protesting her miserable condition — a single woman, singer and poet, taken advantage of and then condemned as immoral — who tries to survive in a man's world. The verses quoted below, taken from a poem from *La chitarra* (p. 388), illustrate a singer's suffering very well and are probably autobiographical. The sadness expressed in these lines, in a style akin to that of poets of the Romantic Period, makes them remarkable:

Quante volte sciogliei la voce al canto	How many times did I intone a song
che di pianger bramai le mie sventure,	while wanting to cry over my misfortunes,
e coi sospir miei rattenni il pianto,	and with my sighs I held back my tears,
sclamando le passate mie venture.	crying out my past adventures.
Ahi, quante volte il mio passato vanto	Oh, how often did I my past honor
mi ramentai fra scene così dure,	recall among such hard scenes,
e quante e quante volte in volto finsi	and how often did I depict content
d'esser contenta e la mia pena vinsi.	in my face, overcoming my pain.
Ridea la bocca e mi piangeva il core.	My mouth was laughing, crying was my heart.
Parlava la lingua, il mio desir tacea.	My tongue was speaking, my longing was silent.
Nel mio riso copriva il mio dolore,	With my laughter my sorrow I covered
e le miserie mie, saggia, ascondea.	and my miseries, smartly, I hid.

The reason why Margherita left Rome for the second time is to be found, I believe, in the fact that she lost the protection of Cardinal Francesco Barberini, because Pope Urban VIII died in 1644 and his nephews were forced to flee to Paris.[77] In her subsequent book, *La tromba di Parnaso* [The Trumpet of Parnassus], Margherita praises the Barberini family.

La tromba di Parnaso, dedicated to Queen Anne of France, comprises a collection of laudatory verses glorifying Anne as well as other members of the royal family and of the French court, especially Cardinal Mazarin. In one of the sonnets addressed to Mazarin, Margherita thanks him for helping her publish her books, referring to herself as *io Costa* [I, Costa, p. 257]. At the end of the volume, Margherita praises the composer Luigi Rossi, his librettist Francesco Buti and the singer Marc'Antonio Pasqualini[78] for the 1647 Paris performance of the opera *L'Orfeo* [Orpheus], in which she sang the part of the goddess Juno, and her sister, Anna Francesca, that of Eurydice. The poems reveal the ambiance of the French court of 1647 through a number of illustrious names, including the king of Po-

---

[77]See note 25.

[78]Antonio Pasqualini (1614–1691), the *castrato* singer, was protected by Cardinal Antonio Barberini. See *NGDMM* 19: 186–87.

land[79] and the queen of England.[80] Sandwiched between these two sections of encomiastic poems are the compositions dedicated to the Barberinis: first, a sonnet on the death of Urban VIII, then one on the death of his sister-in-law, Costanza Magalotti Barberini (who also receives ten additional *ottave*). Cardinal Francesco Barberini is honored with nineteen *ottave*, in which Margherita thanks him for his protection that enabled her to return to Rome in 1644. She implores his mercy as a penitent and mentions that he helped her brother become a soldier, and one of her sisters a nun, rescuing her from an unfortunate life. Margherita will therefore be forever grateful to him. Cardinal Antonio Barberini is thanked with twelve *ottave* for his gift of a gold necklace, upon her presentation to him of a copy of her *Cecilia martire*. These *ottave* are accompanied by a short prose invocation and eleven additional encomiastic octaves.

There follows a set of nine sonnets titled *Saetta prima, Saetta seconda*, etc. ["First Arrow," "Second Arrow," etc.] that, I believe, should be read keeping in mind Margherita's lamentation in *La selva di Diana*, except that the plaint is now applied to the Barberini case. According to Margherita, Urban VIII was respected while he remained in power — now dead, he is scorned and condemned by the vulgar people who deserve to be punished by God for their wickedness. Instead of criticizing Urban, people should be praying to God that the new pope be as pious a sage as was he (p. 265). In the "Ninth Arrow" Margherita utilizes the bees of the Barberini coat of arms to create an elaborate play on words associated with bees in order to glorify her protectors in whom she finds no fault.

The three-act play in verse, *Gli amori della Luna* [The Loves of the Moon Goddess, 1654], is Margherita's last publication. The work is dedicated to Georg Wilhelm, Ernst August, and Johann Friedrich, dukes of Brunswick-Lüneburg,[81] attesting to the poet's stay in Germany, for she mentions in her "Letter to the Reader" that she has not written in Italian for four years while living under a foreign sky. The theme revolves around Diana–Endymion, with a plot based on the rivalry between the two gods, Cupid and Somnus. Diana succumbs to the former, Endymion to the latter, creating a tension between Love and Sleep (or inaction), the two opposing forces commented upon by Sense and Reason. At the end of the play, Love triumphs, for Endymion's resistance falls at daybreak. Although the story of Endymion had reappeared in poetry during the Renaissance, Costa seems to have been the first in Italy to use the theme in a play, but no credit has been given to her in literary dictionaries listing works dealing with that subject. After her, the theme was used by Alessandro Guidi in his *Endimione*, a pastoral play written in 1688 in collaboration with Queen Christina of Sweden, and published in 1692 in a revised form. Pietro Metastasio's scenic serenade *Endimione* (1712), made the topic a popular

---

[79]The same who had invited Margherita, as a singer, to Poland. Wladyslaw IV Wasa (1595–1648), married, in 1645, Maria Luigia Gonzaga, who was under French protection. But he died soon after. See "Ladislao" in *EI* 20: 355–56 and Dulong 327.

[80]Henriette-Marie (1609–1669), sister of Louis XIII and wife of Charles I of England, found refuge with her children in the Louvre. See *LGE* 19: 1116–17 and Dulong 109 and 357–60.

[81]Not Lüneberg, as some critics write.

subject for operas.[82] In the twentieth century, the feminist writer Sibilla Aleramo returned to the theme with her one–act dramatic poem *Endimione* (1923). (One should recall here that Italian women writers contributed to all the various aspects of the theater during the seventeenth century — as actresses, singers, dancers, as writers of religious mysteries, pastoral plays, dramas, tragedies, tragicomedies, librettos for operas and oratorios, and as translators or adapters of Spanish plays for the Italian stage. Some of their works have only recently been studied while others still need to be examined by critics for their historical value.)

Margherita Costa wrote a lot and in a hurry. She made no effort to pare down her work by eliminating repetitions and stylistic imperfections. She adhered to the musical tradition, which permitted greater flexibility in poetry, but a number of the imperfections attributed to her are in fact printing errors. She was accused of composing too many laudatory poems for people of rank, with the hope of gaining favors and protection from them, but the accusation is not always valid, for she also wrote about people living far away or already dead, from whom she could gain nothing and who served only as a literary subject. In all her books, she hyperbolically and humorously stressed her ignorance. In *La chitarra*, for example, she declares that her thoughts corresponded for a while with the Muses, but were void of any talent, so that a deformed monster was born of her writing, comparable only to a crippled and misshaped dwarf. As previously mentioned, such declarations did not gain her the favor of critics, who interpreted them as ostentation, or flaunting, of her ignorance.

Margherita was not ignorant. Her verses betray a knowledge of the major Italian authors: Dante Alighieri, Francesco Petrarca, Ludovico Ariosto, Pietro Bembo, Giovanni della Casa, Francesco Berni, Torquato Tasso, as well as that of the seventeenth-century poets such as Ottavio Rinuccini, Giambattista Marino, Pier Francesco Paoli, Gabriello Chiabrera, Andrea Salvadori, Alessandro Adimari, and others. She was conversant with the Italian women poets that preceded her, and in one of her poems (p. 201), mentions Vittoria Colonna, Veronica Gambara and Margherita Sarrocchi as dwelling in Parnassus, though she hurriedly gives only a few names. She must have read Francesca Turini Bufalini's *Rime* [Verses, 1628], for her poems exhibit some thematic and linguistic similarities that betray such knowledge: the autobiographical complaint against fortune, the description of children using same or similar words (see the notes to the poems given in our anthology). She was conversant with classical mythology and used it frequently in an original way. She even made fun of some heroes of antiquity, as when she warns a desperate lover, ready to commit suicide, not to repeat "the blameworthy stupidity of Curtius" (*non rinnovare . . . / di Curzio la biasmata scioccheria*) of throwing himself into an abyss. Humor, often with a feminist twist, is one of her strong characteristics, as evidenced in examples given in this anthology, in which

---

[82]*DBdOdP* 3: 91–92.

she makes fun of men, either because of their infidelity or because of the restrictions they place on women. In her satire, she is merciless, as when she describes the life of a courtier — full of intrigues, lies, and betrayals — a life unsuitable for an honest person. When read carefully, Margherita's verses reveal original tendencies, both of content and style, as I hope to have demonstrated here in my selection from her vast oeuvre. Her poetic style is recognizable and enabled me to attribute to her an anonymous poem printed in Rome as a leaflet in 1672.[83] I also believe that the manuscript text of *Oh Dio, voi che mi dite,* a song for two voices by *signora Costa,* preserved in the Vatican Library (CHIGI Q. VIII. 177.9), is hers and not her sister's, as Capucci assumed.

According to some critics, Margherita Costa's literary production holds historical value as a documentation of seventeenth-century taste and as a source of information about her contemporaries. I believe, however, that a great number of her poems deserve to be read and studied for their Baroque peculiarities, their originality and their humor, which makes her a unique voice among the Italian women poets of the *Seicento.*

Giovanni Vittorio Rossi (1577–1647), who wrote under the name Necius Erythreus, in his laudatory chapter, in *Pinacotheca,* on the librettist Tronsarelli, records the information that *La catena d'Adone* was composed as a singing competition between Margherita Costa and her rival Cecca del Palude, whose nickname "del Palude" derived from the stagnant waters of the part of Rome where she lived. He claims that Margherita was more famous for her immoral life than for her singing,[84] and in his book *Eudemiae,* he brands her a prostitute, referring to her under the name *Pleura,*[85] a translation into Greek of "*costa*" [side].

Prospero Mandosio (1643–1724), on the other hand, in his *Bibliotheca romana,*[86] sees in Margherita a remarkable seventeenth-century writer versed in different literary genres and lists her books, some of which he owned. He dismisses Rossi's accusations as the malevolent comments of a famous slanderer and states that Margherita was respected by contemporary men of letters (whose names he lists), and even by Ferdinand II of Tuscany and by Cardinal Mazarin.

Similarly Giovanni Mario Crescimbeni, who did not appreciate the Baroque period, nevertheless praises Margherita in his *Comentarj* (1702–1711), describing her as an intelligent woman, well versed, who cultivated diverse literary genres, including the satire, with an ability which, according to him, surpassed that of some of her contemporaries. He concludes his short praise by transcribing a manuscript sonnet by Margherita, in which she states that she spent her best years in studious efforts [*studiose fatiche*] only to be reduced to misery, together with her two daugh-

---

[83]Costa-Zalessow 2010.
[84]p. 150.
[85]p. 86.
[86]pp. 26–28.

ters, by cruel fortune, and thus forced to seek help from a prince (recognizable as a Chigi from the reference to the stars of the Chigi coat of arms). The content of this sonnet corresponds to remarks made by Margherita in her letter to Mario Chigi in 1657.[87] Both of these manuscripts are now preserved in the Vatican Library.

Francesco Saverio Quadrio, writing some thirty years later, lists a selection of Margherita's works, and recalls that she was accused of immorality, though praised by Mandosio and Crescimbeni. Quadrio, however, finds no wisdom in Costa's verses.

Unfortunately, critics historically have been more interested in Margherita's personal "immoral" life than in her work, which they condemned for the many dedications and laudatory poems, and for her apparent self-effacement, interpreted as a personal insecurity of hers, rather than (and more correctly) a shortcoming of seventeenth-century literary stylistic manner.

Alessandro Ademollo, writing in the 1880s, traces some aspects of Margherita's singing career in Rome and in Turin, and her presence in Paris, with attention to her poems dedicated to composers, librettists and singers in *La tromba di Parnaso*. However, he defines her poems as "ugly Italian verses" [*brutti versi italiani*[88]]. Moreover, he considers her "an author of her own stuff and that of others" [*autrice di roba sua e non sua*[89]].

In 1924–1925, Dante Bianchi published a monograph on Margherita, in which he reconstructs her life, as far as possible, by examining the autobiographical references in her poems. Unfortunately, he makes no effort to understand her literary production, dismissing her oeuvre with a few negative remarks, commenting that "no composition is such as to arouse admiration" [*nessun componimento è tale da destare ammirazione*[90]]. He likewise declares that her poetry never improved, "the quality does not change" [*la qualità non varia*[91]], and that the "amount of her pages is completely void of poetic value" [*cotesta congerie di pagine è priva affatto di valor poetico*[92]]. He moreover opines that Margherita best be forgotten. Bianchi saw in Margherita one of the many typically Baroque poets writing on themes used by their predecessors. His comments must be taken as a criticism of Italian seventeenth-century poets in general, rather than only of Costa in particular. Bianchi did not bother to examine how Margherita differs from her contemporaries and thus failed to see her originality. (Not until the late twentieth century did Italian Baroque art and literature receive any serious attention.) Bianchi, however, did point out the affinities between Margherita's *Li buffoni* and the *Commedia dell'Arte*, especially in the peculiarities of some of the characters, their language, behavior, cross-dressing, and the singing, dancing, as well as caning that are common to both. Moreover, the play was written for a specific actor, Bernardino Ricci, *Il Tedeschino*, an unusual attribute.[93] Bianchi concludes his monograph with the hope that further research

---

[87]See Introduction, p. 24.
[88]Ademollo 1884, 37.
[89]*Ibid.*
[90]Bianchi 1924, 28n1.
[91]*Ibid.* 200.
[92]Bianchi 1925, 160.
[93]*Ibid.* 208–10.

on Margherita will be done in archives — a research that will shed light on the intriguing seventeenth-century social life.

Benedetto Croce, writing in the 1930s, considered the *Seicento* a decadent century that did not produce great works of a solid nature such as those of the *Cinquecento*. He dispatches Margherita with the words: "she stands out, above all, for her lack of culture, as she herself declares in very bad verses..." [*risplende soprattutto per la sua incultura, da lei stessa dichiarata in versacci*[94]], and illustrates his opinion with an example taken from the first *Capitolo scherzoso* of *La chitarra*, in which Margherita pokes fun at her limping verses. Croce never saw the humor in that quote, which he, moreover, derived from Bergalli's anthology[95] — not from the original text.

In 1986, Siro Ferrone included *Li buffoni* in his *Commedie dell'Arte*, a book of five plays, published between 1583 and 1641, by five different authors. Thus Margherita received the first modern edition of one of her works, a play which Ferrone interprets as a strange, eccentric, surrealistic comedy — a metaphor for the social and professional condition of actors forced to face the increasing popularity of the improvised *Commedia dell'Arte*.[96]

An important contribution to understanding Margherita's *Li buffoni* is that of Teresa Megale who, in 1988, published an article, "La commedia decifrata: metamorfosi e rispecchiamenti in *Li buffoni* di Margherita Costa," based on archival research done in the Florentine *Archivio di Stato*. Among the Medici documents, Megale discovered Benedetto Guerrini's[97] minutely detailed registry of court payments made to minor employees, that is, to coachmen, grooms, hunters, etc., including physically disabled persons, hunchbacks, dwarfs, deformed and mentally ill, who were kept at court because they were considered "funny." Guerrini's administrative document lists these unfortunate human beings with their deformity next to their names — deformities and names faithfully reproduced in Margherita's comedy. Only the parts of the princess (up to a certain point), of the prostitute[98] and of the female go-between, were invented by the playwright.[99] According to Megale, *Li buffoni* is a play with which Margherita intended to intervene in the general polemics on comic art and in particular to comment on that of Bernardino Ricci. More than a comedy, the work is an anti-comedy in which mockery prevails, accompanied by a dissimulated, playful parody of the court in which the action takes place. The play is a clever trick to disguise the parody of

---

[94]Croce 171.

[95]*Ibid.* 172.

[96]Ferrone 1: 43–44.

[97]Secretary to Ferdinand II, see note 20.

[98]It is intriguing that Margherita chose the name Ancroia for the prostitute, although that name had become synonymous with an ugly, filthy woman, as attributed in a poem by Berni to his servant (see Berni 190–91). Perhaps because Ancroia is close to *troia* [whore]. Originally it was the name of a Saracen queen in an anonymous fifteenth-century poem (see *DBdOdP* 7: 533).

[99]Megale 1988, 65–68.

the Medici court and the matrimonial difficulties of Vittoria della Rovere with her husband, Ferdinand II.[100]

Megale subsequently published two articles on Anna Francesca Costa, followed by the first modern edition of Ricci's book, *Il Tedeschino overo Difesa dell'Arte del Cavalier del Piacere*, for which she provides an ample introduction. These contributions by Megale greatly assist us in understanding Margherita's life and literary works.

Marcella Salvi's article, "'Il solito è sempre quello, l'insolito è più nuovo': *Li buffoni* e le prostitute di Margherita Costa fra tradizione e innovazione," published in 2004, offers more than what the title promises. Aside from examining the feminist tendencies of the prostitute, Ancroia, and her maid in *Li buffoni*, Salvi points out the rebellion of the princess Marmotta against her unfaithful husband, whom she is about to abandon in order to return to her native kingdom of Fessa where women enjoy great freedom and independence from their husbands. Salvi considers these themes to be an overturning, on the part of the play's author, of patriarchal rules governing women. Salvi arrives at the conclusion that Margherita's feminism, as expressed in her comedy, was due to her position as an outsider — a women writer, singer and courtesan trying to establish her place at court. Although Salvi does not mention Megale's contribution (most likely because she was not familiar with it), her interpretation does not contradict Megale's, because Margherita's feminism is present in many of her poems, as is evident in various examples offered in this anthology.

In her book *Women's Writing in Italy 1400–1650*, published in 2008, Virginia Cox briefly comments on Margherita Costa's works, stressing her peculiarities and Baroque extravagance. Cox gives dates of the poet's birth and death as "(1600–1664)"[101] without explaining where she found these precise dates unknown to others. Is it a discovery of new documents on her part or is it just a mistake? She also calls Margherita's narrative poem *Cecilia martire* "a miniature *poema sacro* of four *canti*."[102] Why "miniature"? Because it has only four cantos? But the four cantos comprise 151 pages and represent stylistically the four different phases of the saint's life. Moreover, in "Appendix A," Cox, under the year 1630, lists a *La Santa Cecilia* as published by Costa, adding "(+ 1644 in a revised version)."[103] Well, this work is certainly not Margherita's and her *Cecilia martire* is not a revised version of one of her earlier books. Cox also forgets to mention that Costa's narrative poem "the nine-canto *Flora feconda*" has an additional canto added on at the end, which makes a total of ten cantos. The dramatic version of this work is titled *La Flora feconda*[104] — Cox leaves out the article on p. 243 while she includes it on p. 384. The poem should precede the drama when given in order of publication. These imperfections create confusion — they don't do justice to Costa's work.

In 2010, Natalia Costa-Zalessow was able to attribute to Margherita an anonymous poem in defense of women, printed as a leaflet in 1672, in Rome, which she

---

[100]*Ibid*. 71–72.
[101]Cox 204.
[102]*Ibid*. 220.
[103]*Ibid*. 242.
[104]*Ibid*. 220.

discovered in *Biblioteca Nazionale di Roma,* catalogued under *Miscellanea* 34.0. I.1, n° 20). In the seven stanzas of this poem titled *Doralinda amazzone ai detrattori del valor delle dame: Disfida,* the author accuses men of being arrogant and of spreading lies in claiming that women are cowards. She, being an amazon, challenges them in order to prove *che nell'armi, non che nell'amore / ogni donna d'ogni uomo ha più valore*[105] [that in arms, not less than in love /a woman has more valor (courage) than a man]. By carefully examining the word choice and style of this composition and comparing them with the poetic characteristics of Margherita's published works, Costa-Zalessow concludes that the poem must have been written by Margherita.

Margherita Costa has by now been recognized as a noteworthy writer of her period. She is included in anthologies of Italian women writers edited by Bergalli in 1726, by Ronna in 1843, by de Blasi in 1930, by Costa-Zalessow in 1982, and by Morandini in 2001.[106] She has found a place in literary dictionaries, including the prestigious *Dizionario biografico degli Italiani* (entry by Martino Capucci, 1984) and the *Dictionary of Literary Biography,* Vol. 339: *Seventeenth-Century Italian Poets and Dramatists* (entry essay by Natalia Costa-Zalessow), that appeared in 2008. Margherita's comedy, *Li buffoni,* has received due critical attention along with a modern edition. It is my hope that this bilingual edition of her selected poems will offer readers the opportunity to judge for themselves her originality as a Baroque poet. The verses quoted after the title page of this anthology, in which Margherita declares that the truth about her life and work will certainly be revealed by time, have thus proven prophetic.

NATALIA COSTA-ZALESSOW

BIBLIOGRAPHIES

WORKS BY MARGHERITA COSTA
BOOKS
Istoria del viaggio d'Alemagna del serenissimo Gran Duca di Toscana Ferdinando Secondo. Venezia: n. d. (c. 1630).

La chitarra. Francfort: Daniel Wastch, 1638.

Il violino. Francfort: Daniel Wastch, 1638.

Lo stipo. Venezia: 1639.

Lettere amorose. Venezia: 1639. Reprints: Venezia: Turini, 1643 and 1652.

Flora feconda. Narrative poem. Firenze: Massi & Landi, 1640.

La selva di cipressi. Firenze: Massi & Landi, 1640.

La Flora feconda. Play. Firenze: Massi & Landi, 1640.

Li buffoni. Firenze: Massi & Landi, 1641. (Modern edition, 1986, ed. by Siro Ferrone, in his *Commedie dell'Arte.*)

Cecilia martire. Roma: Mascardi, 1644.

La selva di Diana. Parigi: Craimoisy, 1647.

---

[105]Costa-Zalessow 2010, 80.
[106]See Bibliographies, p. 45.

La tromba di Parnaso. Parigi: Craimoisy, 1647.
Festa reale per balletto a cavallo. Parigi: Craimoisy, 1647.
Gli amori della Luna. Venezia: Giuliani, 1654.

PAMPHLETS

Ottave per l'incendio dei Pitti. Poem. Firenze: Massi & Landi, 1638.
Al serenissimo Ferdinando II, Gran Duca di Toscana, per la festa di San Giov. Battista. Poem.
    Venezia: n. d.
*Al serenissimo principe Gio. Carlo di Toscana, per la carica di generaliss. del mare conferitagli
    dalla M. Cattolica.* Poem. Firenze: Massi & Landi, n. d.
Doralinda amazzone: Ai detrattori del valor delle dame: Disfida. Roma: Giuseppe Corvo, 1672.
    Printed as a leaflet. Poem attributed to M. Costa. (For attribution, see Costa-Zalessow 2010.)

MANUSCRIPTS

In: Biblioteca Apostolica Vaticana: *Cecilia martire* (BARB. LAT. 4069).
___. *Lettera a Mario Chigi* (CHIGI, I. VII.273.21).
___. *Poem: Oh Dio, voi che mi dite* (CHIGI, Q. VIII. 177.9).
Some poems from *Tromba di Parnaso* (CODICES FERRAJOLI 125. ff. 2^r–32^v and 128, pp.
    247–431).
In: Biblioteca Nazionale di Firenze: *Festa reale per balletto a cavallo.*

POEMS IN ANTHOLOGIES, PROSE SELECTIONS, OR WORKS IN COLLECTIONS IN
    CHRONOLOGICAL ORDER

Scielta di lettere amorose, includes a selection of Costa's *Lettere amorose.* Venezia: Bartoli,
    1656, and republished in 1659, 1662, 1671, 1675, 1683, 1687, in Venice by various.
Bergalli, Luisa, ed. *Componimenti poetici delle più illustri rimatrici d'ogni secolo.* Venezia:
    Mora, 1726. Part 2: 149–54.
Ronna, Antoine, ed. "Gemme o rime di poetesse italiane," in *Parnaso italiano: Poeti italiani
    contemporanei maggiori e minori.* Paris: Baudry, 1843, 2: 1025–27.
de Blasi, Jolanda, ed. *Antologia delle scrittrici italiane dalle origini al 1800.* Firenze: Nemi,
    1930. 334–41.
Costa-Zalessow, Natalia, ed. *Scrittrici italiane dal XIII al XX secolo: Testi e critica.* Ravenna:
    Longo, 1982. 146–52.
Ferrone, Siro, ed. *Commedie dell'Arte,* includes Costa's *Li buffoni.* Milano: Mursia, 1986. 2:
    233–359.
Morandini, Giuliana, ed. *Sospiri e palpiti: scrittrici italiane del Seicento.* Genova: Marietti,
    2001. 114–24.

EDITOR'S BIBLIOGRAPHY

Ademollo, Alessandro. *I primi fasti della musica italiana a Parigi (1645–1662).* Milano: Ri-
    cordi, 1884. 36–39.
___. *I teatri di Roma nel secolo decimosettimo.* Roma: Pasqualucci, 1888. 9 n., and 150.
Adimari, Alessandro. *La Tersicore.* Firenze: Massi & Landi, 1637. Modern edition: *Tersicore.*
    Ed. Paola Marongiu. Milano: Res, 2009.
AKL = Allgemeines Künstlerlexicon. München-Leipzig: Saur, 1994. 8: 424–26.

Alone, Roberto. "Tensione tematica e tensione formale in alcune commedie del Seicento." *Studi secenteschi* 12 (1971): 86–87.

Bailey (Bayley), Harold. *The Lost Language of Symbolism*. London: Benn, 1957. 1: 232–33.

Basso, Alberto, ed. *Dizionario enciclopedico universale della musica e dei musicisti: I titoli e i personaggi*. Torino: UTET, 1999. 2: 485–86.

Bellesi, Sandro. *Cesare Dandini*. Torino: Artema, Compagnia di Belle Arti, 1996.

Berni, Francesco. *Rime*. Ed. Danilo Romei. Milano: Mursia, 1985.

Bertière, Simone. *Mazarin le maître de jeu*. Paris: Èditions de Fallois, 2007.

Bettella, Patrizia. *The Ugly Woman: Transgressive Aesthetic Models in Italian Poetry from the Middle Ages to the Baroque*. Toronto: U of Toronto P, 2005.

Bianchi, Dante. "Una cortigiana rimatrice del Seicento: Margherita Costa." *Rassegna critica della letteratura italiana* 29 (1924): 1–31, 187–203; and 30 (1925): 158–211.

Borroni Salvadori, Fabia. *Stefano della Bella illustratore di libri*. Firenze: Biblioteca Nazionale Centrale Firenze, 1976 (Catalogue of the Exhibition held at the Library from Jan. to Apr. 1976).

Brosius, Amy. " 'Il suono, lo sguardo, il canto': The Function of Portraits of Mid-Seventeenth-Century *virtuose* in Rome." *Italian Studies* 63.1 (2008): 16–39.

Capucci, Martino. "Costa Margherita." *Dizionario biografico degli Italiani*. Roma: Enciclopedia Treccani, 30 (1984): 232–34.

Castelletti, Sebastiano. *La trionfatrice Cecilia, vergine e martire romana*. Roma: Stamperia Vaticana, 1724.

Costa, Gustavo. *La leggenda dei secoli d'oro nella letteratura italiana*. Bari: Laterza, 1972.

Costa-Zalessow, Natalia. "Italy as a Victim: A Historical Appraisal of a Literary Theme." *Italica* 45.2 (1968): 216–40.

___. "The Personification of Italy from Dante through the Trecento." *Italica* 68.3 (1991): 316–31.

___. "Fragments from an Autobiography: Petronilla Paolini Massimi's Struggle for Self-Assertion." *Italian Quarterly* 38.147–48 (2001): 27–35.

___. "Margherita Costa." *Dictionary of Literary Biography*, Vol. 339: *Seventeenth-Century Italian Poets and Dramatists*. Ed. Albert N. Mancini and Glenn Palen Pierce. Bruccoli Clark Layman, 2008. 113–18.

___. "Una poesia femminista del 1672 anonima e dimenticata, da attribuire a Margherita Costa." *Esperienze letterarie* 35.4 (2010): 79–85.

Couëtoux, Sophie. "La *vagezza* d'une chanteuse: dans l'intimité du 'Portrait de Checca Costa' par Cesare Dandini." *Revue des Études Italiennes*. New Series. 45.1–2 (1999): 95–107.

Cox, Virginia. *Women's Writing in Italy 1400–1650*. Baltimore: Johns Hopkins UP, 2008.

Crescimbeni, Giovanni Mario. *Dell'istoria della volgar poesia e Comentarj intorno alla medesima*. Venezia: Basegio, 1730. 3: 202.

Croce, Benedetto. "Donne letterate nel Seicento." *Nuovi saggi sulla letteratura italiana del Seicento*. Napoli: Bibliopolis, 2003. 165–82.

DBdOdP = Dizionario Bompiani delle opere e dei personaggi di tutti i tempi e di tutte le letterature. Milano: Bompiani, 1983.

DBI = Dizionario biografico degli Italiani. Roma: Istituto della Enciclopedia Italiana, 1960–.

de Blasi, Jolanda. *Le scrittrici italiane dalle origini al 1800*. Firenze: Nemi, 1930.

DEdLI = Dizionaro enciclopedico della letteratura italiana. Ed. Giuseppe Petronio. Palermo:

Laterza UNEDI, 1966–1970.

Demuth, Norman. *French Opera: Its Development to the Revolution*. Sussex: The Artemis Press, 1963. 64–69.

De Vesme, Alexandre. *Stefano della Bella. Catalogue Raisonné*. Introduction and Additions by Phyllis Dearborn Massar. New York: Collectors Editions, 1971. Vol. 1: Text; Vol. 2: Plates.

Dolfi, Pompeo Scipione. *Cronologia delle famiglie nobili di Bologna*. Bologna: Ferroni, 1670.

DSI = *Dizionario storico dell'Inquisizione*. Ed. Adriano Prosperi. Pisa: Edizioni della Normale, 2010.

Dulong, Claude. *Mazarin*. Paris: Librairie Académique Perrin, 1999.

EB = *Encyclopaedia Britannica*. Chicago: 1973.

EdS = *Enciclopedia dello Spettacolo*. Roma: Le Maschere, 1954–1966. 3: 1555–1556.

EI = *Enciclopedia italiana*. Roma: Treccani, 1933.

Gigli, Giacinto. *Diario romano (1608–1670)*. Ed. Giuseppe Ricciotti. Roma: Tumminelli, 1958. 242.

Index librorum prohibitorum: 1600–1966. Ed. J. M. De Bujanda and Marcella Richter. Centre d'Études de la Renaissance, Université de Sherbrooke. Montréal: Médiaspaul, 2002.

Jombert, Charles Antoine. *Essai d'un catalogue de l'oeuvre d'Etienne de La Belle, peintre et graveur florentine*. Paris: Chez l'Auteur, 1772.

Kemp, Christopher. *Floating Gold: A Natural (and Unnatural) History of Ambergris*. Chicago: The U of Chicago P, 2012.

La Marca, Nicola. *La nobiltà romana e i suoi strumenti di perpetuazione del potere*. Roma: Bulzoni, 2000.

LGE = *La Grande Encyclopédie: Inventaire raisonné de sciences, des lettres et des arts*. Paris: Lamirault, 1886–1902. 19: 1116–17.

Litta, Pompeo. *Famiglie celebri italiane*. Milano: Ferrario, 1839–1840. See "Massimo di Roma, Parte II," in (1840): Fasci. XLV, dispensa 74, tavola VII.

Mamone, Sara. *Serenissimi fratelli principi impresari: Notizie di spettacolo nei carteggi medicei: Carteggi di Giovan Carlo de' Medici e di Desiderio Montemagni suo segretario (1628–1664)*. (Storia dello Spettacolo, Collana diretta da Siro Ferrone, FONTI 3). Firenze: Casa Editrice Le Lettere, 2003.

Mandosio, Prospero. *Bibliotheca romana seu romanorum scriptores centuriae*. Romae: Francisci de Lazaris, filij Ignatij, 1692. Vol. 2.

Marino, Giovan Battista. *La lira*. Ed. Maurizio Slawinski. Torino: Edizioni RES, 2007. 2: 98–102.

Mazzuchelli, Giammaria. *Gli scrittori d'Italia*. Brescia: Bossini, 1750. 2, 2: 1270–71.

Megale, Teresa. "La commedia decifrata: metamorfosi e rispecchiamenti in Li Buffoni di Margherita Costa." *Il Castello di Elsinore* (Quadrimestrale di teatro), 2 (1988): 64–76.

____. "Il principe e la cantante, riflessi impresariali di una protezione." *Medioevo e Rinascimento* 6. 3 (1992): 221–33.

____. "Altre novità su Anna Francesca Costa e sull'allestimento dell'Ergirodo." *Medioevo e Rinascimento* 7.4 (1993): 137–42.

____, ed. Ricci, Bernardino. *Il Tedeschino overo Difesa dell'Arte del Cavalier del Piacere, con l'Epistolario e altri documenti*. (Storia dello Spettacolo, Collana diretta da Siro Ferrone, FONTI 2). Firenze: Casa Editrice Le Lettere, 1995.

Melville, Herman. *Moby Dick*. New York: The Modern Library (Random House), 1950.

Negri, Giulio. *Istoria degli scrittori fiorentini.* Ferrara: Pomatelli, 1722.

NGDMM = The New Grove Dictionary of Music and Musicians. Second Edition, 2001.

Panizza, Letizia and Sharon Wood, eds. *A History of Women's Writing in Italy.* Cambridge: Cambridge UP, 2000. 49–50, 53, and 139.

Papa, Francesco. *Un cardinale di nome Giulio: Il Mazzarino.* Firenze: Atheneum, 2007.

Petrarca, Francesco. *Le Rime* in *Rime Trionfi e Poesie latine.* Ed. F. Neri, G. Martellotti, E. Bianchi, e N. Sapegno. Milano: Ricciardi, 1951. 1–477.

Quadrio, Francesco Severino. *Della storia e della ragione d'ogni poesia.* Milano: Agnelli, 1739–1749. 2: 310.

Rendina, Claudio. *Le grandi famiglie di Roma.* Roma: Newton & Compton, 2004.

Rossi, Giovanni Vittorio (Nicius Erythreus). *Eudemiae libri decem.* Coloniae Ubiorum: Apud Iodocum Karcovium & Socios, 1645.

____. *Pinacotheca.* Coloniae Ubiorum: Apud Odocum Kalcovium, 1648. 3: 147–52.

Russell, Rinaldina, ed. *Italian Women Writers: A Bio-Bibliographical Source Book.* Westport, CT: Greenwood Press, 1994.

____. *The Feminist Encyclopedia of Italian Literature.* Westport, CT: Greenwood Press, 1997.

Salvi, Marcella. "'Il solito è sempre quello, l'insolito è più nuovo': *Li buffoni* e le prostitute di Margherita Costa fra tradizione e innovazione." *Forum Italicum* 38.2 (2004): 376–99.

Sarrocchi, Margherita. *La Scanderbeide.* Roma: Facij, 1606.

Sophocles. *Ajax* in *Electra and Other Plays.* Ed. and trans. David Raeburn. London: Penguin Classics, 2008. 73–123.

Spetri, Vittorio, ed. *Enciclopedia storico-nobiliare italiana,* with *Appendice Parte I–II.* Bologna: Forni, 1928–1935.

Turini Bufalini, Francesca. *Autobiographical Poems: A Bilingual Edition.* Ed. Natalia Costa-Zalessow. Translations by Joan E. Borrelli. New York: Bordighera Press, 2009.

Zolla, Elémire. *The Androgyne: Reconciliation of Male and Female.* New York: Crossroad, 1981.

Zucchini, Maria Cecilia. "Nota all'edizione," in Domenico Mazzocchi, *La catena d'Adone.* Venezia: Vincenti, 1626, Reprint Bologna: Forni, 1969.

TRANSLATOR'S FOREWORD

The verse of Margherita Costa is imbued with the zeitgeist of the Italian Baroque and the influence of its poets — the *marinisti,* or Marinists — followers of Giambattista Marino (1569–1625) who opposed the classical Petrarchan tradition that had dominated poetic production throughout the Renaissance. Seeking a dramatic shift in technique, the Marinists emphasized the use of exotic metaphor, hyperbole, antithesis, alliteration, consonance, assonance, wordplay and witticism to create what Marino defined as '*meraviglia,*' or the 'marvel' of surprise/wonder/awe, for the reader. Like their contemporaries in the fine arts (Caravaggio and Bernini), these poets sought to draw the audience into the action of the art form and, towards that end, introduced new themes and aesthetic definitions aimed at engaging reader involvement. *Seicento* poetry thus embraces a wide variety of subject matter, poetic conceit and prosodic novelty.

Margherita's verse challenges the translator to capture its Baroque attributes and, at the same time, to preserve the poet's unique voice through the various metric forms she employs. In our anthology, these include mainly the sonnet, the *ottava rima* stanza, the *canzonetta* and the idyll. (Margherita titles several sections of her works with the term '*capitolo,*' which traditionally describes a poem in *terza rima* — as that of Dante's *Divina Commedia* — a rhyme scheme originally used for allegorical or moral poetry, and later adopted during the Renaissance for Italian satirical poetry. Her *capitolo,* however, alternatively comprises stanzas in *ottava rima.*) While Margherita adheres to the meter and end-rhyme patterns of imitative forms well established by the seventeenth century within the Italian literary tradition, her skillful use of internal rhyme, alliteration, consonance and assonance, and her deft manipulation of tone allow her to enhance the affective strength of an individual poem.

As a poetic invention, the sonnet is attributed to Giacomo da Lentini (c. 1215–c. 1250), who flourished within the Sicilian School of poets during the first half of the thirteenth century. Perfected and made popular by Francesco Petrarca (1304–1374), the form was much prized and imitated throughout the Renaissance (and beyond), first in Italy and later in France, Spain and England. In her use of the Petrarchan sonnet, Margherita conforms to the structure codified by Pietro Bembo (1470–1547) — fourteen lines, each in *endecasillabi* (eleven syllables), the first eight lines grouped into two *quartine,* or quatrains, to form two stanzas of four lines each, with a fixed end rhyme of ABBA + ABBA or ABAB + ABAB; the remaining six lines divided into two *terzine,* or tercets, of three lines each, in which the poet is allowed a more liberal end-rhyme pattern. (During the Renaissance, no deviation was acceptable within the rigid rhyme scheme of the quatrains.) Although Margherita accepts Bembo's model, one need only compare a few of her sonnets to realize her accomplishment in achieving startlingly different registers of emotion from poem to poem. In "On the Death of Giovanni Vidoni" (pp. 68–69) from *La chitarra,* for example, she evokes the leaden affect brought about by grief, conveyed through consonant-laden lines, an alliterative "d," and the repetition of the syllable "on" to echo the surname of the deceased and to suggest, through an assonant "o," the mourner's accompanying sighs. Conversely, her witty

"Beautiful Woman to Her Lover Who Would Throw Himself into the River" (pp. 76–79) and "To the Same Lover" (pp. 78–79), both from *La chitarra,* display Margherita's *sprezzatura,* her haughty confidence in her abilities to conquer hearts. The language of these sonnets, peppered with colloquial expressions together with an air of flirtatious familiarity towards the lover and his histrionic threats of suicide, draws the reader into the game of courtship and its affectations while simultaneously conveying Margherita's recognition of the duplicity of the courtier and his penchant to 'fib.' In "Fifth Arrow" (pp. 262–65) from *La tromba di Parnaso,* Margherita rails with righteous indignation against political power-brokering, building drama into the sonnet with her direct address to a personified Rome and with her call to the ancient Greco-Roman goddess of justice, Astrea, to mete out death as would the deus ex machina of classical tragedy. These examples offer only a sample of many strategies cleverly adopted within the sonnets and throughout Margherita's oeuvre so that the voice of her poetic 'I' might range across the scale of human emotion — from sorrow and despair to flirtation and frivolity, from serious admonition to teasing irony (especially when advising other women on the pitfalls of love), from self-indulgent lament (in blaming her misfortunes on a star-crossed Destiny) to objective self-scrutiny (in naming her outspoken verse as a likely cause for her reduced circumstances). The skill with which she achieves such range is moreover obvious in her use of *ottava rima.*

Although some evidence of the *ottava* may be found in Italian poetry before the *Trecento,* Giovanni Boccaccio (1313–1375) elevated and defined the form for narrative verse with his *Filostrato* (c. 1335–1339), considered the first literary work in *ottava rima.* The form realized its perfection with the *Orlando furioso* (1516) of Ludovico Ariosto (1474–1533) and the works of Torquato Tasso (1544–1595). The metrics of the *ottava* require lines of eleven syllables arranged in eight-line stanzas with end rhyme of ABABABCC. Within this fixed pattern, Margherita proves adept in shaping the tone of her poem to fit its content. The strength of her *ottave* can be felt, I believe, in her sensitivity to sound in choosing vocabulary for a desired effect and in her successful use of prosodic devices to vary the tonal properties of the text — talents that free her long works from monotonous rhythm that may otherwise deaden the reading. Margherita's *ottave* record a variety of her lived experience: her despair over an unwanted pregnancy in "Woman, Far from Her Lover Tirsi" (pp. 58–61) from *La chitarra;* her anguish in discovering her wounded husband in "Tirsi Stabbed" (pp. 180–89) from *La selva di cipressi;* her reverence for and deference before nobility in "The Alps: To the Royal Lady of Savoy" (pp. 224–25) and in "From the Honors Received in Paris" (pp. 244–45) both from *La selva di Diana;* her pure enjoyment of song and vocal improvisation in "To Lavinia Buratti" (pp. 226–29) from *La selva di Diana;* her piety before religious sacrifice (throughout *Cecilia martire*); her cold-eyed appraisal of her life, literary fortune and the politics of the times in "Hapless Elisa" (pp. 188–203) from *La selva di cipressi* and elsewhere throughout her works. To create formal tone, Margherita often employs within her introductory stanzas an invocation to the Muse — as in *Cecilia martire* (p. 204) — to elevate and to refine her poetic 'instrument.' To that end, she likewise utilizes anaphora — the repetition of a word or phrase at the beginning of each line or stanza — as in "To the Queen of France" (pp. 254–55) from *La tromba di Parnaso*. To convey serious intent, she frequently relies on alliteration and consonance — as with the extraordinary line "*donna danno, dolor, doglia predice*" (p. 157) in "Woman, Despairing Over Her Lost Beauty" (pp. 154–65) from *Lo stipo*. To sustain reader interest, long poems are punctuated by antitheses, often contrasting metaphors or imagery in unexpected juxtapositions of light with dark or fire with ice, to achieve chiaroscuro coloration. Rhetorical devices also add dimension to Margherita's *ottave* in building suspense and hastening the action from stanza to stanza, thus encouraging reader participation. For example, interjections and spoken monologue break the surface of the narrative and lend immediacy and an element of surprise — both when the autobiographical 'I' expresses doubt about personal motives and actions, or pleads with Fortune for aid — and when the 'I' represents another speaker, as when Almachius orders his henchman to behead Cecilia (pp. 216–19) from *Cecilia martire: Canto II,* or when the saint herself invites the flaming waters and venomous monsters to torture her the more, so that she may earn her place with God (pp. 214–17) from *Cecilia martire: Canto I*. Dialogue is employed to heighten dramatic effect — as in the exchanges in "Tears of the Alp" (pp. 172–81) from *La selva di cipressi,* where a personified Italy, Alp, and the rivers Dora and Po denounce to one another the carnage of war and its damage to their natural environments.

In a lighter vein, Margherita adopts the *canzonetta* to amuse the reader, often with pungent observations of the vagaries of love. The Italian *canzonetta*, literally 'little song,' traces its origins to the Sicilian School of poetry, but is also closely allied to the secular vocal piece of the same name, both rising to great popularity during the last two decades of the sixteenth century. Unlike the sonnet or the *ottava*, with their fixed metrical and end-rhyme requirements, the *canzonetta* as a metric form allows the poet freedom to vary meter by alternating *versi brevi*, or 'short lines' — those from three to seven syllables — with *versi lunghi*, or 'long lines' — those from eight to eleven syllables — and to place rhymed and unrhymed lines in no fixed pattern. Italian *canzonetta* poetry of the *Seicento* is heavily influenced by the verse of Gabriello Chiabrera (1552–1638), who revived the Sicilian form and also drew inspiration to fashion new models for his *canzonetta* from the works of the French Pléiade poets of the Renaissance and from classical literature — his aim to create a simple verse form that would invite musical accompaniment and that could be sung. Margherita's canzonets display her versatility in achieving delightful and humorous poems that may easily be set to music, as was often done during the *Seicento* with poems in this genre. The canzonets selected here from *Il violino* (pp. 130–35) are filled with the poet's playful spirit. Others, however, as in the selections from *La chitarra* (pp. 86–91), carry a serious message beneath the apparent humor. In "To Lovers" (pp. 86–89), for example, Margherita presents a short poem of three strophes, each strophe comprising four short lines [*versi brevi*] followed by a rhyming couplet in hendecasyllabic lines [*versi lunghi*] — an end rhyme of abbaCC. While the short lines indicate the dangers of falling in love, the final couplets, with their greater syllabic length, hammer home a pragmatic warning about the personal cost of amorous entanglements. Especially noteworthy is "To Women" (pp. 88–91), which employs a final couplet to chime with the word '*filare*' positioned as the last word of each strophe. The insis-

tence of that final infinitive injects the tonal device of irony — one of Margherita's
signature strengths — where the true message of the poem lies beneath the words to
contradict what is actually stated. I find this *canzonetta* exceptional in its successful
fusion of form with content, its rhyme and meter mocking and overturning, with
sparkling wit, an entrenched male viewpoint of the time — that women are put on
the earth solely 'to spin.'

In composing her idyll, Margherita would have been fully conversant with
those of Giambattista Marino's *La Sampogna* (1620), a work comprised of idylls
on mythological and pastoral topics. The form mixes lines of *endecasillabi* [eleven
syllables], *settenari* [seven syllables], and *quinari* [five syllables], organized freely
in stanzas of no fixed pattern. End rhyme is left to the poet's discretion, and lines
may be rhymed or unrhymed. Within the classical tradition, the idyll describes a
bucolic setting — its tranquil, innocent, 'idyllic' life sentimentally invoked and un-
folding in a dreamlike atmosphere. Margherita, however, utilizes this metric form
to convey much different subject matter, even to encompass aspects of human suf-
fering. Most effective is "Beautiful Woman to Other Women" (pp. 84–87) from *La
chitarra*. Here, Margherita's autobiographical 'I' achieves an irony more trenchant
than that enforcing her sonnet of the same title (pp. 82–85) or her *canzonetta* "To
Women" (pp. 88–91), and deeply derides societal pressure on women to find their
purpose within the domestic circle. Autobiographical themes embedded within the
idylls from *Il violino* likewise achieve strong emotional registers. In "Gift of Her
Poems to Ferdinand" (pp. 92–95), for example, Margherita vocalizes her struggle
up from lowly beginnings, her passion to write and her humility about her po-
etic accomplishment. In "Woman Lamenting Her Dead Lover" (pp. 122–25) and
in "Mother to Her Daughter Fallen Ill" (pp. 124–31), she reveals painful feelings
of powerlessness in the face of life's harsh but inevitable blows. Most unusual is her
"Mother to a Son Born Female and Then Changed to Male" (pp. 116–23) which,
as Costa-Zalessow suggests, carries the poet's feminist protest that the child pos-
sessed of male, not female, gender is promised the more fortunate life. In her use
of the idyll, Margherita additionally experiments with a poetic 'I' that embodies a
male persona. She is preceded in this endeavor by Laura Terracina (1519–c. 1577)
and by Isabella Andreini (1562?–1604), celebrated actress of the commedia dell'arte
— the first Italian female poets to adopt a male voice and point of view within
their works. In "The Rape of Lilla" (pp. 98–109), we hear from the rapist himself,
who excuses his violent act because of the irresistible beauty of the 'nymph.' Here,
the purported 'idyllic' setting is unmasked to reveal, in a present-tense descrip-
tion, the blow-by-blow assault. In "The Lover of an Ugly Woman" (pp. 108–15), the
male speaker's preposterous declarations unveil the distortion of reality in viewing
woman as object. In "Her Lover, Having Seen Her Letter to Another" (pp. 94–99),
extreme statements of blame by the jealous male disclose his underlying misogyny
and his equation of woman with personal property, if but 'deadly merchandise.'

The meter and end rhyme of the various lyric genres employed by Margherita
serve to endow her poems with a musicality that is further enhanced by her atten-
tion to the entire soundscape of her text. An accomplished and sought-after *vir-
tuosa*, she would undoubtedly have brought a trained ear to the composition of her

written works. In rendering her poetry into English, I have felt it exceedingly important, therefore, to attend to the very musical quality of her verse. While keeping a close eye on content, I have likewise kept an ear attuned to the aural properties of the Italian original and have sought to capture some aspect of its musicality within the translated version.

The Italian word 'sonetto' (a derivation of the Provençal 'sonet,' diminutive of 'son'), once signified 'melody' or a poem accompanied by music. Although destined to shed its musical component, the sonnet as a poetic form — with its strict metrical and end-rhyme pattern — continues to create a kind of music in words and challenges the translator in several ways: to recreate the fixed end-rhyme pattern of the *quartine,* to find full-rhyme sound equivalents for the Italian's full end-rhyme sounds, and to reproduce regular meter. In rendering Margherita's sonnets into English, I have first attempted to recreate the ABBA + ABBA end-rhyme pattern utilized in most of her *quartine.* Where not possible, I have alternatively utilized the ABAB + ABAB pattern, also acceptable as a rhyme scheme for the *quartine* during the *Seicento.* In translating her *terzine,* I have taken the liberty to stray from the original's end-rhyme pattern while yet producing a consistent rhyme for the translation and one that would have been acceptable in Margherita's day. When challenged in reproducing the original's full end-rhyme sound, I have sought a slant rhyme for my English counterpart. In doing so, I hoped to suggest some of the original soundscape. To reproduce meter, I have employed an eleven-syllable line, if possible, to respect the Italian *endecasillabi,* but have more frequently utilized a ten-syllable line in iambic pentameter, preferred in English poetry. Because the Italian hendecasyllabic line always stresses its tenth or penultimate syllable, the ten-syllable English line, which stresses its last syllable, closely reproduces the rhythm of the Italian from line to line.

In approaching the translation of Margherita's *ottava rima* stanza, my objective, as with the sonnet, has been to preserve the resonance of the original and the pleasure that rhyme and meter afford to the ear. I have therefore consistently adhered to the stanza's end-rhyme requirements of ABABABCC, relying on slant rhyme to suggest the full end-rhyme sounds of the original. In reproducing meter, I have alternated eleven-syllable with ten-syllable lines, which I feel blend easily together to sustain rhythm. This practice allowed me to keep close watch on content while still retaining important prosodic features of the source text within the English version.

Margherita's *canzonette* present the translator with a further challenge: to capture the particularities of their end rhyme and meter as these change from strophe to strophe and from poem to poem. In translating her *canzonette,* I have held closely to the end-rhyme pattern of the originals. To reproduce meter, and to distinguish in the English translation the long lines [*versi lunghi*] from the short [*versi brevi*], I have first attempted to match the syllabic line lengths of the original. If not possible, I have sought a meter in English to suggest these variations. Where the original text employs a hendecasyllabic line, I have consistently reproduced in English either an eleven-syllable or ten-syllable line. For the short lines of the original text, I have employed in most instances a line of eight syllables or shorter in English. Thus, although some lines of the translation do not meet the exact definition of *versi brevi* (lines from three to seven syllables), they indicate to the reader of English the position of short lines within the Italian text.

My approach to the translation of Margherita's idyll has been similar to that towards her *canzonetta*. As a poetic genre, the idyll leaves end-rhyme pattern to the discretion of the poet, and rhymed and unrhymed lines are likewise permissible. Line length may vary, as well, from line to line and from stanza to stanza. In translating this verse form, I have held in almost all cases to the end-rhyme patterns of the source text. In reproducing meter, I have employed either an eleven-syllable or ten-syllable line in English to represent the use of *endecasillabi* in the source. To reproduce *settenari,* I have employed, wherever possible, a seven-syllable line and, where not possible, I have employed in nearly all instances either a six-syllable or eight-syllable line in English. For the *quinari* or five-syllable lines of the source, which I found most difficult to replicate in English, I have first attempted to create a line length shorter than six syllables and, if not possible, have settled on a six- to eight-syllable line.

I have likewise endeavored to capture within the English translation other prosodic devices that often feature in particular lines or stanzas of the original — such as those of alliteration, consonance and assonance. As alliteration and consonance are hallmarks of Margherita's works, I have given these my closest attention. My first priority in reproducing alliteration has been to replicate within the target text the same consonant employed by Margherita. For example, to recreate the bold onomatopoeia of her sonnet "To a Lover Departing the City in Pouring Rain" (pp. 238–39) from *La selva di Diana* — with its alliterative "p" mimicking the patter of raindrops — I have made onomatopoeia the prominent feature of the translation, positioning the sound of "p" within the target text close to where it appears within the source. If unable, in other poems, to utilize the exact consonant employed in the original, I have substituted another within the translation in order to mark for alliteration or to suggest the overall consonance within a line or a stanza. Because I find assonance more difficult to reproduce, I have replicated vowel sounds only where the original shows purposeful use of the device.

To preserve some of Margherita's syntactic nuance, and to move my translation closer to the source text, I have allowed word order inversion — such as verb-noun or noun-adjective placements — into my English counterpart. I have also attempted to recreate, where possible, Margherita's use of internal rhyme (when two or more words rhyme within a single line of verse), as well as her use of crossed rhyme (when words in the middle of each line cross over to rhyme with those in the middle of another) — devices which echo the Baroque predilection for complex patterns of sound. In making these translation decisions, I wished to create for the Anglophone reader a subtle reminder of the historical context of Margherita's poetry within the Western canon.

The verse of Margherita Costa presents us with a marvelous kaleidoscope of emotion — gaiety, pride, erotic desire, despair, hope, lament, piety, remorse, anger and many other aspects of mood including those of self-reflection and self-scrutiny. Projected through the prism of her poetry is a composite picture of a singular, albeit multi-faceted personality. Margherita allows her reading audience — and we are her first in almost four hundred years to enjoy selections from all of her books of verse — to enter into her experience as a woman of various roles: *virtuosa,* courtesan, sister, lover, wife, mother and, above all, writer attempting to achieve recognition and respect for that endeavor. Margherita's poetic 'I' gives voice to her energetic spirit as she engages with her times and with personal struggles. Through her sorrowful as well as her joyful tones, we recognize bravery as well as vulnerability. It is my hope that this first translation of Margherita's work might serve the poet's own hope: that through her writings we may come to know her 'feelings, loves and deeds' and the truth of what must certainly have been a most remarkable life.

JOAN E. BORRELLI

NOTE ON THE ITALIAN TEXT

The text of the poems is based on Margherita Costa's books of verse, published between 1638 and 1647, of which no modern editions exist. All obvious printing errors were eliminated from the original text. The punctuation, accents, and apostrophes were updated. The spelling was made uniform and modernized. Double consonants were eliminated where unnecessary, as in *viddi > vidi.* Single consonants were doubled as in *fabro > fabbro,* as needed. The unnecessary letter *h* was eliminated. The Latin *t* was changed to *z,* as in *gratioso > grazioso,* and *et > ed.* The use of prepositions with definite articles was made uniform where possible: Margherita uses all possibilities: *a'l* and *al, a i, ai* or *a', a gli, agli,* and *agl'* (before all vowels). She uses *lo, i, li,* and *gli,* not according to modern standards, but as needed to achieve the required count of syllables. These characteristics were common among her contemporaries. Some of the long, descriptive titles of her poems were shortened.

POEMS by MARGHERITA COSTA
Selected from Seven of Her Books

THE GUITAR (1638)

THE VIOLIN (1638)

THE CABINET (1639)

THE CYPRESS GROVE (1640)

THE MARTYR CECILIA (1644)

DIANA'S WOODS (1647)

THE TRUMPET OF PARNASSUS (1647)

POESIE di MARGHERITA COSTA
Scelte da sette dei suoi libri

LA CHITARRA (1638)

IL VIOLINO (1638)

LO STIPO (1639)

LA SELVA DI CIPRESSI (1640)

CECILIA MARTIRE (1644)

LA SELVA DI DIANA (1647)

LA TROMBA DI PARNASO (1647)

FROM: *THE GUITAR* (1638)

FROM: CAPITOLI

Woman, Far from Her Lover Tirsi, and Pregnant
. . . .

    Thus in my womb, this memento in place,
formed from your viscera and my delight,
loosens my rein on tears, lets pain increase,
has me scatter my words to the winds' flight.
When I think he, in sweeter ambience,
should greet his trials and toils, his own by right,
I weep for the innocent's anguished life,
for my distress, for yours, his father's strife.

    I am disturbed, while I yearn for this boy,
to have to give birth to him on this soil;
a new Ascanio, mid fires of Troy,
denied by you his every good by will.
I pray that on my breast, newborn, he'll die
so I'll not see him bound in greater ill,
and when, oh God, within my womb I feel him,
child do I call him of my every harm.

    Ah, what misfortune and what bitter fate
makes me mother to misfortunate son?
What pleased the Heavens to alter my state?
What luck, bent on my peril, led me on?
Oh poor innocent, you are born for what?
To counsel you in life, who'll be the one?
Your mother leaves you, proves to be your rebel.
From father you're cut off by a star cruel.

    Unhappy orphan, where then are they gone,
those things of grandeur you would gladly know?

DA: *LA CHITARRA* (1638)

DAI: CAPITOLI

Donna all'amante Tirsi, lontana da lui e gravida[1]
. . . .
        Il pegno poi, ch'è posto nel mio seno,
delle viscere tue, dei miei contenti,
m'acresce il duol e scioglie al pianto il freno
e fa ch'io sparga le mie voci ai venti.
E se poi penso che in altro sereno
dovrà godersi i propri danni e stenti,
dell'innocente piango il crudo affanno,
le mie miserie e di te padre il danno.
        Pargoletto lo bramo e poi m'annoia[2]
d'averlo a partorir su queste arene[3]
qual nuovo Ascanio[4] all'incendio di Troia
disredato[5] da te d'ogni suo bene.
Bramo che nato appena in sen mi moia
per non mirarlo involto in maggior pene,
e se talvolta in sen lo sento, oh dio,
figlio lo chiamo d'ogni danno mio.
        Ahi, qual sventura e qual acerbo fato
mi rende madre a sventurato figlio?
Qual piacque al Cielo di cangiarmi stato?
Qual sorte mi condusse a te al periglio?
O povero innocente, a che sei nato?
Chi fia ch'al viver tuo porga consiglio?
La madre t'abbandona e t'è rubella.
Al padre t'allontana iniqua stella.
        Infelice pupillo, e dove sono
quelle grandezze che goder dovei[6]?

---

[1]While the first part of this poem, in *ottava rima*, is a lamentation on the absence of her lover, it concludes with the realistic despair of the woman who is expecting an illegitimate child. Both mother and child are condemned to a miserable destiny. A common problem, but here it appears for the first time as a literary theme in poetry written by Italian women. See also Introduction, p. 27.

[2]*m'annoia*: mi dispiace.

[3]*arene*: terra, mondo.

[4]Ascanius, son of Aeneas, lost his paternal inheritance when Troy was destroyed.

[5]*disredato*: diseredato.

[6]*dovei*: dovevi.

Despite your innocence, she has no pardon,
mean Fortune? Do the gods have none to show?
Where is your father's rich gift to you, son —
the trophy that he swore he would bestow?
He enriched you with spoils possessed of his,
to dispossess you of what you possess.

Beautiful Woman, in Fun, to Other Women

A lovely woman must also be wise
not to take just one lover, as a rule.
With one love at a time, you have no peace;
even worse, you'll be taken for a fool.
To live for a single good, at your demise,
to bear the torch for one heart over all
is such disgrace, there's no excuse to find,
unless, of course, you want to lose your mind.

Further, you'll see beside you, ever near,
a most despondent lover, desperate,
who with his howls, shouts, hurt, many a tear,
will give you only angry bread to eat;
and to exchange your joy, its songs and laughter,
for life lived fretfully in worried state,
is pain without an end, is a real hell —
a ship at sea, no captain at the sail.

To lose your freedom and your friends' embraces;
to lose your youth, even the life you own;
out of your wits, disdain past happiness;
experience extremes with no help shown;
to follow the shade of a shadow and its traces;
midst others' joy, to suffer only scorn,
is madness without match, ardor unworthy,
vileness of soul and a heart's poverty.

What hope is left for a locked-away beauty!
What does golden hair matter, shining skin!
Spirit and pride, what use then can they be,
if those gifts fall prey to oblivion?
For in the end, as years pass quickly by,
youthfulness fades, carried off by the wind;

Dunque alla tua 'nnocenza alcun perdono
ria Fortuna non ha, non hanno i dei?
Dov'è del padre tuo quel ricco dono
che giurò di donar a tuoi trofei?
Dunque chi t'arrichì delle sue spoglie
or delle spoglie tue fia che ti spoglie.

Bella donna di scherzo alle donne[7]

Deve la donna bella esser sagace
a non amar un sol amor per volta.
Chi ama un solo amor non ha mai pace
e dagli più sarà tenuta stolta.
Provar per un sol cor l'ardente face,
viver per un sol ben da sé disciolta,
obbrobrio è tal, che non si può scusare,
se non con dir colei vuol impazzare.

Oltre che sol vedersi sempre avanti
un amante languente e disperato,
che con urli, con gridi, duoli e pianti
sol ti faccia mangiar pane arrabbiato,
e 'n cambio di gioir fra risi e canti,
viver vita infelice in dubbio stato
è pena senza fine, è vero inferno,
è nave in alto mar senza governo.

Perder la libertà, perder gli amici,
perder la gioventù, la propria vita,
disprezzar forsennata i dì felici,
provar gli estremi, senza nulla aita,
d'un'ombra seguitar l'ombra e i vestici,[8]
fra le gioie penar d'ognun schernita,
è pazzia senza pari, è indegno ardore,
viltà d'un'alma e povertà d'un core.

Che mai più può sperar chiusa bellezza!
Che val dorato crin, fronte d'argento!
A che serve spirto e fierezza,
s'in preda dell'oblio giace il talento?
Mancano gli anni e al fin la giovinezza
cade languente e se la porta il vento,

---

[7]For comment, see Introduction, p. 28.
[8]*vestici*: vestigi, orme.

so that the only fame your name will have
will be not that of lady but of slave.
　　　What's more, the whole world says: "She can't find anyone
but him. That's why she's with him round the clock."
They form about you a certain opinion,
and in their circles you're made the laughingstock.
Thus, having a lot of lovers, in conclusion,
promotes your worth, and good to good will flock;
for beauty that's valued most, with most appeal,
is one that all are trying their best to steal.
　　　Whatever no one likes is left discarded.
A lovely woman needs no hand at the rein,
for if not seen by others as well regarded,
she hides the best rewards of her domain.
To see yourself by many lovers courted,
to be the heart's desire of every man
is joy that will allay all agony,
where unseen beauty is ugly by decree.
　　　"For you, this one lies dying. That one's on fire."
Oh, how the heart adores hearing the claim.
But beauty that satisfies a sole desire,
with a perceived lack of beauty stamps her name.
To see not one, but more than two expire,
and still to boast: "No one escapes my aim!"
is joy that will any obstacle conquer,
where paltry beauty wages paltry war.
　　　To keep the faith, be faithful to the core,
is vain extravagance, insanity
put in one's mind by others, and the error,
unrecognized, becomes their own blind folly.
Laws placed on women are nonsense. Furthermore,
naughtiness offends not, were none to see.
Women, do as you will, for if love please,
laws do no good unless the heart agrees.

onde si lascia poi nome alla fama
di miserabil schiava e non di dama.

Oltre ch'il mondo dice: "e le persone
colei non trova[9] e però sta con quello,"
e forman di te certa opinione
che nei circoli servi per zimbello.[10]
L'aver dimolti amanti, in conclusione,
dinota il merto e 'l bello fa più bello,
ché quel bello val più ed ha più stima
che da molti n'è cerco[11] far rapina.[12]

Quel che non piace sol si lascia stare.
A bella donna non richiede il freno,
ché se vista non è d'altri stimare
s'oscura ai merti suoi ogni sereno.
Il vedersi da molti corteggiare,
veder ch'ognun la porta impressa al seno
è gioia tal, ch' ogn' altra pena ammorza,
ma la bella rinchiusa è brutta a forza.

Oh, quanto gode un cor sentirsi dire:
"questo muore per te, quell'altro avvampa."
Una beltà ch'appaga un sol desire
di povera bellezza il nome stampa.
Più d'uno e più di due veder languire,
e poter dir: "da me nessun la scampa,"
è tal gioir ch'ogn' altra cosa atterra
e sol poca beltà fa poca guerra.

L'osservar lealtà, l'osservar fede
è vana opinione, folle pazzia,
ch'altri si pone in testa e non s'avvede
del proprio errore e della sua follia.
Non offende quel mal che non si vede.
Il dar legge alle donne è sciocheria.
Ognun faccia a suo modo, ch'in amore
poco giovan le leggi senza il core.

---

[9]*non trova*: non riesce a trovare.
[10]*zimbello*: oggetto di scherzo e risa.
[11]*è cerco*: è ricercato.
[12]*rapina* rima con *stima*: assonanza (rima imperfetta).

To a Woman Mortally Wounded by Her Lover
for Having Refused Him a Kiss

Be sure to kiss your men, oh lovely women,
so as not to endure a mortal wound
and see your joys to tears and to pain driven,
or without both your love and life be found.
Never for ready cash are kisses given;
never from any kiss will wrong rebound;
and if in sincere faith you give a kiss,
to men in need, a peck is almost bliss.

Kissing is really nothing but a pact
of a true peace and of friendship sincere.
To kiss is courtesy, a noble act;
a real kiss is diplomat to Amour,
and further, if refused outright, in fact,
just might reduce your life to murder's flare.
Listen, oh lovely women — don't be too proud;
even by girls, kissing is quite allowed.

So kiss and kiss again and do not fear
to ruin any aspect of your beauty.
From her, lovely but cruel, who has paid dear,
take heed, at least — avoid such cruelty.
For just one kiss refused, as you see here,
with mortal wound she lies, deprived of pity,
since, miserly, she begrudged one request,
to find her heart in twain, bludgeoned her breast.

Foolish one! Tell me, why would you deny
a kiss to him, living on fire for you?
Despite his pain, cruel girl, did you enjoy
a joke at his expense, martyr him so?
No woman deserves love if she lacks pity,
for where no mercy dwells, love does not do.
If one is rude, beauty will not suffice.
So learn well, ladies, or else pay the price.

Woman, go kiss and kiss. Don't dramatize:
"I just don't feel like kissing you, idol mine."
Deny a kiss and you may realize
your death; refuse the kiss and pay the fine.

***Per una donna mortalmente ferita dall'amante
per avergli rifiutato un bacio***[13]

    Baciate, o donne belle, i vostri amanti,
se non volete di mortal ferita
ridur le vostre gioie in duoli e pianti
e restar senza amore e senza vita.
I baci non si danno per contanti,
né per baciar altrui si va fallita,
e per il bacio di sincera fede,
poca è molta mercede a chi lo chiede.

    Baciar al fin non è se non un patto
di sincera amicizia e vera pace.
Il darlo è cortesia e nobil atto,
è ministro d'Amor bacio verace,
e tanto più quanto il negarlo affatto
riduce l'altrui vita a mortal face.
È vanità, credete, o donne belle,
ché lice[14] il bacio ancor fra le donzelle.

    Baciate e ribaciate e non temete
di far oltraggio alla vostra beltate.
Dalla bella e crudele omai prendete
esempio a non usar tal crudeltate.
Per un bacio negar, voi la vedete
giacer ferita, priva di pietate.
E per esser avara a un sol diletto,
porta trafitto il cor, piagato il petto.

    Ah folle, dì, perché, perché negare
un bacio a chi per te vivea nel foco?
Forse, cruda, godevi al suo penare
e ti prendevi il suo martire a gioco?
Donna senza pietà non si dèe[15] amare,
ch'amor non ha con l'impietate il loco.
Non giova l'esser bella a chi è scortese,
e impari oggi ogni donna alle tue spese.

    Bacia, bacia, meschina, e non più dire:
"Non ti voglio baciare idol mio."
Provi, negando un bacio, il tuo morire
e d'un bacio negato paghi il fio.

---

[13]For comment, see Introduction, p. 28.
[14]*lice*: è lecito.
[15]*dèe*: deve.

Better a thousand kisses than death's surprise,
as too blindly do men to kiss incline.
Best one kiss when just to kiss is his plea,
than too stiff a pride's excessive vanity.

FROM: **SONNETS**

Beautiful Woman to Her Lover Departed for Spain

Return, return my love, for I, in horror
of dark of night, hour by hour, rant and curse.
Return, beautiful idol mine — I want first
and only you, to stay my burning ardor.

How can it be but that I must, my treasure,
adore you? — though I know I'll prove the worse;
for by your beauty's golden mail coerced,
poor me, by true love I'm enchained the more.

Return, return, my heart, for all my pains
grow greater yet, encourage my harsh fate
to threaten my very life with tragic scenes.

Have mercy — open to me your heart's gate.
Return, at least, to make my hopes serene,
for I am, without you, a prey to death.

Beautiful Woman, Doubting Her Lover, Addresses Her Heart

My heart, why hope, why sigh, to what aspire?
The one of whom you dream you'll not ensnare.
Happy, perhaps, about my pain and torture,
you hope to pluck light from the starry sphere?

Hope not for peace, although his bright eyes gyre
to mock haughtily, jeering at your ardor.
Fool that you are, those archer's eyes, with humor,
make fun of you, death's prey of your desire.

With dulcet laugh, he laughs at your distress,
his soul only rejoicing in your torment.
To cause more pain, he turns to you his face.

Megli'eran mille baci e non languire,
ché troppè del baciar cieco il desio.
È meglio un bacio a chi baciar sol brama
che mille vezzi di superba dama.

DAI: **SONETTI**

Bella donna all'amante partito da lei per la Spagna[16]

Torna, torna, mio ben, ch'io negli orrori
di tenebrosa notte ognor vaneggio.
Torna, bell'idol mio, che te sol chieggio,[17]
per raffrenar i miei cocenti ardori.

Come vuoi, mio tesor, ch'io non t'adori,
benché conosca d'appigliarmi al peggio,[18]
mentre di tua beltà l'aurato freggio
m'astringe, ahi lassa, ai miei veraci amori?

Torna, torna, mio cor, che le mie pene
s'acrescon sì che la mia dura sorte
minaccia al viver mio tragiche scene.

Aprimi, per pietà, del cor le porte,
ritorna omai a consolar mia spene,
ch'io sono, senza te, preda di morte.

Bella donna parla al suo cuore diffidandosi dell'amante[19]

Mio cor, che fai, che speri, a che sospiri
per chi preda non è dei tuoi pensieri?
Forse trar dalle stelle i lumi speri,
vago del mio penar, dei miei martiri?

Non sperar pace, benché i lumi giri
ridendo agli ardor tuoi con modi alteri,
scherzan, folle che sei, quegli occhi arcieri
per far preda di morte i tuoi desiri.

Arride al tuo dolor il dolce riso,
rallegra l'alma sua nel tuo tormento
e, per farti penar, ti volge il viso.

---

[16]The longing for the lover's return expressed in this sonnet was a common theme in the *Seicento*.
[17]*chieggio*: chiedo (desidero).
[18]*appigliarmi al peggio*: deriva da: *al peggior m'appiglio* (Petrarca, CCLXIV, 136).
[19]In this sonnet, a woman addresses her heart and warns it not to hope, because the man she loves is smiling at her only in jest, happy to see her suffer.

Arrogant towards your hurt, he lives content.
With vain smile, all in fun, he will dismiss
your hopes, that on the air, the wind, are spent.

Beautiful Woman to Her Unfaithful Lover
Ungrateful one, done is at last my torment.
No longer do I feel the pain, the torture,
and neither will I turn an eye, an ear,
to your false and perfidious deportment.
To all my joys I return, to contentment.
Fled are the plaintive calls, sighs you'd once hear.
My soul returns to accustomed desire,
clamors not to the winds with more lament.
Nor in your faithfulness, your charming air
will I place trust (though faithful I remain),
nor do I covet any sign of mercy.
Instead, I see a false, a faithless man,
as nature made you, beneficiary
of the cruel heart and crude soul of a boor.

On the Death of Giovanni Vidoni
Displaced from your own self, displaced from me,
in dreaded death you lie now, my Vidon.
Drowned are your lovely eyes, their splendor lovely,
within death's shadow, by dark fate undone.
Already leaden and so dull, your beauties,
where once I saw them shine in you, are gone.
And I, brimming with hurt, awash in woes,
my life's brief time with difficulty earn.
My eyes pour forth their light in mournful liquid
to slake the ardor that at heart I hide;
yet more tears seem more ardor to create.
Wherefore, my saddened soul, by body weighed
and desperate, spirit without a heart,
is left a prey to earth, ward of the world.

Superbo del tuo duol, vive contento
e, con folle scherzar di van sorriso,
cede le tue speranze all'aria, al vento.

Bella donna all'amante infedele[20]

Son pur finiti, ingrato, i miei tormenti,
non sento pene più, né più martiri.
Né mai fia che le orecchie o gli occhi giri
agli tuoi falsi e perfidi andamenti.

Ritorno alle mie gioie, ai miei contenti,
fuggon da me gli pianti e gli sospiri.
L'alma ritorna ai soliti desiri,
né più si lagna o si querela ai venti.

Né più dei vezzi tuoi, né di tua fede
mi curerò giammai, benché fedele,
né bramo più da te nulla mercede.

Già ti conosco un falso, un infedele,
che natura ti fe' per farti erede
d'un animo villan, d'un cor crudele.

Per la morte di Giovanni Vidoni[21]

Vidon, tu giaci e nell'orror di morte
da me diviso, a te diviso stai.
Sommerse il bel splendor dei tuoi bei rai
nelle tenebre sue l'oscura sorte.

Le tue bellezze, già livide e smorte,
non sembran come un tempo le mirai.
Ond'io, piena di duol, colma di guai,
procaccio al viver mio le ore più corte.

Versano i lumi miei doglioso umore
per strugger quell'ardor, ch'al cor nascondo,
ma più nel pianto mio cresce l'ardore.

Onde il mio spirto afflitto, il mortal pondo[22]
disperato, senz'alma e senza core,
lascia in preda alla terra, in cura al mondo.

---

[20]The theme of this sonnet is a declared freedom from the chains of love – a popular theme that will reach its apex with Metastasio's *La libertà*.
[21]Note the personal participation of the poet in lamenting the death of a friend.
[22]*pondo*: peso (corpo mortale).

Beautiful Woman Gazing at Her Lover during Rain

Not a wind stirred, and turbid were the skies,
the sun eclipsed by the cloud-laden air,
that day when my own Sun, brilliant and clear,
hurled suddenly at me his scorching rays.

Two ardent flames they were, so bright, his eyes
set fire my soul, that I could not be sure
I would yet live; nor to live do I care,
if without comfort for my miseries.

Oh Love, either give aid or from my heart
douse my lust's torch, extinguish raw desire;
no joys appease me, if not that delight.

For beauty such, I would gladly expire,
but for a tomb, his lovely breast I'd choose,
where already my spirit, buried, lies.

To the Same Lover

To laughter I had turned my old refrain,
and was from Love's enlacements free and loose;
but now, entangled in your love, alas,
I see by your bright eyes my heart is slain.

To gaze at you, my love, my joy is one,
wrapped in a thousand joys, of paradise;
but should you part, deprive me of your beauties,
my spirit from my breast you'd flay again.

Do not depart, my Sun, if I must stay,
for I to pain and grief will rest a prey,
and I'll ready my death as you take leave.

For in your chains am I entwined so tightly,
I follow with my thoughts your every move,
and with each thought, unknot each hope of love.

To the Same Lover

If my mouth laughs, my heart weeps inwardly.
If my tongue speaks, my soul's voice is shut out.

Bella donna mirando l'amante mentre piove[23]

Era torbido il cielo e senza venti
l'aere nebbioso, ed era il sol oscuro,
quando il mio vago sol, lucido e puro,
avventò verso me raggi cocenti.

E furono i lumi suoi due fiamme ardenti
che m'arser l'alma, ond'io non m'assicuro
di viver più, né viver più mi curo
se conforto non hanno i miei tormenti.

Amor, o tu m'aita o il crudo affetto
dal cor mi svelle e spegni l'empia face,
ché goder non si può senza diletto.

Per sì vaga beltà morir mi piace,
ma per tomba vorrei quel vago petto
ove l'anima mia sepolta giace.

Al medesimo[24]

Rivolto avea gli antichi pianti in riso,
dagli lacci d'Amor libera e sciolta,
ed ora, ahi lassa, agli amor tuoi rivolta
mi vedo il cor dagli tuoi lumi ucciso.

S'io ti miro, mio bene, il paradiso
mi par goder, fra mille gioie involta,
ma se tu parti e tua beltà m'è tolta,
dal petto il spirto mio resta diviso.

Deh, non partir, mio sol, che s'io qui resto,
resto in preda agli affanni ed alle pene,
e la mia morte al tuo partir appresto.

Son così avvinta nelle tue catene,
che seguo col pensiero ogni tuo gesto
e col pensier dispero ogni mia spene.

Al medesimo[25]

Se ride la mia bocca, il cor si duole.
Se parla la mia lingua, l'alma tace.

---

[23]Typical of the Baroque is the juxtaposition of the darkness of the gloomy day outside and the light of the lover's eyes that provoke a flame of passion.
[24]In this sonnet, the lover beseeches her beloved not to depart from her, for his departure will cause her great suffering, even death. The theme of departure will repeatedly be used by Margherita.
[25]The contradictory, visible and invisible faces of love are well expressed here.

My brow cries war, but to peace turns my thought.
The words falsify the reality.

  Oh my bright Sun, don't doubt you're loved by me.
Though faking ice, in true fire lies my heart,
pretends to scorn love, though to Love devout,
and seeking, wanting you, appears to flee.

  Through pretense of disdain, the ways are real
to draw a fickle heart to firm intent:
when in love, sometimes show it's scorn you feel.

  My heart cloaks with a laugh, a smile, its torment,
and with feigned vanities, its woe conceals,
so that, in place of hurt, appears content.

Beautiful Woman, Fallen Ill, Far from Her Lover

  Far away from my love, weakened and wan,
my life, spun round to death, languishing lies;
its span of hours to briefest hour flies,
vanishing with an occidental sun.

  Already has my rosy hue grown dim;
already, my bright eyes their portals close;
thus do my fortune and my fate dispose
that I, so harrowed, be so far from him.

  My soul from body I've nearly untied;
already do my speech, my spirits fail,
and from my love I hope no more for aid.

  Depart then from my breast, beautiful soul,
for with my Sun departed from my side,
eclipsed let be my lucky star as well.

Beautiful Woman, as Lorenzo de' Medici Lies Sick

  Wait, Parca, why this deed? That noble thread
Heaven has not conceded that you cut.
Not yet will you such progeny uproot,
nor will Death on such prey be let to feed.

La fronte chiede guerra, il pensier pace.
La verità smentisce le parole.

Non creder ch'io non t'ami, o mio bel sole,
il cor si finge un ghiaccio e in fuoco giace,
finge sprezzar amor, d'Amor seguace,
mostra fuggirti e te sol chiede e vuole.

Il finger disprezzar son veri mezzi
per trar un cor fugace al proprio intento:
s'ama talvolta e par che si disprezzi.

Veste il mio cor di riso il suo tormento,
copre gli affanni suoi con finti vezzi,
e 'nvece di dolor mostra contento.

Bella donna inferma lontano dall'amante[26]

Dall'idol mio lontana, egra e languente,
giace la vita mia rivolta a morte
e corre al viver suo le ore più corte:
s'invola[27] dall'occaso in occidente.

Già son del volto mio le rose spente,
già gli miei lumi serrano le porte,
così vuole il mio fato e la mia sorte,
ch'io lungi dal mio ben viva dolente.

Dal corpo ho quasi l'alma dissunita,
già mi mancan gli spirti e la favella,
né dall'idolo mio più spero aita.

Pàrtiti dal mio petto, anima bella,
mentre il mio sol da me fece partita,
s'eclissi ancor la mia propizia stella.

Bella donna per la malattia di don Lorenzo de' Medici[28]

Ferma, Parca, che fai? Quel nobil stame[29]
non t'è dato troncar, il Ciel non vuole.
Non lice ancor spiantar sì nobil prole,
né che di preda tal Morte si sfame.[30]

---

[26]The theme of departure that can lead to death has its variation in this sonnet. The woman is close to death because her beloved is far away.
[27]*s'invola*: fugge.
[28]On Lorenzo de' Medici, see note 62 of Introduction (p. 30).
[29]*stame*: filo della vita.
[30]*si sfame*: si sazi.

Turn elsewhere now to satisfy your need,
as the Eternal Sun is resolute;
for, of those lovely limbs, genteel repute,
the earth, insatiable, would stem its greed.

And you, put down your scythe, oh haughty Death,
for such glory is not yet granted you
to fly, proud one, the black flag you unfurl.

Never will fate decree that noble Arno
be heir to so much pain, that night so cruel
enshroud a sun of such merit and faith.

Beautiful Woman, Indignant, to Her Lover

The more you plead, you wretch, I harden more.
Your pledge I shun, and your love I disdain,
and from my foot pry the unworthy chain;
to your plaints I no longer give a care.

Without you, life seems easy to endure,
and my heart pines not to see you again,
but finds repose within the breast of one
whose soul's more beautiful and more secure.

I loved you once, and that I don't deny.
My life, gifted to you, ingrate, you spurned,
while I'd no thought that scorned by you I'd be.

But when I saw myself by you so scorned,
that other thoughts of love were fantasy,
to a more grateful love my soul I turned.

Beautiful Woman to Her Lover, during Rain, as He Departs from Her

In pity for my torment and my pain
does Jove disturb with water your departure;
yet you depart, and wish upon me languor,
without a worry for the wind and rain.

Joy and content I, towards your parting, feign,
yet, as you part, I feel my death draw near,

Rivolgi in altra parte le tue brame,
così comanda e vuol l'eterno Sole,[31]
ché di sì vaga salma e gentil mole
ancor l'ingorda terra non ha fame.

E tu ferma la falce, o Morte altera,
ch' or di tal gloria a te non si concede
spiegar, superba, l'orrida bandiera.

Né fia giammai ch'il nobil Arno erede
resti d'un tanto duolo, e sì ria sera
adombri un sol di tanto merto e fede.

Bella donna di sdegno all'amante[32]

Se più tu piangi, iniquo, io più m'induro,
disprezzo l'amor tuo, sdegno tua fede,
sciolgo l'indegno laccio dal mio piede
e degli pianti tuoi poco mi curo.

Il viver senza te non mi par duro,
né più di rivederti il cor mi chiede,
ch'in altro petto si riposa e siede
spirto di te più bello e più sicuro.

T'amai, no'l[33] niego, e della vita mia
largo dono ti feci, anima ingrata,
né stimai ch'io da te sprezzata sia.

Quando mi vidi poi da te sprezzata
e ch'altri amor tenei per fantasia,
rivolsi l'alma ad altro amor più grata.

Bella donna all'amante mentre pioveva ed egli voleva partire da lei[34]

Pietoso del mio duol, del mio tormento,
turba Giove con l'acque il tuo partire,
e tu pur parti e mi vuoi far languire,
e poco curi l'acqua e meno il vento.

Fingo del tuo partir gioia e contento,
e provo al tuo partir il mio morire,

---

[31]*eterno Sole*: Dio.

[32]In this sonnet, a woman refuses to forgive her former unfaithful lover because she has found a more faithful lover.

[33]*no'l*: non lo.

[34]The lover's despair at her beloved's departure is reinforced by the rain outside and is expressed by using words with the harsh sound of the letter *p*, to imitate the sound of raindrops hitting a hard surface.

nor do I dare display how much I suffer,
how, before you, I feel all senses drain.

    With eyes cast down, I go through my good-bye,
that my ill-begot passion you'll not see there
within my soul, by my heart locked away.

    Raw Love and a pitiless jealousy
within me wage extreme, pitiless war,
with blows to fell my heart, soul, without mercy.

To Prospero Cechini, Praising His Surgery in Healing the Broken Leg of Her Brother

    May Heaven, brave Cechino, in our days,
make prosper your fine intellect so bold;
while, with the tools of surgery that you hold,
you treat the wounds of one who, injured, lies.

    Your knowledge all other knowledge belies;
in cloisters, courts, your works are manifold;
it's rare to see a spirit so well skilled
as yours, or one among us here so wise.

    Your face displays to me a heart sincere;
your mouth issues good news I wait to hear;
you seem, throughout, an angel bona fide.

    Your fame takes wing unto the farthest stars,
and every spirit proud, soul virtuous,
by your spirit and virtue, is denied.

Beautiful Woman, in Fun, to Her Lover Who Would Throw Himself into the River

    I've left you, Tirsi, without your consent,
as I, at Ponte Mollo, had declared.
Now you would break your neck, I hear it said,
won't take yourself in hand, be a bit patient.

    If death you would now choose, don't be imprudent,
more so because you'll die unsatisfied;

né palesar ardisco il mio martire
ch'avanti a te tutta mancar mi sento.

    Addio, ti dico e, con le luci[35] a terra,
cerco coprir il mio malnato ardore,
che dentro l'alma il cor rinchiude e serra.

    Gelosia dispietata e crudo Amore
mi fanno estrema e dispietata guerra,
l'un mi colpisce l'alma e l'altra il core.

A Prospero Cechini lodando la sua chirurgia
con occasione che sana d'una rottura di gamba al fratello di lei[36]
    Prosperi[37] il Cielo la tua mente audace,
valoroso Cechino, ai tempi nostri,
mentre che tratti gli taglienti rostri[38]
alle piaghe di chi ferito giace.

    Al tuo saper ogni saper soggiace,
son pien delle opre tue gli atri e i chiostri,
e così saggio fra di noi ti mostri
che mai si vide un spirto sì sagace.

    Si scorge alla tua fronte il cor sincero,
spira alla bocca tua grazie novelle
e sembri nell'aspetto un angel vero.

    Vola la fama tua fino alle stelle;
ogn'alma virtuosa o spirto fiero,
al tuo spirto e virtù rimane imbelle.

Bella donna di scherzo all'amante che si vuole buttare nel fiume[39]
    Il mio partir da te, senza licenza,
Tirsi, ti lasciai detto a Ponte Mollo.[40]
Or sento dir che vuoi romperti il collo
e che non vuoi pigliartelo in pazienza.

    S'uccider tu ti vuoi, l'è inavvertenza,
e tanto più che non morrai satollo.[41]

---

[35]*luci*: occhi.
[36]An encomiastic poem written in gratitude to the doctor who treated the poet's brother.
[37]*Prosperi*: gioco di parole con il nome di battesimo del dottore.
[38]*taglienti rostri*: ferri che tagliano (strumenti chirurgici).
[39]This sonnet and the next one are humorous compositions in which the poet uses colloquial expressions.
[40]*Ponte Mollo*: colloquial name for Ponte Milvio, in Rome.
[41]*satollo*: sazio.

and if love drives you to your suicide,
folks will simply remark: "Look, how indecent."
     Turn back, fool that you are; regain composure
and set aside this crazy thought of yours,
and live, if more of life is in your stars.
     Recall that you're a noble cavalier,
that in the water you would drown and bob,
just to be roasted: "Too tied to his job."

To the Same Lover

     You tell me: "I will take Death as my consort,"
and that you burn, you languish, you're consumed,
you'll drown yourself, hang yourself in some room;
your love for me grows hourly, you exhort.
     I'm already familiar with a sort
of feigned compliment and a sort of steam
that issues from a false heart with a custom
to fib more than a courtier at court.
     Yet if you cannot suffer that self-harm,
on a sure footing, come to where I am,
for you'll find I've strength to endure your darts.
     But if I find your declarations perjured,
a pain equal to each I'll have delivered,
and you will then see clearly my dark thoughts.

Beautiful Woman at Her Lover's Departure

     Soul of mine, you depart, and it is clear
you'll leave me here alone and so abandoned.
When you are gone, who'll then come to my aid,
console me if your thought for me should alter?
     Amidst my hopes, hope turns into despair;
my soul flies from me as you go ahead.
I dare not, without you, utter a word,
but hope only to die from all my dolor.

E s'amor ti darà l'ultimo crollo,
dirà la gente poi: "guarda indecenza."
    Torna, folle che sei, torna in te stesso
e cangia il forsennato tuo pensiero,
e vivi, se di viver t'è permesso.
    Ricordati che sei buon cavaliero
e che nell'acqua moriresti allesso,[42]
onde si potria dir: "stroppia mestiero."[43]

Al medesimo
    Il dirmi: "io vuò,[44] per te, darmi la morte"
e ch'ardi e che ti struggi e ti consume,
e ch'appiccar ti vuoi, gettare a fiume,
e che sei nell'amarmi ognor più forte,
    già conosco che sono certa sorte
di complimenti finti e certo fume,[45]
ch'esce dal falso cor, ch' ha per costume
di finger più ch'un cortigiano in corte.
    Pur se non puoi soffrir tuoi crudi mali,
vien dov'io sono, con il piè securo,
che troverai la tempra agli tuoi strali.
    E se qui m'ha condotto il tuo spergiuro,
il mio ti renderà le pene uguali,
e vedrai chiaro il mio pensiero oscuro.

Bella donna nella partenza dell'amante[46]
    Tu parti, anima mia, ed è pur vero
che qui mi lasci abbandonata e sola.
Chi fia che più m'aita o mi consola,
se tu lungi da me cangi pensiero?
    Fra le speranze mie sperar dispero,
l'alma col tuo partir da me se n' vola,
non oso senza te formar parola
e sol dal mio dolor la morte spero.

---

[42]*allesso*: lessato (affogato).
[43]*Stroppia mestiero*: eccede il mestiere ("il troppo stroppia").
[44]*vuò*: voglio.
[45]*fume*: fumo.
[46]This sonnet is another variation on the theme of departure, but here with a realistic twist — a woman in an empty house talking to the empty bed.

I linger in your nest, stare at each wall
only to weep; and the innocent bed
in pain I caress, in a sultry fever.
     Promise that it will be, my handsome idol,
a shelter for us both, that with great care
your soul, in pity, to my breast you'll speed.

Beautiful Woman to Her Lover in His Unrequited Love for Another Woman

     Upon a slab of marble, sad and low,
and far from my desires so long you've lain;
yet you console my past hurt with your pain,
for just to see you fixed like stone, I glow.
     Where you love truly, I, only for show,
a love with false plaints, sighs for you, did feign.
I now gloat at your despair for that woman,
as not an inch she'll move for your love's woe.
     Oh, how unequal is yours from my state:
I revere noble soul — you, a vile woman.
Lover beloved am I — in scorn you dwell.
     You live despised. I live in honored style.
I live within the breast of one who's given
his heart. You live in a breast profligate.

Beautiful Woman to Her Lover Passionate for Another Woman

     Tirsi, immobile and in suffering clad,
before me you appear, stock-still in place,
and with your tearful eyes, your pallid face,
among the living seem a living-dead.
     A river, I observe, your bright eyes shed,
while from your breast you exhale horrid lays.
Tell me the reason for your maladies;
wherefrom springs this motif of yours so languid?
     Ah, well now, a new ardor does, I see,
afflict your mind, my disloyal amour;
within her image lies amorous torment.

M'aggiro entro il tuo nido e queste mura
piangendo miro, e l'innocente letto
dolente premo, fra dolente arsura.
 Deh, fa', bell'idol mio, che sia ricetto
ad ambe due, con più pietosa cura
torna l'anima tua dentro il mio petto.

Bella donna all'amante innamorato d'altra donna ma non riamato[47]

 Sovra un tronco di marmo, afflitto e lasso,
te ne vivi da lungi ai miei desiri,
e col tuo duol consoli i miei martiri,
mentre io godo vederti quasi un sasso.
 Tu vero amante sei, io sol per spasso
finsi di trar per te pianti e sospiri,
or godo, ché per altra tu deliri
e ch' ella per tuo amor non muova un passo.
 Oh, quanto è differente il nostro stato:
io nobil spirto e tu vil donna adori,
amata amante io son, tu sei sprezzato.
 Tu vivi fra disprezzi, io fra gli onori.
Io vivo in sen di chi 'l suo cor m'ha dato,
tu vivi in sen di dissoluti amori.

Bella donna all'amante appassionato d'altro amore

 Tirsi, nel duolo involto e quasi privo
di movimento avanti a me ti stai,
e con pallido volto e mesti rai,
mi sembri fra mortali un morto vivo.
 Dai lumi già sgorgar ti veggio[48] un rivo,[49]
esalando dal petto odiosi lai.
Deh, dimmi la cagion degli tuoi guai
e donde vien sì languido motivo.
 Ah, ben m'avveggio che novello ardore
il petto t'ange,[50] disleale amante,
per altra imago ti tormenta amore.

---

[47]This sonnet, as well as the following, depict a woman observing her former lover now in love with another woman.
[48]*veggio*: vedo.
[49]*rivo*: fiume.
[50]*ange*: opprime.

Ah, yes, it's true that you, inconstant, traitor,
have turned to her your still inconstant heart,
while with me you're congealed, diamond and ice.

Beautiful Woman to Her Lover in Parting

Life of my life, tell me, can it be so,
you'd part from me with no word of good-bye,
demonstrate not one worry for my worry,
nor soothe my doubtful thoughts before you go?
    I'm terse with every cavalier in tow,
for where my desire lies, I show quite frankly;
and as for my vulnerability,
I'm left prey to the god of bow and arrow.
    Nearby hearts' blaze, hourly, I freeze to ice.
My hurt's my glee, as hurt gnaws me within.
I break each tie; yours ties me in a vice.
    Cruel laws of Love! Adored by everyone,
I flee them all, as you alone entice.
You gloat, you brute, that for you I'm undone.

Beautiful Woman to Other Women

Women, now that you've heard in sundry tales
the vagaries of love, with its delights,
its pain and its afflictions and its trials,
its false hope, its irrefutable spite;
    of love's empty contentment you've heard well,
the crazy inanities of its thought,
its paltry sweetness, more its bitter pill,
through which each woman's hope has come to naught.
    Let us no more pursue desire so vain,
and let not one more woman for love pine;
the god of bow and arrow let us shun.

Sì, sì, ch' è vero, o perfido, incostante,
ad altra hai volto l'incostante core
e meco sei di ghiaccio e di diamante.

Bella donna all'amante che parte[51]

Vita della mia vita,[52] ed è pur vero
che da me parti senza dirmi addio,
né mostri affanno dell'affanno mio,
né pur consoli il dubbio mio pensiero.

Io muta resto ad ogni cavaliero,
e chiaro rendo, ahi lassa, il mio desio
e, di me stessa già posta in oblio,
mi rendo preda al faretrato arciero.[53]

Al fuoco d'ogni cor ognor m'aghiaccio.
Gioisco d'ogni duol e il duol m'accora.
Ogni legame scioglio e 'l tuo m'allaccio.

Cruda legge d'Amor! Ognun m'adora,
ognun io fuggo e sol per te mi sfaccio,
e tu godi, crudel, ch'io per te mora.

Bella donna alle donne[54]

Donne, ch'avete udito in vari accenti,
le fortune d'amor, coi suoi piaceri,
le sue pene, i suoi affanni, i suoi tormenti,
le fallaci speranze e i scorni veri,

udito avete i suoi vani contenti,
il folle vaneggiar dei suoi pensieri,
le sue poche dolcezze, i molti stenti,
in cui non fia che mai più donna speri.

Lasciate di seguir sì van desio,
né più donna vi sia che voglia amare,
anzi, sprezziamo il faretrato iddio.

---

[51]Another version on the theme of departure, but here the man is indifferent, while the woman is still sentimentally attached to him.

[52]*vita della mia vita*: an expression made famous by Tasso.

[53]*faretrato arciero*: Cupido.

[54]In this sonnet, in the idyll of the same title that follows it, and in the canzonet *Alle donne*, which is given after *Agli amanti*, the poet uses three different poetic meters, but the same subject, to poke fun at the idea that women should stay at home and work the needle and spindle. See Introduction, p. 28.

No, no, women, no more, no more this pain.
The art of love leave to oblivion.
The only art for us is but to spin.

FROM: **IDYLLS**

Beautiful Woman to Other Women

Women, once done with the grand tour
of all my torments and unpitied pain,
I came to be in this terrain
to make some peace, in part, with my past torture;
but having just arrived, alas,
pitiless Love, with beauty new,
enflamed my heart (such as I'd come to rue);
hence into a thousand ifs,
condemned to torture and lies
I returned, poor me, hurting and plaintive,
a prey to fortune cruel, to my demise.
I'd lived as lover beloved,
and often proved, although ensnared, entwined,
to live a felicitous life;
yet again, alas, I tried
to love one love alone, handsome and cruel.
I gave my faith, and with my faith my life,
to one who, faith betrayed, led me to grief.
I once lived felicitously;
midst thousands of delights, to my content,
did I walk haughtily, a beauty proud.
But then did I witness, alas,
my hopes hurled down,
my pride collapsed.
I witnessed myself, though I would not have guessed,
precipitate to my own precipice.
And yet did Love, insatiate,
bind me again more tightly in his snares,
and with more vicious torture and harsh pain
he cinched me in a violent chain;
he slashed my soul and he pierced through my heart.
And here did I prove death's chill,
unpitied ardor as well,

No, no, donne, non più, non più penare,
l'arte del far l'amor vada in oblio,
ché l'arte nostra è solo di filare.

DAGLI: **IDILLI**

Bella donna alle donne

Donne, dopo il gran giro
dei miei tormenti e dispietate pene,
me ne venni in queste arene
per racquietare in parte il mio martiro,
ma, lassa, appena giunta,
il dispietato Amore
di novella beltà m'accese il core,
onde fra mille affanni
di nuovo a reo martire
tornai, misera me, fra duoli e pianti,
preda di ria fortuna, al mio morire.
Già vissi amante amata
e più volte provai, fra lacci involta,
viver vita felice,
e ancor, lassa, provai
amar solo un amore, beltà crudele.
Donai la fede, e con la fé la vita,
a chi della sua fé m'ha poi tradita.
Vissi felice un tempo,
e fra mille piaceri ai miei contenti,
superba me n'andai di mia beltade.
E poi, lassa, vid'io
dirupar mie speranze,
cadere i pregi miei.
Vidi, quando che men io mi credea,
precipitarmi al precipizio mio.
Né di ciò sazio, Amore
di nuovo ai lacci suoi mi rese avvinta,
e con più reo martire e cruda pena
mi cinse aspra catena,
mi ferì l'alma e mi trafisse il core.
Qui provai gel di morte,
ardor spietato,

and faithless lies, and fraudulent deceit,
thanklessness and a clench tyrannical.
Where now, in snare so fierce no longer caught,
I'll share with you this thought.
Women, in the end, I resolve
to turn from everything I was involved in,
do nothing else except to spin;
for when it is said and done,
all other enterprise will spell our ruin.
A woman I was born, and thus
each vestige of our use I'll don,
and choose, as my one pastime,
needle or spindle, to pass my time upon.
Yes, yes, women, you must now make
your sole desire and itch
to spin or else to stitch.
And since just spinning's left to our behalf,
let's drop all else. Let's all pick up the distaff.

FROM: CANZONETS

To Lovers

      Nobody vaunts
of beauty's thrill
without a fill
of sighs and plaints.
For Love wants tears mingled with his contents;
brief joy at thousandfold torments' expense.
      No one can say
without some pain:
"Love, I sustain,
is trouble-free."
For Love wants tears and he wants sighs from all.
There's never been a joy without a toll.
      Who'll have a fling
its pain will prove,
and for that love
feel they're expiring.

fede mentita, frodolente inganno,
tirannico rigor, pensier ingrato.
Onde, or sciolta da laccio così fiero,
vi dico il mio pensiero.
Donne, al fin mi riduco
di lasciar ogni stile, ogn'altro affare,
e sol darmi al filare,
poiché conosco al fine
che l'altre imprese son nostre rovine.
Donna nacqui e di donna
vestir mi voglio ogn'uso,
e sol sarà mio spasso
spassarmi ora con l'ago, or con il fuso.
Sí, sì, tutte volgete
il pensiero e il desire
al filare e al cucire.
E giacché di filar solo ci tocca,
lasciamo ogn'altro affar, prendiam la rocca.

DALLE: CANZONETTE

Agli amanti[55]

    Nessun si vanti
goder beltà,
se pria non dà
sospiri e pianti.
Vuò le lagrime Amor nei suoi contenti,
paga un breve gioir mille tormenti.
    Nessun più dica
senza dolor:
"Io godo amor
senza fatica."
Vuò le lagrime Amor, vuol gli sospiri,
non vi fu mai goder senza martiri.
    Chi vuol gioire,
provi il penar,
e per amar,
provi il morire.

---

[55]Love is both joy and torment, but the poet describes it with light, musical verses.

For being cruel, in love, is charity.
There's never been a joy without a fee.

To Women

    Women, because I've lived awhile
to sample love, its fickle snare,
its iciness mixed with its flare,
its disdainful, ungrateful style;
this truth I know full well — you'll find
that, in love, all your logic's blind:
thus, over love I'll not grow thin;
I savor nothing but to spin.
    A common fate we women bear —
to don some unattractive cloak
and sit and spin until we croak —
is gifted us from every star;
if needle, spindle we'd refuse,
our use as women we would lose:
so I'll toss business in the bin,
for all I crave to do is spin.
    You'll find you're much less tired, distrait,
if you pick up spindle or thread,
and you'll not have a day to dread,
though it be any day in May;
for any hour will be well spent
if with a needle you're content:
therefore, happily I'll begin
to take up stitching and to spin.
    Up, up, women, all you beauties!
Turn your minds unto the thought
of the one pose for which we're wrought,
for such is written in the stars;
neither, when richly dressed, deride
clutching the distaff at your side:
we're born to this affair akin,
to stitch, sew, and, of course, to spin.
    And with more beauty to our name,
along with light and ready heart,
let's thus our days and hours allot,
for what is lost we will reclaim.
Yes, women, certainly you would

Ch'in amor è pietà l'esser crudele,
non vi fu mai goder senza querele.

Alle donne

    Donne mie, poi ch' ho provato
dell'Amore il folle laccio,
il suo fuoco col suo ghiaccio,
il suo stil scortese e ingrato,
io conosco, a dirvi il vero,
ch'in Amor cieco è il pensiero:
onde più non voglio amare,
ma sol godo di filare.

    Alle donne è dato in sorte,
fin dal cielo e dalle stelle,
di vestir abito imbelle
e filar fino alla morte;
e chi sdegna l'ago e il fuso
della donna perde ogn'uso:
ond'io lascio ogn'altro affare
e sol bramo di filare.

    Men fatica e men disagio
ci darà il fuso e 'l cucire,
né del giorno avrem martire,
benché sian giorni di maggio;
ché ben spesa fia quell'ora
che con l'ago si dimora:
ond'io lieta prendo a fare
il cucire col filare.

    Su, su, tutte, donne belle,
rivolgete omai 'l pensiero
allo stil nostro primiero,
ché così voglion le stelle;
né sdegnate in nobil manto
di portar la rocca accanto:
ché di tutte è il proprio affare
il cucire col filare.

    E se più belle noi siamo,
con più lieto e pronto core
dispensiamo i giorni e l'ore,
ch'il perduto racquistiamo:
sì, sì, donne, se volete,

take spinning as your only good:
for woman's work, through thick and thin,
you must agree, is just to spin.

di filar solo godete,
ché la donna sol dèe fare
l'esercizio del filare.

FROM: *THE VIOLIN* (1638)

FROM: IDYLLS

Gift of Her Poems to Ferdinand II, Grand Duke of Tuscany

Today, as all bow at your feet
to pay respect, oh Sire,
and with merited gifts
show you obedience —
among such a rich throng,
with my songs rough and bare,
today, as humble servant do I, too,
offer as small homage my gift to you.
. . . .
With this page pure and white
that's tinted with dark ink
I come, my hand not replenished with gold.
No treasure do I hold,
no silver cup, no vessel aureate.
I bring my gift ornate
but nude of any jewel,
a gift impoverished, bare —
before your feet I humbly lay it there.
Stripped of every real good, I offer, Sire,
this very small effect of my affection;
and given that I cannot give
a gem precious and rare —
of my impoverished songs,
of my powerless pen,
of my rough intellect, of all I heed,
to you, my royal Sire, the reign I cede.
And I, as anyone, deserve
to be with thanks received,
though I can't offer you what I'm denied
by my impoverished star,
for from my day of birth,
Heaven arrogantly

DA: *IL VIOLINO* (1638)

DAGLI: **IDILLI**

Dono delle sue rime a Ferdinando II, Gran Duca di Toscana[56]
    Oggi, ch'ognun s'inchina
agli tuoi piedi, o Sire,
e con dovuto dono
ubbidienza ti rende,
fra così ricco stuolo,
di rozzi e nudi carmi
umile ancella in questo giorno anch'io
t'offro in picciol omaggio il dono mio
. . . .
Con questa pura carta,
d'oscuri inchiostri tinta,
vengo, non con la man ripiena d'oro,
o di ricco tesoro,
o di coppa d'argento, o vaso aurato.
Porto il mio dono ornato,
ma nudo d'ogni gioia,[57]
povero e nudo dono,
umile agli tuoi piè cedo e condono.[58]
Spogliato d'ogni ben, Sire, io ti porgo
questo picciol effetto del mio affetto,
e giacché dar non posso
gemma pregiata e rara,
dei miei poveri carmi,
della mia debol penna,
del rozzo ingegno mio, d'ogni pensiero,
a te, regio signore, cedo l'impero.
E come ogn'altro io devo
esser da te gradita,
benché non t'offra quel che mi diniega
la mia povera stella,
ché fin dai miei natali
il cielo, a me protervo,

---

[56]In this idyll, Margherita, although addressing Ferdinand II, does not fail to mention her luckless life and her "rough" style.
[57]*gioia*: gioiello.
[58]*condono*: dono, rimetto.

handed me not a shred,
and did, with harsh and harrowing affairs,
further oppress, alas, my months and years.
Poor was I born and live
poor yet, and without joy;
miserable do I
draw breath, in cruel pain, to languish and sigh.
Beggar am I of goods,
a laughingstock of luck,
oppressed by fate full of iniquity —
what can you have from me?
. . . .
So take, pityingly,
this very paltry fruit
of my musings austere;
and though my destiny
permits me naught but this,
pray indulge your desire
upon my written words, pure and sincere,
expressed on a bare page
by dark ink marks scratched out in a black smear.
. . . .

Her Lover, Having Seen Her Letter to Another, Admonishes Her Harshly

       Disloyal, treacherous,
what more can I foresee
of your deceitful arts?
With what trick, wicked woman,
with those deceiving eyes
will you betray and compromise?
. . . .
Oh wicked sex, fraudulent and so cruel!
Alas, certainly nature
bears you into the world
only for man's distress.
You're born for this alone —
to render most unhappy,
if you can trick him, every hapless man.
You boast, with no constraint,

di ciò nulla mi diede.
Anzi, con duri e disperati affanni
m'ha sempre oppresso, ahi lassa, i mesi e gli anni.
Povera nacqui e vivo
povera ed infelice,
miserabil respiro,
e sempre in crudo duol languo e sospiro.
Mendica d'ogni bene,
bersaglio di fortuna,
oppressa da destino iniquo e rio,
che donarti poss'io?
. . . .
Prendi dunque, pietoso,
questo picciolo parto
dei miei rozzi pensieri,
e giacché la mia sorte
altro non mi permette,
appaga il tuo desire
dei caratteri miei, puri e sinceri,
espressi in nuda carta
da foschi inchiostri mal vergati e neri.
. . . .

Amante, dopo aver visto la lettera della sua donna a un altro[59]
    Perfida, disleale,
che più veder poss'io
delle arti tue mentite?
Con qual inganno, iniqua,
con quai mentiti rai
più tradir mi potrai?
. . . .
Iniquo sesso, frodolente e rio!
Ahi, che solo natura
vi partorisce al mondo
per strazio dei mortali.
Solo, solo nascete
per ridurre infelice
ogn'infelice ch'ingannar potete.
È solo il vostro vanto

---

[59]Idyll written in imitation of misogynous compositions.

to lie and to betray,
to damage everyone,
to reduce every soul
to dolorous and everlasting plaint.
Oh lying company,
or else cruel enemy
Heaven on us bestowed,
and for support, oh God,
to each man's mortal life,
such mortifying harm
and everlasting condemnation showed.
Oh unlucky and wretched,
whose foot the evil snare
with barbarous chain cinches and takes hold.
Oh miserable heart
that does in her confide.
Oh sorry man is he
who from monster so harsh
hopes for trustworthy guide.
Oh sex, horror of earth!
Sex impious, perverse.
Sex, just a nest of lies —
a deadly nest of deadly merchandise.
Oh tongue, forever ready
to scorn and to deceive.
Oh tongue, you do not dare
to offer up your diction
without deceiving with a feigned affection.
You, you, mendacious mouth,
you swore, liar, that I
was your hope's certitude,
your fire, your very ardor —
that I was life to you, your heart, your good.
. . . .
Oh beautiful but cruel,
of beauty undeserved.
Ah, how it does misspeak,
that angelical face,
that tantalizing smile,

il mentire, il tradire,
il danneggiare altrui,
il riducere ogn'alma
in sempiterno e doloroso pianto.
O compagnia bugiarda,
anzi, cruda nemica,
ch'il cielo a noi permesse[60]
e per sostento, o dio,
d'ogni vita mortale
sì mortifero danno
a nostro danno eternamente elesse.
Oh, infelice e meschino,
a cui laccio sì reo
con barbara catena il piede accinge.
Oh, misero quel core
ch'in donna si confida.
Oh, dolente colui
che da mostro sì crudo
spera sicura guida.
O sesso, orror del mondo!
Sesso perverso ed empio.
Sesso nido d'inganni,
nido funesto di funesti danni.
O lingua sempre avvezza
a schernire, a mentire.
O lingua che non osi
proferir i tuoi detti
senza mentir i simulati affetti.
Tu, tu bugiarda bocca
mi giurasti, mentita,
ch'io ero la tua spene,[61]
il tuo fuoco, il tuo ardore,
la tua vita, il tuo core, ed il tuo bene.

. . . .

O bella ma crudele,
bella di beltà indegna.
Ahi, quanto in te disdice
quell'angelico volto,
quel lusinghiero riso,

---

[60]*permesse*: permise, conferì.
[61]*spene*: speme, speranza.

that glance of your bright eyes in haughty charm,
that celestial and yet dissembling form.
Ah, Heaven should have shaped
within deepest abyss
a monster of you, fierce,
and had your lovely limbs
draped with a horrid shroud,
and within Stygian shade
made you a shadow, miserable, sad.

. . . .

I will retain true fame
of all your false pretenses,
and I'll declaim in pain and as your martyr
that, just because I loved you,
betrayed by you, pitiless, I expire.

The Rape of Lilla

      Loose-limbed and nude she lay,
the young and lovely Lilla,
while with her naked flank,
the dew-kissed floral bed
she caressed in sleep's abandon, quietly.
Some strands of golden hair
into a necklace twined
around her pure white throat,
all of the rest dispersed
with little care and art
to veil, as if by chance,
her most private and venerated part.
There wafted subtly
a zephyr in a breath
of air, gentle and clear,
and with the whisper of crystalline fountain,
the goddess bountiful, kind friend to earth,
her comely bosom fraught with leaf and flower,
reclined to lend the ground a petal shower.
And for a canopy of subtile ardor,

quel giro dei tuoi lumi altero e vago,
quella celeste e simulata imago.
Ahi, che doveva il cielo
nel centro degli abissi
farti mostro d'orrore.
Dovea la vaga spoglia
vestir d'orrido manto,
e, fra l'ombre di Stice,[62]
un'ombra farti, misera e infelice.
. . . .
Sarò verace fama
dei tuoi falsi pensieri,
e dirò nel mio duol, nel mio martoro,
che, sol perché t'amai,
senza pietà da te tradito, io moro.

Violamento di Lilla[63]

     Scinta e nuda giacea
Lilla, la giovinetta,
e con il nudo fianco
i rugiadosi fiori
in sonnachioso oblio, quieta, premea;
e dell'aurato crine
fatto in parte monile[64]
alla candida gola,
l'altro tutto disparso
con poca cura ed arte,
copria quasi per gioco
la più remota e riguardevol parte.
Quivi soavemente
zefiretto spirava
aura soave e cara,
e al mormorio di cristallina fonte,
la bella dea,[65] dell'orba quiete amica,
gli prestava, vezzosa, il vago seno
carco di frondi e fior sul bel terreno.
E sotto manto di soavi ardori,

---

[62]*Stice*: Stige.
[63]For comment, see Introduction, p. 29.
[64]*monile*: collana.
[65]*bella dea*: Flora (goddess of spring, flowers and blossoms).

with their amorous charms,
the cupids wove a cover;
whence I, just on the scene,
alas, rested my gaze
on beauty so disarming.
Stock-still and half-alive
I stood, midst shock and hope,
finding no words but these to say as well:
"Behold, with your own eyes,
how sun in shadow lies."
Made bold by such avid desire was I
led by desire to die —
to die, since lusting for relief, ah yes,
I lost myself, I lost my life, alas.
With footfall light and careful
towards her (so lovely, graceful),
I now draw near my goal,
poor me, to my own precipice eternal.
Intent, I fix my eyes
on her angelic face
and with my muted sighs, missives of pain,
to Love I plead for aid, silent, alone.
Then with a trembling hand,
from her silvery breast
I lift the teasing veil,
discover there, oh God,
two yet-ripening plums
at which, upon their harvest,
I crave to quench my thirst.
Tempted to glimpse beyond to greater treasure,
alas, the one I'd die for,
(too weak to tell how) I gazed in a thrall
at the tangible reason for my fall.
My two eyes, eager now
to see more hidden things,
upon the lovers' font
with longing looks did fasten —
on that coveted font

con amorosi vezzi,
la coprivan gli Amori,[66]
onde io, che giunto appena,
rivolsi, ahi lasso, i lumi
a cotanta bellezza,
immoto e semivivo
restai fra tema e speme;
né seppi altro formar che dire anch'io:
"Venga chi veder vole[67]
giacer all'ombra il sole."
Pur fatto ardito, l'avido desire
mi condusse a morire,
a morir sì, poiché sperando aita
perdei me stesso, ahimè, perdei la vita.
Con lieve e lento passo
vèr la vezzosa e bella,
misero me, m'invio
per fare eterno il precipizio mio.
Intento affisso i lumi
all'angelico volto
e con muti sospir, messi del duolo,
chiamo in aiuto Amor, tacito e solo.
Poi con mano tremante,
al bel petto d'argento,
svello importuno velo
e scorgo, e miro, oh dio,
due immaturi pomi,
ch'accorli[68] già mi chiama
l'assettata mia brama.
Pur vago di mirar maggior tesoro,
ahi lasso, ch'io mi moro,
né forza ho pur di dir come mirai
la soave cagion degli miei guai.
Avidi gli occhi miei
di mirar più nascoso,
al fonte degli amanti
affissaron gli sguardi
alla fonte bramata,

---

[66]*Amori*: Amorini, puttini.
[67]*vole*: vuole.
[68]*accorli*: accoglierli.

where each man's heart is fed
by Love, the luring and merciless god.
Just there, spurred on to see more, I admire,
between two mounds of silver,
her treasured conch shell brimming full of joy
that, in a golden filigree
woven by Love's own hand
and burrowed as by chance,
lay wanton in its lair.
Treasure of Love, so precious and so dear!
Here do I lock my eyes —
then I fall silent; then my sighs;
and by a new emotion now oppressed,
I sense in the next instant,
my strength build while my heart deserts my breast.
I sense in every vein
a shiver of cold fear
when, in that gelid state, a fire new
enflames me through and through.
I feel myself gain force and don't opine
on my new frenzy, on this force of mine.
Then finally it's out of my hands
to override myself,
when such burning desire
(as I'm about to faint)
cuts through all fear to loosen my restraint.
Little by little, I lean close
and with my arms at her arresting breast
I bind her in a snare,
and with both feet I fasten her feet down.
Next, with so parched a thirst,
on those lips roseate
I place, languidly, my now breathless lips.
I squeeze, bite, do not kiss,
and taste and fear and do not dare to taste
the joy I sigh for, and my dulcet rest.
Oh God, now she awakes,
my lovely enemy.
With a rigorous shove, armed with disdain,
she slips from me and she declaims:

ove ciba ogni core
il lusinghiero e dispietato Amore.
Quivi, quivi mirar più intento ammiro,
fra due basi d'argento,
conchiglia di tesor, colma di gioie,
a cui di fila aurate
per man d'Amor tessute
facean, quasi per scherzo,
lascivetto riparo.
O tesoro d'Amor, pregiato e caro!
Qui gli occhi affisso e miro
e taccio e poi sospiro;
e tutto oppresso da novello affetto,
sento ch'in un istante
vigor m'acresce e manca il cor nel petto.
Sento per ogni vena
scorrer freddo timore,
e nello stesso giel del nuovo foco,
tutto ardendo m'infoco.
Forza mi sento far, né so che sia
il mio nuovo furor, la forza mia.
Alfin non più in mia mano
è il superar me stesso,
ma l'infocata voglia,
mentr'io mi vengo meno,
tronca d'ogni timor l'invido freno.
M' inchino a poco a poco,
e delle braccia al leggiadretto petto
fatta lenta catena,
con le mie piante le sue piante accingo,
e con avida sete,
sulle labbia[69] rosate,
poso, languente, l'anellanti labbra.
Stringo, mordo e non bacio,
e godo e temo e di goder non oso
il sospirato mio dolce riposo.
Oh dio, ecco si desta
la bella mia nemica,
e tutta di rigor, di sdegno armata,
da me si scioglie e dice:

---

[69]*labbia*: labbra.

"Oh swindler most unworthy
of my virginal flower —
like this, within the forest
you'd thrust yourself on nymphs?
Like this, like this, seduce me,
while I, by sleep oppressed,
careless, poor me, unlucky,
distracted lay, replenishing my rest?
Ah sleep, the evil reason for my ills —
that dubious, false death
of miserable mortals!"
She, having spoke, haughtily
takes to her heels to flee,
and fleeing, she disdains me,
and disdaining, destroys me.
But Love, who had been lurking
to see all that would pass, stayed close, intent,
and lent me wondrous wings
in pity for my pain and for my torment.
Emboldened thus, and fierce,
pressed forward to the prey
I flung myself, my mind avaricious.
And when I reached that beauty,
with such sensual ardor
I clutched her to my chest,
eager no more to suffer her disdain.
I clasped her to my breast
and with my arms twined tight around her waist,
in one smooth, languid motion
the lovely fruit of love I plucked in haste.
She, scornful in demeanor,
feigned a desire to flee,
but fleeing, held instead
tight to my waist and breast.
She twisted herself so indolently,
exactly at that moment,
as though she might have said:
"Enjoy, enjoy, my heart, for I enjoy."
Haughty yet, she denied me
her beauty to assess,
then turned to me her face

"O truffatore indegno
del mio pudico fiore,
così, così nei boschi
si fa forza alle ninfe?
Così, così tradirmi,
mentre dal sonno oppressa
riposando giacea,
trascurata, infelice, di me stessa?
Ahi sonno, empia cagion degli miei mali,
morte dubbiosa e finta
dei miseri mortali!"
Ciò detto il piè veloce
muove, superba, e fugge,
e fuggendo mi sprezza,
e sprezzando mi strugge.
M'Amor, che di nascoso
il tutto a rimirar si stava intento,
mi prestò le ali aurate,
pietoso del mio duol, del mio tormento.
E fatto ardito e fiero,
alla forza, alla preda
sospinsi il sitibondo mio pensiero.
Onde la bella e cara
giunsi e con molle ardire,
sotto il mio seno accolta,
avido di non più restar schernito,
al petto mio la strinsi;
e con le braccia avviticchiata e stretta,
con moto egro e soave
il bel frutto d'amor rapisco in fretta.
Ella sdegnosa in vista
fingea voler fuggire,
e nel fuggir stringea
il mio petto, il mio seno.
Si distorcea con neghittoso modo,
e nello stesso tempo
quasi che mi dicea:
"Godi, cor mio, ch'io godo."
Mi negava, superba,
di mirar sua bellezza,
e poi volgeami il viso

all flushed in lovely hues, in every tint
of amorous joy, of sweet happiness.
At first, she pushed me from her,
then kissed me, then bit harder,
then almost weakened, slack,
surrendered in embrace;
and damp with perspiration overall,
in meek and feeble voice,
sighing, did she exclaim:
"Oh God, enough of torture —
let go, traitor, let go, for I expire."
Whence I, again on sensual theft bent,
with much sweeter content,
with equal joy and with equal desire,
with a more gentle ardor, with more leisure
reaped yet again the beauty of love's pleasure.
With cinnabar's rich colors
beautiful Lilla scattered
the lascivious flowers.
Then having bathed at a clear spring
her breast, her bosom and her dewy face,
after my nuptial promise
she turned and from me suddenly did race.
And I, all full of smiles,
sustained a dulcet hope,
believed as happy lover to enjoy her,
believed that I'd renew the same amour
with my belovèd sun, my own dear one.
Oh God, I hoped in vain!
Lilla I saw no more;
Lilla — the cruel and proud.
She gave herself to others — in embrace
captured them, traitress, with treacherous noose.
And now she flees and hates me;
all my good she negates me.
Love, here does my life stand,
by you brought to its end!
Lilla, Lilla ungrateful!
Like this, like this, you'd let
one who adores you perish —

tutto da bel pallor fregiato e tinto
d'amoroso gioir, lieta dolcezza.
Da lei mi sospingea,
poi baciava e mordea,
e quasi afflitta e lassa,
mi si rendeva in braccio,
e tutta di sudor disparsa e molle
con lenta e flebil voce
sospirando sclamava:
"O dio, non più martoro,
lasciami, traditor, lascia, ch'io moro."
Ond'io di nuovo al vago furto attento
con più dolce contento,
con egual gioia e con egual desire,
con più riposo e più soave ardore
colsi di nuovo il bel piacer d'amore.
Di vaghi e bei cinabri[70]
sparse la bella Lilla
i lascivetti fiori.
E al chiaro fonte poi
lavato il petto, il seno e 'l molle volto,
con pegno d'imeneo
da me volse il bel piè nudo e disciolto.
Ond'io tutto ridente
restai fra dolce speme
e di goder credei felice amante.
Credei di rinnovare i miei contenti
con l'amato mio sol, caro mio bene.
O dio, ch'in van sperai!
Lilla più non rividi,
Lilla la cruda e fera
ad altri si donò, ad altri in braccio
cinse, l'infida, dell'infido laccio.
Ed or mi fugge e schiva,
e d'ogni ben mi priva.
Amore, ecco mia vita,
solo per te finita!
O Lilla, o Lilla ingrata!
Così, così consenti
che pera chi t'adora,

---

[70]*cinabri*: colori rossi.

whose soul is yours, you'd thus to death relinquish?
Is this the kind of mercy
you repay for my love?
Like this, like this, you keep
the faith you swore to me?
Oh female wild and crude!
Oh monster impious, of pity nude,
would you then have me die? Then die I will,
to give you joy, to still your troubled soul,
and with my death thus quell
your base desire, though so unmerciful!
I die, I die for you –
ruthless, perfidious – I die, yet dying,
I cry out Lilla, Lilla.
I die, cruel Lilla. I die and adore you.

The Lover of an Ugly Woman Lauds Her Ugliness

      My ugly one, beauty above all beauties —
beauty, for each desire of mine
you pleasure beyond joy
and, bare of any beauty, make me pine.
What wagging tongue mendacious
mocks your valid qualities?
Who veils over your advantages?
Who steals away, my Sun, your lovely splendor?
Who calls it only folly my sweet ardor?
Why too must I, ungrateful,
scorn you whom others detest —
disdain your homely countenance,
if from your homeliness I live so blest?
And what of it, if your two eyes
(not sparkling darkly) turn to me and gaze,
for of such a pale-blue color
is their glance (squinting and sullen)
like two prettily turning charms
when you, gazing, say to me: "Burn, for I burn"?
Can it drag much on my longing
if your locks, golden no longer,
scintillate silvery rays,
if silver be to my liking,

e chi l'alma ti diè vorrai che mora?
È questa la mercede
che doni all'amor mio?
Così, così mi osservi
la fè che mi giurasti?
O fera troppo cruda!
O mostro d'impietà, di pietà gnuda,
vuoi ch'io mora? Morrò, sarai più lieta,
quieta l'anima inquieta,
e della morte mia
sazia tua voglia dispietata e ria!
Moro, spietata, io moro,
perfida, sì ch'io moro e nel morire
Lilla, Lilla pur chiamo.
Moro, Lilla crudel, moro e t'adoro.

Amante di donna brutta loda le sue bruttezze[71]

      O bella, brutta mia, più d'ogni bella,
bella ch'il mio desire
rendi pago di gioie
e nuda di beltà mi fai languire.
Qual mentitrice lingua
biasima i pareggi tuoi?
Chi t'oscura i tuoi vanti?
Chi ti toglie, mio sole, il bel splendore?
Chi folle chiama il mio soave ardore?
Perché, perché debbo io,
s'altri ti sprezza ingrato,
disprezzare i tuoi sprezzi
s'io degli sprezzi tuoi vivo beato?
Che mi fa, se i tuoi lumi
non sfavillanti e neri a me rivolgi,
ma di color celeste
in bieco e torvo guardo
vezzosetti li giri,
e mirando mi dici; "ardi, ch'io ardo."
Che preme alla mia voglia
ch'il tuo crin, non più d'oro,
splenda raggi d'argento,
se l'argento mi piace,

---

[71]For comment, see Introduction, p. 29.

if I yet value your silvery treasure?
What care I, my very own,
that your face glints not with sheen
of the whitest ivory or of candid snow,
if my heart is so enticed and lured the more
by an Egyptian-like woman's
Moorish face of tints and colors rustier?
What's it matter, life of mine,
that your ever-laughing lips
show your gums lacking a few —
and, instead of ruby-reds to vermilions,
you've a mouth of caverns strewn about with thorns?
Why must I feel any torment
that your teeth of alabaster,
smudged as dark as ebony,
hour to hour more black I see;
if your teeth entice me thus, is it a sin
to enjoy and to admire their malformed grin?
What regretful groan must I
sound about you, my hope dulcet,
if your throat, just barely glimpsed
underneath a goiter's lump
(gift of unjust fate), bulges with profound weight?
What repentance will I ever
have to love you, oh my beauty,
(beauty, yes, though all the others
of your beauty so deny you),
if your horrifying chest with bumps replete,
(its heavily-hanging breasts,
novel pockets full of love),
spattered with a brassy hue, is my retreat?
What repugnance might there be
that would have my soul recoil
if I see that your rough hand
lacks the cleanliness of white,
if for me your roughness increases allure,

s'io prezzo ancor d'argento il suo tesoro?
Che mi curo, mio bene,
s'il volto non hai sparso
di bianco avorio e candidata[72] neve,
se più m'alletta e mi lusinga il core
quel d'egiziaca[73] donna
volto morato e ruggino[74] colore?
Che mi pesa, mia vita,
che la bocca ridente
raccolta pur non sia
e invece di cinabri e bei rubini,
sia sparsa di tane fra foschi spini?
Qual deo[75] sentir tormento
ch' i denti alabastrini
d'ebano oscuro e nero
coperti ognor rimiri,
se m'allettan così, se così godo
di rimirare il mal composto modo?
Qual rammarico io devo
avere, mia dolce speme,
se l'adombrata gola
di globo[76] invido e rio
iniquo fato in maggior peso opprime?
Qual pentimento mai
avrò d'amarti, o bella,
bella sì, benché ognuno
di bellezza ti privi,
s'il tuo spianato e inorridito petto,
fra due caduti pomi
nuove tasche[77] d'amore,
sparso di color d'oro è mio ricetto?
Qual ripugnanza fia
che mi ripugni all'alma
se della rozza mano
non miro il bel candore,
se la rozzezza tua più mi lusinga,

---

[72]*candidata*: bianca.
[73]*egiziaca*: dell'Egitto.
[74]*ruggino*: rugginoso (colore della ruggine).
[75]*deo*: devo.
[76]*globo*: gozzo.
[77]*tasche*: attrattive.

and if Love (as your hand becomes filthier)
makes me kiss it, makes me squeeze it all the more?
What disgust must I admit to
that you, skyward like a novel cypress
stretch, tall and sublime,
if your proud summits as such,
parched with thirst for love, require that I climb?
Why must I unduly fret
if your shoulders, undulating
with their humps so high and broad,
can but bear a lighter load?
Why, if somebody should scoff
and declare that you're a crooked, deformed case,
must I cease my adoration
if you seem to me a godsend
from the god of love, his page in plainer dress?
For what reason must I moan
if your corrugated chest
(almost an uncharted sky)
I discover scattered over
by a rash of oozing, scabby stars in swarms,
if as boatman I'll be rowing through their storms?
Why must I show a distaste
if your lovely font of love,
underneath a hairy hedge,
drop by drop from dripping springs
forms a putrid stream of liquid in excess,
if I more so craving live
there to fill my lover's craving
where others refuse to sip (what's to me dear)
at that earthy font, though not tranquil and clear?
Why in blushes must I be
if lopsidedly you place
your lopsided feet and to the right you keel,
if almost as humble servant
with each bending step you bow to me and kneel?
Have I not the greatest treat
from your most lopsided mien
that on bowing to your bowing I am keen?

s'Amor, quanto è più sozza,
fa ch'io la baci più, fa ch'io la stringa?
Qual disgusto ricevo
che verso il ciel, quasi novel cipresso,
t'allunghi, o bella lunga,
se le altere tue cime,
sitibondo d'amor, convien ch'io giunga?
Ché mi deve dar pena
se la tua spalla inbelle
di peso altero e grave,
regge soma soave?
Perché s'altri ti scherne
e che sei storpia e disconciata dice,
devo non adorarti,
se del bendato dio[78]
mi sembri, o bella, il paggio di valice?[79]
Di che devo dolermi,
s'il tuo crespato seno,
quasi un cielo novello,
sparso tutto rimiro
di rugiadose e sanguinose stelle,
s'io nocchiero mi fo di sue procelle?
Perché devo sdegnarmi
ch'il bel fonte amoroso
sotto l'irsuta siepe
stilli dalle sue vene
putrida vena di soverchio umore,
s'io più bramoso vivo
di cibar la mia brama,
del rifiuto d'ogn' altro, a me sì caro,
al rozzo fonte, non sereno e chiaro?
Qual rossor devo avere
ch'inegualmente porgi
l'inegual piante e 'l destro fianco chini,
se quasi umile ancella
ad ogni chino passo a me t'inchini?
Anzi, maggior dolcezza
dall'inegual tuo modo,
lieto, nel tuo chinar mi chino e godo.

---

[78]*bendato dio*: Cupido.
[79]*paggio di valice* (valigia): paggio (servitore) che accompagnava il padrone in viaggio.

What's it to me if, without talent or art,
sloppy always I observe you,
if, sloppy, the more you lure me,
if I love sloppy your every sloppy part?
What annoyance might I feel
of your inarticulate tongue
if you, in pronouncing words with hesitation
(novel stutterings of love)
interruptedly, give me less aggravation?
Rather, I'm far happier
when your indignations, your defects betraying,
you let loose mixed up, like macaronic sayings.
Why must I make accusations
that you're inexpert, of intellect devoid,
if in your inexpert way
you, at your most foolish, are to me less crude?
Why must I turn to escape you,
if your foul way of life
is reflected everywhere
and, like a merciful sphere,
shows to me just bit by bit
the foul churnings of your unseen viscera?
I've at least no grounds to fear
that with surplus pounds you'll prove to me too weighty.
Your emaciated frame I much condone:
the most savory meat lies closest to the bone.
Therefore, my own Sun unique,
(beggar though you be of splendor),
star of mine bereft of light,
beauty mine bereft of beauty,
eyes of mine bereft of shine,
my own treasure, though you be despoiled and poor —
in my love, enjoy and hope; know well that there
in your ugliness, all beauty I adore.

Ch'importa a me che senza ingegno ed arte
sciatta sempre ti scorgo,
se sciatta più m'alletti,
se sciatta ammiro ogni tua sciatta parte?
Qual noia fia ch'io senta
della non sciolta lingua
se tu nel proferir dei detti tuoi,
d'amor balba[80] novella,
con interrotto dir meno m'annoi?
Anzi, più lieto sono
mentre gli sdegni tuoi, gli tuoi difetti
confusi sciogli con tuoi mozzi detti.
Perché ti deo tacciare
di non esperta e d'ogni spirto ignuda,
se l'inesperto stile
ti fa, quanto più sciocca, a me men cruda?
A che ti deo fuggire
se la tua laida vita
riluce in ogni loco,
e, qual sfera pietosa,
delle viscere occulte
mi mostra i laidi moti a poco a poco?
Almen temer non devo
che di soverchio peso al sen mi pesi.
L'estenuato tuo biasmar non posso,
ch'il meglio della carne è accanto all'osso.[81]
Dunque, mio sol novello
d'ogni splendor mendico,
mia stella senza luce,
mio bel senza beltade,
miei lumi senza rai,
mio dispogliato e povero tesoro
godi dell'amor mio e credi e spera,
ch'ogn' altro bello io nel tuo brutto adoro.

---

[80]*balba*: balbuziente.
[81]Dal proverbio *La meglio carne è quella d'intorno all'osso*.

Mother to a Son Born Female and
Then Changed to Male by Nature

My charming little one,
my precious and dear son,
soul of my heart, life of my life, so fair —
baby not once but twice born to the world,
beneath propitious, favorable star.
Daughter — your lovely name you turned to son;
son — just when I had issued you
from my womb's viscera,
unclad but with proud beauty decorated,
I then discover, see,
despite the laws of nature,
with lovely, virile soul you're animated!
Exalted miracle
of Heaven and of earth!
To you in swaddling clothes,
the Holy Font bestowed
the pretty name Maria Vittoria;
you now claim victory
in altering your sex,
and glad, as Ferdinand,
you enjoy that proud name
to your eternal, everlasting glory.
Just how did it take hold,
belovèd little one,
within your tiny breast,
the fecund blossoming
that seconded you with your fertile fate?
As now, dear baby boy,
I see so changed in you
your posture and your style,
your voice, emotion in your tender plaints,
your face, tender caress,
the turn of your bright eyes, your lovely semblance.
Babbling throughout the day,
you seem happy to tell me:

Madre al bambino nato femmina e
poi dalla natura convertito in maschio[82]

    Vezzosetto mio bene,
pargoletto[83] mio caro,
anima del mio cor, vita mia bella,
parto due volte partorito al mondo,
da tua propizia e favorevol stella.
Figlia, ch'in figlio hai volto il tuo bel nome,
figlio, che già ti diedi
dalle viscere mie
dispoglia imbelle alteramente ornato,
ed or ti scorgo e miro,
ad onta di natura,
di bell'alma virile inanimato!
O miracolo altero
del cielo e della terra!
Tu, che già nelle fasce
ti diede il Sacro Fonte
il vago nome di Maria Vittoria,
or la vittoria porti
di cangiare il tuo sesso
e lieto di Fernando
godi l'altero nome
a tua perpetua e sempiterna gloria.
Come, come campeggia,
mio pargoletto amato,
nel pargoletto seno
il germoglio fecondo
che ti permette il tuo fecondo fato.
Come, bimbo mio caro,
cangiare in te rimiro
i portamenti e l'arte,
la voce e i moti delle molli piante,
il viso e i molli vezzi,
il girar dei tuoi lumi e 'l bel sembiante.
Balbettando ad ognora
par che lieto mi dici:

---

[82]For comment, see Introduction, pp. 29–30.
[83]The word *pargoletto* was repeatedly used by Turini Bufalini in reference to her sons and grandsons: *vezzoso pargoletto, dolce pargoletto, pargoletto gentile* (Turini Bufalini, poems 50, 104, 122).

"Mother, to sweeter life
I've changed life's way and I return to life."
And, brimming full of love's amorous joy,
to your sweet little breast you clasp me close,
offer me loving charms
with a more wise and a more virile face.
Oh son, to me so welcome —
son of my thoughts inspired —
son of all I'd desired —
son of my joy, of every hope of mine,
and of this Tuscan land heavenly omen.
Oh benevolent Fortune
of genteel destiny —
Oh protectress divine
of my felicitous boy —
Oh stars of the great sky
who gifted such great mercy
upon my baby's birth —
my humble thanks I offer.
And I, made bold by gift of such largess,
I pray you, Heavens and benevolent gods,
that my fortunate boy
may find a secure haven
with other demigods.
I pray that you bestow
to such a noble soul
a noble fate, immortal;
that under pleasant mantle
of your graces and gifts,
you harvest the sweet fruit
which from your gracious hands
in my hands happily by day grows ripe;
that his beautiful spirit
henceforth with more divine garments you drape.
Oh lucky baby boy,
a boy who among mortals,
with communal regard
will well regarded be.
What lovely girl who upon you might gaze

"Madre,[84] in più dolce vita
il viver ho mutato e torno in vita."
E, tutto colmo d'amorosa gioia,
mi stringi al vago e leggiadretto petto,
mi fai vezzi amorosi
con più sagace e più virile aspetto.
O figlio, a me sì grato,
figlio dei miei pensieri,
figlio dei miei desiri,
figlio del mio gioire, d'ogni mia spene,
mostro celeste delle toscane arene.
O benigna Fortuna
di cortese destino,
o protetrice dea
del mio parto felice,
o lumi del gran giro,
che di sì gran mercede
i miei parti dotate,
umil grazia vi rendo.
E fatta ardita da sì largo dono,
vi prego, o cieli, e voi benigni dei,
ch'il parto fortunato
abbia sicuro nido
tra gli altri semidei.
Concedete, vi prego,
a così nobil alma
nobil stame immortale;
e sotto il grato manto
di vostre grazie e doni,
accogliete il bel frutto
che dalla vostra mano
nelle mie man ognor lieto germoglia,
e 'l bel spirto fatale
vestite omai di più celeste spoglia.
O bimbo fortunato,
bimbo, che fra mortali
con riguardo comune
riguardevol sarai.
E qual beltà fia mai che ti rimiri

---

[84]These verses are similar to: *Mi ridi e miri e par che in tua favella* /*dica: "madre* . . .
(Turini Bufalini, poem 50).

could then, without your beauty,
live but in pain throughout her painful days?
What mortal soul so proud,
once having seen your lovely eyes' resplendence,
would choose not to adore you;
and who, in that bright splendor
could hesitate to shed
a flood of bitter tears as consequence?
What tongue loosened and twisting,
but negligent to praise you,
could form a praise that's true, or speak true speech?
What heart so petrified,
once conquered by your charms,
would not surrender gladly to Love's torch?
Who, from those bright-hued cinnabars
of your vermilion lips
nectars of love would taste,
could be left but to languish
with a heart so enamored and so pierced?
What haughty girl could see your hair
of gold, by breezes tousled, teasing, pliant,
and not declare: "I now expire
in subtle dolor, dulcet torment."
And that beautiful hand,
depriving dawn of all luminous candor —
who could but look upon that noble feature
and not find herself twined
in a sweet servitude, bound in sweet chains,
not find herself undone by lover's pains?
Ah, every soul so crude,
every spirit so proud,
by those charming and lucent eyes of yours
will find her heart pierced through,
will find her soul oppressed by lover's woes.
Yes, yes, my dulcet heart,
for solely by your beauty
each one will be left vanquished;
and each, from your fair face —
each heart (though ever shrewd,
though each so wise, in love experienced),
will have, my lovely idol, dulcet death.

senza per il tuo bello
viver dolente fra dogliosi giri?
Qual anima sì fera
potrà tuoi vaghi e risplendenti lumi
mirar senza adorarti,
e per il bel splendore
non disparger dolente
dagli occhi lagrimosi amari fiumi?
Qual lingua scioglierassi
che senza le tue lodi
formi in verace dir lode verace?
Qual cor così impetrito
sarà che dai tuoi modi
vinto non ceda all'amorosa face?
Qual da quei bei cinabri
della vermiglia bocca
trarrà cibo d'amore
che priva non rimanga
dell'invaghito ed impiagato core?
Chi potrà 'l tuo crin d'oro,
superba, vagheggiar disparso al vento
senza dirti: "io mi moro
in soave dolor, dolce tormento."
E della bella mano,
che l'alba priva d'ogni bel candore,
chi potrà rimirar la nobil parte,
senza restare avvinta
in dolce servitù, dolce catena,
senza disfarsi in amorosa pena?
Ahi, ch' ogn' alma più cruda,
ogni spirto più fiero
dai tuoi lucenti e vezzosetti rai
porterà 'l cor trafitto
e l'alma oppressa d'amorosi guai?
Sì, sì, dolce mio core,
che dalla tua bellezza
ognun resterà vinto,
e dal tuo vago volto
ogni cor più sagace,
ogni più saggio e più scaltrito ardire
trarrà, bell'idol mio, dolce morire.

Live, then, even more happy
about your genteel fate,
and more so for Heaven and your good luck
with a miracle touched you
amidst all other mortals —
fashioned you as a new omen of beauty.
Rejoice then, enjoy, hope
to be of every virtue
a unique sign in our fine century.

Woman Lamenting Her Dead Lover

He's gone, alas, he's gone,
my heart's idol, my own.
Gone, therefore, is my life.
Who'll come to give me aid here in my grief?
It's gone, all of my good, all of my joy.
Would that I, too, could die.
Oh Tirsi, beautiful soul —
where, where do they exist
your eyes so luminous?
Where is your loveliness?
Where do you leave me now,
with no mercy for all my pain, no justice?
Spirit, breath of my being —
how could you thus expire,
oh God, how breathe your last while I've breath yet,
and not snuff out from my poor heart my spirit?
Ah Death, unfair and cruel,
how did you dare, pitiless,
cut down so fine a stalk,
uproot from my own heart my very soul?
Ah, fraudulent, fierce Death,
how, from that lovely face,
did you block off the light?
Over his lovely lips
flecked with their ruby hues,
how did you pull a shadow-veil, ungrateful?
And, on those spoils of his, so prized and noble,
how did you sate, crude Death,
your craven thirst, ever insatiable?

Vivi dunque più lieto
del tuo fato cortese,
e già ch'il cielo e tua benigna sorte
per miracol ti diêro
nel centro dei mortali,
e ti fêr di beltà novello mostro,
godi felice e spera
esser d'ogni virtude
unico mostro nel bel secol nostro.

Donna che si duole dell'amante morto[85]
  È morto, ahi lassa, è morto
l'idol del cor mio.
È morta la mia vita.
Chi mi darà nel mio dolore aita?
È morto ogni mio bene, ogni mia gioia.
Anch'io convien che moia.
O Tirsi, anima bella,
e dove, dove sono
i tuoi sì vaghi lumi?
Dov'è la tua beltade?
Dove così mi lasci,
senza aver del mio duol giusta pietade?
O spirto del mio seno,
come spirar potesti
senza ch'io spiri al tuo spirare, o dio,
dal mio misero cor lo spirto mio?
Ahi, morte iniqua e ria,
come osasti, spietata,
di troncar sì bel stame,
di torre al petto mio l'anima mia?
Ahi, frodolente e fiera,
come da quel bel volto
oscurasti la luce?
Come la bella bocca,
sparsa dei bei rubini,
d'oscuro velo ricopristi, ingrata?
Come l'ingorda e sitibonda voglia
saziasti, infida e cruda,
di così degna e sì pregiata spoglia?

---

[85]Perhaps excessive in tone, but it is Baroque and well written.

And you, Heaven unkind,
why did you give permission?
Why, with such haste from such a charming breast,
did you chase off his lovely soul?
. . . .
Oh you, my griefs perverse,
my pains and all my anguish,
I pray you, please unloose
the harsh knot, undeserved,
that binds my youthful years,
and, midst pitiless hurt, real agonies,
put me to death as well, you, tears and sighs.

Mother to Her Daughter Fallen Ill

My loving, little girl —
my baby so adored, of my own womb —
like this, like this, I see,
my charming, little beauty,
that with your tears you give a languid sigh.
Like this, from your bright eyes
I see the light grown faint,
and of your marvelous mouth
that would justly cast scorn
at coral's deepest crimson,
I see become so pallid
those truly luscious lips.
Like this, the pretty pinks,
once in your cheeks so delicate and fine,
I see a little languished;
about your pain they give a warning sign.
Your beautiful, blonde hair
tangled in gold confusion,
I see tumble, alas,
over your silvery brow.
Your soft and pretty breast,
that many times you'd press against my own,
with its thousandfold charms,

E tu, cielo scortese,
perché permesso l'hai?
Perché sì tosto a sì vago petto
scacciasti la bella alma?
. . . .
O mie perverse doglie,
mie pene e miei tormenti,
voi sciogliete, vi prego,
il duro laccio indegno
degli anni miei più vaghi,
e, fra spietati duoli e rei martiri,
uccidetemi voi, pianti e sospiri.

Madre alla bambina inferma[86]

Pargoletta amorosa,
delle viscere mie parto adorato,
così, così ti miro,
vezzosetta mia bella,
sparger col pianto il languido sospiro.
Così dei tuoi bei lumi
veggio il lume adombrato,
e della bella bocca,
che già scorno facea
al purpureo corallo,
rimiro impallidite
le lascivette labbia.
Così le vaghe rose
del leggiadretto e delicato viso
languidette rimiro,
e del tuo duolo, ohimè, mi danno avviso.
Il vago e biondo crine
quasi in matassa d'oro
cader ti scorgo, ahi lassa,
sull'argentata fronte.
E 'l molle e vago petto,
che già solea nel tuo materno seno
stringer fra mille vezzi,

---

[86]A mother's despair at seeing her little girl enervated by illness is expressed here with tenderness. The poet stresses the close relationship between mother and daughter. As far as I know, it is the first time that an Italian woman poet addresses a daughter and her illness. See also Introduction, p. 30.

I see oppressed, and feel
from this feverish dolor, scalding poison.
Idol of my own soul —
focus of all my thoughts —
life of my very life —
the light of my own eyes —
who cloaks over your splendor?
Who now attacks you with so fierce an ardor?
Just as with halting voice you try to speak,
my languid, little dear one,
it's then of pain and of complaint you learn.
Just as your smiling liveliness breaks through,
with painful tears, alas, you overflow.
Oh lovely, little girl,
how it weighs on my soul
when, with your voice so pained,
"Mother" to me you call,
and with sweet, charming ways
to share your hurt, alas, you pull me in,
and point to me, there in your pains, my own;
then, with delicate arms,
offer a weak embrace.
Daughter, to me so welcome —
daughter of all my joys —
joy of all my contentments —
shelter of my repose —
and so the dulcet cause for my harsh torments.
Like this, in these, your years
of tender youth, I see
that, breathless, you are fading.
I witness you destroyed,
oh dainty, little dawn
of days felicitous.
When will there reappear
in you, your loveliness —
lovely, gracious and graceful,
amorous little girl?
Beauty, yes, yes, my beauty,
be that, in your fair face,
I'll see once more your loveliness revive —

oppresso scorgo e sento
da febbrico[87] dolor, caldo veleno.
Idol dell'anima mia,
scopo dei miei pensieri,
vita della mia vita,
luce degli occhi miei,
chi copre il tuo splendore?
Chi mi t'offende di sì fiero ardore?
Appena a balbettar muovi la voce,
languidetta mia cara,
che di dolerti e di lagnarti impari.
Appena il tuo bel riso, allegra, scocchi,
ch'in doloroso pianto, ohimè, trabocchi.
O bella pargoletta,
quanto m'opprime l'alma
la tua voce dolente
quando "madre" mi chiama,
e con tuoi dolci vezzi
a pianger il tuo mal, lassa, m'inviti,
e nelle pene tue la mia m'additi.
Poi con le molli braccia,
languente, m'accarezzi.
O parto, a me gradito,
parto delle mie gioie,
gioia dei miei contenti,
nido del mio riposo,
dolce cagion degli aspri miei tormenti.
Così, così negli anni
acerbetti io ti miro
anelante languire.
Distruggere io ti veggio,
o leggiadretta aurora
dei miei giorni felici.
Quando sarà che torni
in te la tua bellezza,
bella, vaga, vezzosa
fanciuletta amorosa?
Sì, sì, bella mia bella,
che nel tuo vago volto
risorger rivedrò la tua beltate.

---

[87]*febbrico*: febbricoso, febbrile.

so that, my proud belovèd,
on your resplendent head
I'll see much merrier that lovely treasure
gathered in plaits of gold entwined at leisure.
And from those dulcet lips
deep-hued in cinnabar,
content once more I'll drink, my girl so dear,
a draft of their sweet nectar.
And from your face so fair,
happy, will I enjoy
an air much lighter, more serene and clear.
My pallid, little one,
tell me, tell me, my darling,
what pain so fierce and crude
does now enshroud your splendors?
Ah, what cloud of ill-luck
shadows your face, darkens its brilliant colors?
Oh you, for each of my harsh pains
the gentle restoration.
You fail, I die — no hesitation.
You shriek, I take my life.
You weep, and in your wailing
I feel my soul distill.
You moan, tearfully telling of your hurt —
I, moribund, exhale my very heart.
Daughter, daughter belovèd —
daughter of my privations
and of my lamentations.
Oh pale lovely, of all loveliness bare.
Lovely are your bright eyes,
but, dark with pain, obscured.
Lovely your lips and mouth,
but colorless and dull.
Lovely your breast and lovely your fair face,
but this injurious ill
does now each lovely trait of yours erase.
Heaven, or You who can,
make her lovely again
as once you made her so.
Concede, oh kindly Heaven,
that in the end I'll see

Sì, mio sostento amato,
che del tuo crine aurato
rimirerò più lieta il bel tesoro
accolto in vari groppi in treccia d'oro.
E dalle dolci labbia,
sparsi dei bei cinabri,
contenta suggerò, bimba mia cara,
il nettare soave.
E dal tuo vago viso
goderommi, felice,
aura più lieta, più serena e chiara.
Pallidetta amorosa,
dimmi, dimmi, cor mio,
qual duol sì fiero e crudo
opprime i tuoi splendori?
Ahi, qual nube importuna
del tuo bel volto oscura i bei colori?
O, d'ogni aspra mia pena,
mio soave ristoro.
Tu langui ed io moro.
Tu gemi e io m'uccido.
Tu piangi, io nel tuo pianto
l'anima mia distillo.
Tu sclami, lagrimosa, il tuo dolore,
io, moribonda, esalo il proprio core.
O figlia, o figlia amata,
figlia degli miei stenti,
figlia dei miei lamenti.
O bella esangue, o d'ogni bel spogliata.
Son belli i lumi tuoi,
ma dal duolo oscurati.
È bella la tua bocca,
ma scolorita e smorta.
È bello il tuo seno e 'l vago viso,
ma dall'invido male
ogni più vago e bel gli vien reciso.
O Ciel, o tu che puoi,
rendila bella e vaga
qual di già la rendesti.
Concedi, o Ciel cortese,
ch'io la miri omai

what I saw her to be.
Sustain the tender foot
that, so weakened before me here, files past.
Give breath to the bright spirit
that, pale and languid, nearly breathes its last.
And since, from my own womb, those lively limbs
you gifted once, in pity,
please grant comfort to her, relief to me,
for as she fades away, I fade and die.

FROM: **CANZONETS**

Contented Lover to His Woman

　　　　Eurilla, your glances
are sweet sparks that thrill me,
that in sweet darts skillfully
menace like lances.
It pleases,
the flame does —
it's good for me to smart:
keep torching and scorching my ardent heart!
　　　　Eurilla, I die here.
I'm happy to perish.
To languish, I cherish —
it's sweetness to suffer.
Inviting,
delighting,
the pain, the desire:
keep torching and scorching my soul afire!
　　　　Eurilla, you never
will see in my breast
the ardor desist,
or less of love's fever.
This life's become
welcome,
the pain and the hurt:
keep torching and scorching my ardent heart!

qual di già la mirai.
Sostenta il molle piede
ch'indebolito avanti a me raggira.
Dona spirto al bel spirto,
che quasi esangue, ohimè, languendo spira.
E giacché dal mio sen le vaghe spoglie
le donasti, pietoso,
permetti a lei conforto, a me ristoro,
ché mentre ella si langue, io languo e moro.

DALLE: **CANZONETTE**[88]

Amante contento alla sua donna

Eurilla, i tuoi sguardi
son dolci faville
ch'in dolci scintille
m'avventano i dardi.
Mi piace
la face,
mi giova l'ardore:
colpisci, ferisci l'ardente mio core.
Eurilla, mi moro
e godo morire,
m'è dolce il languire,
soave il martoro.
M'alletta,
diletta
la pena, l'affetto:
colpisci, ferisci l'ardente mio petto.
Eurilla, non mai
vedrai nel mio seno
l'ardor venir meno,
mancare i miei guai.
M'è vita
gradita
la pena e 'l dolore:
colpisci, ferisci l'ardente mio core.

---

[88]The three *canzonette* given here have been chosen as examples of the poet's ability to write verses that flow rapidly.

Lover Enjoying the Jests of His Woman
        You, lovely smiles
when merciful
or when disdainful
entertain —
enjoy! It's plain
that I enjoy your smiling at my pain.
        You, lovely taunts
that so rejoice
as you go slice
and slay with mercy —
confess! You see,
I yearn for you to taunt me playfully.
        You, dulcet ways
that my heart's core
with dulcet ardor
you enflame —
admit! You're game
that I'm glad when you goad me without shame.

Lover to His Woman's Hair
        Golden tresses,
whether bound
or unwound,
you entwine me —
tighten not
on your net:
no more strings, for pity's sake.
        Lovely hair,
from my heart
to my foot,
a snare you make —
no more plaiting,
no more strings, for mercy's sake.
        Aureate skeins,
with your chains
free of pains,
you squeeze me, taut —
no more trappings,

Amante che gode degli scherzi della sua donna
     Vaghi risi,
che pietosi
e sdegnosi
mi piacete,
deh, godete,
ch'io mi godo ch'al mio duol sempre ridete.
     Vaghi scherzi,
che gioite
e ferite
con pietate,
deh, mirate,
ch'io sol bramo ch'al mio mal sempre scherzate.
     Dolci modi,
ch'al mio core
dolce ardore
m'accendete,
deh, godete,
ch'io gioisco che di me gioco prendete.

Amante ai capelli della sua donna
     Trecce d'oro,
che raccolte
e disciolte,
mi legate,
non stringete
sì la rete,
non più lacci, per pietade.
     Vago crine,
ch'il mio seno
tieni in freno
col mio piede,
non più nodi,
non più lacci, per mercede.
     Fila aurate,
ch'in catena
senza pena
mi tenete,
non più groppi,[89]

---

[89]*groppi*: viluppi.

no more wrappings,
no more strings, please have a heart!

non più agroppi,[90]
non più lacci, se volete.

---

[90]*agroppi*: avviluppamenti, avvolgimenti.

FROM: *THE CABINET* (1639)

FROM: TOP DRAWER: RED CARBUNCLES AND DIAMONDS

To Vittoria della Rovere, Grand Duchess of Tuscany
     Returned is the Age of Gold unto the world.
On Arno's shores, the oak, her precious boughs
and leaves to Heaven lifts that, rife with gold,
on our desires placid shade she bestows.
All golden wealth the universe may hold,
through her alone, is restored unto us,
and at the sight of oak, one of such beauty,
hearts fill with joy, souls with tranquillity.
     Wherever acorns grow, from there flees peril
along with pain that trails felons pernicious,
and flung afar scattering into exile
go fears, regrets, and portents ominous.
Away from the Age of Acorns turns as well,
laden with turbid apprehensiveness,
the brow of Discord, while Deceit together
with Damage flies, vanishing into air.
     The violent blows of Mars no more are heard,
nor the disdainful rivalries of War,
nor with hair bristled, foot halted on guard,
does one detect Terror whistling with Ire.
The vengeful Furies, restraining instead
their tumults harsh, condemn punishments bitter.
And through the acorns whispers just the trace
of friendly Peace and loving Happiness.
     The grass enwraps herself with emerald,
and pretty flowers enrich themselves with gems.
With rubies does the rose her lap enfold,
and diamonds' rich distinctions the lily claims.
Violet, king of the day seems, clad in gold,
and jasmine has, from dawn, her diadems.

DA: *LO STIPO* (1639)

DAL: PRIMO CASSETTINO: CARBUNCOLI E DIAMANTI

A Vittoria della Rovere, Gran Duchessa di Toscana[91]
Fatto ha ritorno il secol d'oro al mondo.
In riva all'Arno preziose foglie
erge rovere[92] al cielo, che d'or fecondo,
placide ombre ministra all'altrui voglie.
Onde solo per lei rieda giocondo
quant' oro l'universo in sé raccoglie,
e di sì bella rovere all'aspetto
gioisca il core e si tranquilli il petto.

      Ove le ghiande son, fugge il periglio
e la pena che segue i rei nocenti,
e lungi si disperdono in esiglio
i timori, i rammarichi, i portenti.[93]
Dal secol delle ghiande altrove il ciglio,
formidabil di torbidi spaventi,
rivolge la Discordia, e in un col Danno,
lontano il volo suo spiega l'Inganno.

      Non s'odono di Marte i fieri insulti,
né di Bellona le sdegnose gare,
né con rigido piè, con crini inculti,
l'Ira in un col Terror s'ode fischiare.
Condannano, frenando aspri tumulti,
l'ultrici[94] Furie le lor pene amare.
E solo tra le ghiande evvi spirante
la Pace amica e la Letizia amante.

      Vestesi l'erba di smeraldi intorno,
e di gemme arricchisconsi i bei fiori.
La rosa di rubini ha 'l grembo adorno,
e 'l giglio di diamanti ha ricchi onori.
Par la viola all'oro il re del giorno,
e 'l gelsomin dall'alba ha i suoi tesori.

---

[91]According to Margherita, Vittoria della Rovere brought peace and harmony to Florence and established a new "golden age." Reference to the *secol d'oro* was a recurring theme in Italian literature (see G. Costa). In octave 4 and 5, the poet shows off her ability to describe nature in an animated way.
[92]*rovere*: albero dello stemma della famiglia della Rovere.
[93]*portenti*: fatti straordinari.
[94]*ultrici*: vendicative.

Sweet violet is with amber nicely tressed,
and pearls in fragrant sprays enlace the frost.
        Through pleasing vales, precious silver enhances
the course of rivers to run and so resound.
The trees in rivalry ready their dances
in concert with the breezes' peaceful sound.
Crystal to sapphire joyous turn the seas,
while nymphs, a hundred hundredfold are found
with crowns of the pearlescent marguerite,
in lively dance about upon bejeweled feet.
        All thanks to the grand oak that now adorns
with boughs felicitous our Tuscan fields,
and in whom courtesy and grace sojourn,
for now the Fates grant joy to our appeals.
Hatred and Time desist and suffer scorn.
Clipped wings retracted, Envy likewise yields.
In Iron's Age, our fair Etruria
delights in golden years of a new era.
. . . .

FROM: **Third Drawer: Gold and Pearls**

Truth Addresses the Lovely Tuscan Ladies
        Fair goddesses of Arno at Flora's breast —
the fire of noble hearts, Italy's splendor,
light of the world amid the starry host,
of Love's beautiful blaze a welcome ardor,
numen, omen of beauty manifest,
of every glory, virtue, the true honor —
the truth to you (as I am she, the Truth),
I raise up as a throne here of your worth.
        Not from lands distant or Aegean abysses
come I to you, your vantages to stain,
but from my travels, earthly goddesses,
I carry truth into Tuscany's reign.

D'ambre la mammoletta ha vago il crine
e con spirti d'odor perle ha per brine.
      Corrono i fiumi per l'amene valli
con risonante, prezioso argento.
Gli alberi in gara apprestano i loro balli
al suono placidissimo del vento.
In zaffiri tramutano i cristalli
gioiosi i mari, e cento ninfe e cento
di margherite incoronate stanno,
e con gemmato piè le danze fanno.
      Mercé della gran rovere, ch'adorna
coi suoi felici rami toschi prati
ed in cui grazia e cortesia soggiorna,
ch'a noi di nostra gioia arrecan i Fati,
il Tempo, e l'Odio, cede e se ne scorna.
Chiude l'Invidia i vanni suoi tarpati,
e nel secol di ferro Etruria[95] bella
gode degli anni d'or l'età novella.

. . . .

DAL: **TERZO CASSETTINO: ORO E PERLE**

La Verità alle belle dame toscane[96]
      Belle dive dell'Arno a Flora in seno,
splendor d'Italia, ardor d'ogn' alto core,
luce del mondo in celeste sereno,
del bel fuoco d'Amor gradito ardore,
mostro[97] d'ogni beltà, nume terreno,
d'ogni gloria e virtù verace onore,
a voi la Verità, ch'io quella sono,
innalzo qui dei vostri pregi il trono.
      Non da Biarmi o dall'Egeo profondo,[98]
per macchiar vostri vanti a voi ne vegno,
ma dal mio giro, o belle dee del mondo,
porto la verità sul tosco[99] regno.

---

[95]*Etruria*: Toscana.
[96]Speaking through the voice of *La Verità* [Truth], the poet praises the many excellent qualities of Tuscan ladies, but at the same time exposes various beauty tricks that *La Bugia* [Falsehood] attributes to them.
[97]*mostro*: sommo grado.
[98]*Non da Biarmi o dall'Egeo profondo*: non da lontano e non dall'abisso.
[99]*tosco*: toscano.

Disheartened by the burdensome distresses
of my impious foe's wicked design,
I'm now haughtily desirous to show
Flora's fair face and charms to loving Arno.
     Let wicked Falsehood hide and henceforth silence
the lying words of her prevarications,
lay bare before your eyes her mad impudence,
not load you down with her disfigurations.
Fake is her talk, double her countenance;
of amour's wiles, vast are her affectations,
and with makeup, an artful artifice,
she tints her lips and masks over her face.
     Wicked towards you, she lets up on her bit
and at your aureate hair, your hands of snow,
your cheeks of cinnabar and bosom white,
she — cruel, unbridled — lets her insults flow,
pretends your clear complexion's not quite right,
your charm but fakery (though it's not so),
and claims your beauty, your neatness, to be
an artful artificiality.
     You, rich in brio, pomp and self-respect,
grace, spirit, manners, whimsicality,
go forth haughty about your lovely aspect,
not masking over what is true with lie:
among you, fake things earn but disrespect.
Neither does there exist a Tuscan beauty,
(as each of you this cruel liar would dare
accuse), with made-up face and tinted hair.
. . . .
     Your locks' true gold, your alabaster breast,
bosom of snow, of ebony your brow,
your ruby lips, forehead of ivory cast
and framed by sweet curls dangling down just so,
roses your cheeks and your glance piqued with lust,
(through roses, lilies, does your charmed smile go),
lumen of all splendor Heaven-bestowed,
of all embellishment, soft spheres' abode.

Ed abbattendo sotto grave pondo
dell'empia mia nemica il rio disegno,
altera scoprir voglio, all'Arno amante,
le vaghezze di Flora e 'l bel sembiante.
    Celi l'empia Bugia, racquieti omai
del suo mentito dire i falsi detti,
soggiacia il folle ardire ai vostri rai,
né scarichi sopra voi i suoi difetti.
Ella solo ha due volti e finti lai:
di menzogne d'amor vari ha gli affetti,
e di mistura, artificioso avviso,
tinge le labbra e mascherato ha 'l viso.
    Sol l'empia, contro voi disciolse il freno,
e con l'aurato crin, la man di neve,
le guance di cinabro,[100] il bianco seno,
la ria tracciò mal castigato e lieve;
finse non chiaro il vostro bel sereno,
e 'l vostro vago e bel d'ogn' arte greve,
e d'artificio artificiosa cura
chiamò vostra beltà, vostra lindura.
    Voi, che ricche di brio, fasto, fierezza,
grazia, spirto, maniera e bizzarria,
ne gite altere di vostra bellezza,
non ricoprendo il ver con la bugia,
da voi che l'artificio si disprezza.
Né v'è tosca beltà che fatta sia,
ardì questa mendace di dar nome
di finto volto e simulate chiome.
. . . .
    Qui d'oro il crine, d'alabastro il petto,
di neve il seno, d'ebano il bel ciglio,
il labbro di rubin, d'avorio il tetto,[101]
del bel giro di lui tra dolce artiglio,[102]
guance di rose, guardo lascivetto,
vezzoso riso tra le rose e 'l giglio,
lumi d'ogni splendor dal ciel dotati,
soavi giri d'ogni bello ornati.

---

[100]*di cinabro*: rosse.
[101]*tetto*: fronte, viso.
[102]*artiglio*: nell'uso raro di dito, *dolce artiglio*: boccoli di capelli (che circondano il viso).

Beautiful, polite, clever, with each deed
so neatly done, each art, custom, motif;
visage ornate without ornaments' need;
comeliness no adornment need contrive;
beauty sans artifice cosmetic-made;
lovely complexion naturally alive;
mannered desire and ladylike effect;
wise will bent to the wish to show respect.

    In custom civilized, in carriage graceful;
ornately donned even in simple dress;
brio luxurious and ways genteel;
subtle in speech, in song harmonious;
magnanimous in thought, splendid in style;
in all good-hearted works, a pridefulness;
breeding unique, affection unvanquished;
gold hair, bosom of pearl and diamond blest.

    Joys, laughter, pleasure, contentment and charm
are but in Tuscan beauties surely found.
Let Falsehood sing, others to disaffirm,
for Fame's already spread the word around.
Elsewhere let wicked Falsehood ply her harm,
profit with lies upon a liar's ground;
for Flora to her clan makes the truth clear,
and Tuscan land is an empire sincere.
. . . .

    Yes, yes, enjoy henceforth, you beauties Tuscan,
in spite of her, the honors that are yours,
and let her declarations, false and vain,
be turned back by your beauty to blind horrors.
With you I intend always to remain.
I'll hold back her disfavors and her snares,
and with my face unveiled, in boldness proud,
I'll make her fib about every false word.

Belle, garbate, accorte, e con lindura
ogn'opra, ogn'arte, ogn'uso, ogni motivo,
ornato volto senza orpellatura,[103]
leggiadro aspetto d'ogni acconcio privo,
beltà senza artificio, opra o mistura,
vago color sol del suo bello vivo,
manieroso desir, tratto di dama,
sagace voglia d'ossequiosa brama.
    Portamento leggiadro, uso civile,
ornato addobbo[104] di semplice ammanto,[105]
gala, sfarzoso brio, modo gentile,
soave detto, armonioso canto,
magnanimo pensier, splendido stile,
d'ogn' opra di gran core altero vanto,
cortesia non usata, invitto affetto,
oro il crin, perle il sen, diamante il petto.
    Gioie, risi, piacer, contenti e vezzi
sol nelle belle tosche han fermo il nido.
Canti pur la Bugia gli altrui disprezzi,
che già spiegò di lor la Fama il grido.
Altrove empia Bugia mentir s'avvezzi,
procacci al suo mentir bugiardo lido,
ché Flora ai parti suoi discopre il vero,
ed è 'l suol tosco verdadiero impero.
. . . .
    Sì, sì, godete omai, belle toscane,
ad onta di costei, dei vostri onori,
e le sue voci menzoniere e vane,
avvolga il vostro bello in ciechi orrori.
Con voi mi sarò sempre, e a voi lontane
terrò di lei l'insidie e i disfavori,
e col volto svelato, in puro ardire,
ogni suo falso dir farò mentire.

---

[103]*orpellatura*: abbellimento.
[104]*addobbo*: ornamento.
[105]*ammanto*: vestito.

from: Fourth Drawer:
Amethysts, Lapis Lazuli and Turquoises

Author's Response to Paganino Gaudenzio
　　　Alas, Rome never granted the bright fortune
to all my prayers, and if the truth be told,
there's nobody who, in his native town,
ever enjoys contentment in his soul.
If Rome called injury and plunder down
upon herself, plotted many a brawl,
to hope for else but these neither could I,
than my misfortune, my own injury.
　　　Destined was Rome to deal out only exile
to the great, noble Scipioni clan,
and with their very lives also in peril,
the Ciceroni, too, with harsh luck ran.
No less did the Camilli those claws feel
of Fortune, who sees good and bad as one.
Wicked numen, with both of her eyes blind,
tries to poke fun but causes harm in kind.
　　　That men in Rome were wont to flare with love
upon my glance, the fact I won't deny,
that from amorous lightning they'd dissolve
at the darts fulminating from my eye;
but those hearts burn with fire that's make-believe,
fabulous flash expended easily.
Rome, used to its real ardors, pays no mind
to hearts of lovers in amour that's feigned.
　　　Venus, from whom the Romans claim their birth,
desires no other woman on her soil,
and though no beauty's equal to her worth,
she disdains sharing any of her spoil.
Neither would Rome, from my frail song plucked forth,
devoted to her, eternity cull,
if with valor (to which all virtue bows),
she's the sole site of thousands of Apollos.

DAL: **QUARTO CASSETTINO:**
AMETISTE, LAPISLAZZULI E TURCHESI

Risposta dell'autrice a Paganino Gaudenzio[106]

Ah, che liete venture unqua non diede
Roma ai miei voti, ché, se 'l ver si dice,
entro la propria sua nativa sede
non v'è spirto che goda alma felice.
E se Roma a se stessa e danni e prede
nelle sue rissa ordì poco felice,
altro sperare non potevo anch'io,
che le sventure mie, ch'il danno mio.

    Fu Roma destinata a dare esiglio
ai generosi, nobili Scipioni,
e della vita loro anco il periglio
corser con aspro fato i Ciceroni.
E i Camilli non men soffrir l'artiglio
di lei[107] che gli empi in un confonde e i buoni.
Invido nume ha ciechi i lumi sui,
né sa scherzar se non offende altrui.

    Io già non negherò ch'altri al mio sguardo
non avvampasse nei romani campi,
e delle luci al fulminante dardo,
non si sciogliesse in amorosi lampi,
ma favoloso è 'l foco ond' i cor ardô,[108]
e facile la vampa ond'altri scampi.
Usa ai veri ardor suoi Roma non cura
dei cori amanti la mentita arsura.

    Venere, ond' i romani ebber natale,
non brama ch'altra donna ivi risieda,
e, benché a lei non sia bellezza uguale,
sdegna comun con le altre aver la preda.
Né fia che Roma, del mio plettro[109] frale
dovuta a sé, l'eternità richieda,
se con valor, ch'ogni virtù pareggia,
ella è di mille Apolli unica reggia.

---

[106]For comment, see Introduction, p. 30.
[107]*di lei*: della Fortuna.
[108]*ardô*: ardono.
[109]*plettro*: ispirazione poetica.

Helicon's garden's surely blest with flowers
and, as eternal springtime there abounds,
today, to reach Flora's time-honored shores,
did destiny concede to me the grounds,
where Arno gazes on its regal bowers
much less bejeweled with waves than with diamonds.
And all those born on Etruria's hills
are offspring from whom every virtue spills.

     To make my life here, Gaudenzio, I yearn,
wherein dwells royal patronage and where
one is by new Augustus called upon
for works of fame using unique endeavor.
Let Rome the others' welcome seat remain,
for Heaven's grace rains down upon me here
to drink from Arno my eternal measure.
Straying from Tiber's coast is Costa's pleasure.

FROM: **FIFTH DRAWER: AMBERS, CORALS AND SAPPHIRES**

Beautiful Woman Laments Her Fortune
     Tell me, cruel Fortune, tell, pitiless one,
the purpose of the gifts you gave to me?
To make me luckless, more than anyone?
Why did you, from my works, strip yours away?
Why decorate me with your riches when
against my riches you let your wings fly?
And why, when my locks of thick hair you held,
with cruel destiny did you pluck me bald?

     Tell me, what good's it to me, if your wheel
you tilted in my favor, if your splendor
you turned to favor me, held it there still,
to have me by all hearts and souls adored?
Why then my beauty, to the world known well,
did you make haughty with plentiful ardor,

S' Elicona ha di fiori orto beato
e ivi eterna primavera abbonda,
oggi a ragion m'ha conceduto il fato
giunger di Flora all'onorata sponda,[110]
ove l'Arno si mira il regio prato
di diamanti ingemmar vie più che d'onda.
E quanti parti han dell'Etruria i colli,
tutti esser di virtù chiari rampolli.

Qui, Gaudenzio, bram'io trovar mia vita,
ove son regi mecenati e dove
le anime altrui novello Augusto invita
a far d'opre di fama uniche prove.
Sia Roma ai voti altrui sede gradita,
ché qui 'l ciel per me sue grazie piove
per bere in Arno eternità verace.
Lo scostarsi dal Tebro a Costa piace.

DAL: **QUINTO CASSETTINO: AMBRE, CORALLI E ZAFFIRI**

Bella donna si duole della Fortuna[111]
Dimmi, Fortuna ria, dimmi spietata,
a che dei doni tuoi già mi dotasti?
Per farmi più d'ogn'altra sfortunata
e le opre in me dell'opra tua spogliasti?
A che dei pregi tuoi rendermi ornata,
se contro i pregi miei le ali spiegasti?
E con le ciocche in man dei folti crini
calva rendesti gli empi miei destini?

Dimmi, che pro mi fia, se la tua rota
a mio favor girasti, e i tuoi splendori
vèr me volgesti e a favorirmi, immota,
mi festi ardor delle alme, ardor dei cori?
E se la mia beltade al mondo nota
già rendesti superba in mille ardori,

---

[110]*di Flora all'onorata sponda*: a Firenze.
[111]These *ottave* are autobiographical. The poet addresses Fortune and demands to know why she was gifted with poetic talent only to be abandoned in her struggle to follow a chaste life (Diana) and develop her intellect (Pallade = Pallas Athene), when she was condemned to serve only Venus and be scorned. Margherita laments her fate, but at the end of her composition, she declares that time will reveal her true calling — that of a poet.

and with spirit, virtue and rich design
render my nature with talent so fine?
· ·
      What use to me, if with Pallas' thought
you gifted me, and with Diana's heart,
if through the goddess of pleasures illicit
I'm made shadow ignited, prey to fright?
Why give me emotions so resolute
if but Amour my actions motivates,
if with this, that burdensome task in sway,
you cast my days upon blameworthy way?
      What can I do, if with my thought, alas,
only Diana's steps and path I track,
if I place hope in the actions of Pallas,
and if to imitate those two I seek,
when the cruel archer, Cupid, son of Venus,
makes my eyes drowsy, my thought overtakes,
then Venus (of the two, sworn enemy),
makes of my chaste desire immodest prey?
· ·
      What use to me, from goddess of all beauty
to have tribute so rich, and in my face
perceive in each one of its charms, so haughty,
all charm and beauty gathered in one place?
What good do virtue, spirit and pride do me,
greatness of soul, greatness of thought apace,
if then my virtue, value and allure
the jealous, wicked Fame would so obscure?
      Fame, to my detriment, spread on your wing
Venus' works — she holds me at her bosom —
with those of Cupid and his obscene yearning;
tell everyone of those forbidden whims;
claim I'm alone guilty of others' sinning
and pluck out the leaves only from my limbs;
the actions of my fate do not excuse,
but only the shame of my gifts accuse.
      What can I do? What blame then do I merit
about my deeds, if luck iniquitous

e di spirto, virtù, di pregi ornata
rendesti di natura opra in me grata?
. . . .
    Che mi val che di Pallade i pensieri
già mi donasti e di Diana il core,
se per la dea d'illeciti piaceri[112]
mi festi ombra d'ardor, preda d'orrori?
A che rendere in me moti sì fieri,
se solo i moti miei motiva Amore,
e sotto l'uno e l'altro grave incarco,
desti ai miei giorni il biasimevol varco?
    Qual opra tratto, ohime, se col pensiero
sol di Diana seguo i passi e le orme,
e di Pallade i moti, e in lor mi spero,
e d'imitarle cerco in varie forme,
se di Venere il figlio, il crudo arciero,
soprastà al mio pensier, miei lumi addorme,
e della dea già delle due nemica,
mi fa in casto desir preda impudica?
. . . .
    Che mi val della dea d'ogni bellezza
aver ricco tributo, e nel mio volto
scorger altera d'ogni sua vaghezza
ogni più vago e bello in me raccolto?
Che mi giova virtù, spirto, fierezza,
animo grande a gran pensier rivolto,
se mia virtù, miei pregi e 'l bello mio
adombra nume[113] invidioso e rio?
    Dispiega a danno mio, volante Fama,
le opre di quella dea ch'in sen m'accoglie,
e in me, del dio bendato oscena brama,
tra il volgo spande d'illecite voglie,
e me sol rea dell'altrui colpe chiama,
e sol dai rami miei svelle le foglie,
né del mio rio destino i moti scusa,
ma solo ai pregi miei le onte raccusa.
    Che vi posso fare io? Qual colpa deggio[114]
aver delle opre mie, s'iniqua sorte

---

[112]*dea d'illeciti piaceri*: Venere.
[113]*nume*: la Fama.
[114]*deggio*: devo.

leads me to this, if to an obscene seat
my star's assigned and to death worried thus?
Well do I know my fault — well I concede
that only to reproach swing wide my doors.
What can I do if my sail is so spun
and by Love, Fortune, Fate, Heaven thus blown?
    Denied that our fate individual
prevail, we cannot move against our star
which turns by directions of Divine will,
nor from high astral storms can we fly far.
For where Fortune would place our ship in battle
against destiny's waves cruel and unfair,
the pilot is not served by act or skill,
for rock envious rips away his sail.
. . . .
    Great goddess of the stars, oh you who bring
to us from lucent spheres the ornate day —
friendly fate, star to me most gratifying,
turn round at last from the spheres' starlit way;
turn, oh nocturnal goddess, a more pleasing
mantle of gold for me mined from your quarry.
Since I cannot in your beautiful font
wash myself clean, please conceal my affront.
    Reveal, oh numen, unto my foes common,
my prayers and the effects of my chaste thought.
Point out to them my spirit that's not wanton.
Reveal my heart, unto your thoughts devout.
Unveil, friend of my works, oh kindly numen,
the pure and burning love of mine so felt.
You who perceive my heart, please have them see
honest desire they find not there in me.
    I, more than any other, yearn to arm
my right hand with your darts, and through the forests
to chase, fleet of foot, the wild sylvan swarm
and haughtily to fell ferocious beasts,
no arrow more than mine faster to harm

a ciò mi porta e nell'osceno seggio
assise la mia stella in cura a morte?
Ben l'error mio conosco e ben m'avveggio
che sol del biasmo mio s'apron le porte.
Ma che poss'io, se 'l destinato telo[115]
m'avventa Amor, Fortuna, il Fato e 'l Cielo?

    A noi non è permesso il suo destino
predominar, né contro nostra stella,
che gira ai cenni del voler divino,
dei pianeti fuggir l'alta procella.
Ch'ove Fortuna il combattuto pino[116]
lascia tra le onde a sorte iniqua e fella,
non giovan del pilota i moti e l'arte,
ché sdruce[117] invido scoglio a lui le sarte.[118]

. . . .

    O gran dea delle stelle,[119] o tu, ch'ornato
il giorno porti di lucenti spere,[120]
a me più grata stella, amico fato,
rivolgi omai dalle stellate sfere,
volgi, notturna dea, vèr me più grato
l'aurato manto delle tue miniere.
E giacché non poss'io nel tuo bel fonte
bagnarmi, ahi lassa, in me ricopri le onte.

    Discopri, o nume, al volgo mio nemico,
del casto mio pensier gli effetti a voto.
Nota lo spirto mio non impudico.
Scopri il mio core ai tuoi pensier devoto.
Svela, benigno nume, alle opre amico,
di puro ardor l'affetto mio già noto.
E tu, ch'il cor mi scorgi, a lui fa prova
dell'onesto desire, ch'in me non trova.

    Più d'ogn' altra bram' io la nobil destra
armar dei dardi tuoi e tra le selve
seguir con ratto piè fiera silvestra
e altera saettar feroci belve,
né più di mia saetta altra più presta

---

[115]*telo*: dardo.
[116]*pino*: nave.
[117]*sdruce*: strappa.
[118]*sarte*: vele.
[119]*dea delle stelle*: Diana.
[120]*spere*: sfere.

than any shot by others to deep woods.
But what's the use, if my ungrateful star
condemned me to the arrows of Amour?
     He alone armed my hand in infancy,
since I sucked cowardly at breast to raise
maternal lymph; henceforward, tenderly,
in sweet disport my body spent its days;
nor to another's light did I, childishly,
than to amorous Venus' turn my gaze;
true path of other light I did not find
while prattling in embrace of archer blind.
     I don't deny that to studies and art
I then turned with my heart and with my mind;
that I did set the love-goddess apart,
and that her son's blind ardor I declined;
that of disdain I felt, the major part
of blame, to pitiless Love I assigned.
So what! If then at work, my mind insane
followed only their undertakings vain.

· ·

     Enjoy, troublesome one, go and expand,
mendacious Fame, your feathers that defraud;
submerge my name with others' you have drowned,
each with resplendent light, in that abode.
In league with fate and destiny conjoined,
batter each of my virtues, wicked god;
your shrieking clamor I no longer heed.
Instead, I hand my fate to Time, my guide,
     and Truth, who daughter is to Time, one day
will make my feelings clear, and how I lived.
In my face, no flourishes on display,
let be unveiled light of my eyes once hid,
and let scorn from my name be wiped away,
the iron bite of my shame dissipated.
Treat thus my thought alike, and let Truth have
revealed my heart's loves were enslaved by Love.
     So go exclaim, cruel one, and criticize
as you see fit — I grant your words no space.
My mind already does its past excise —
attends, awaits its hoped-for future place.

fia, che scocchi altro braccio e si rinselve.
Ma che poss'io s'il mio pianeta ingrato
solo ai dardi d'Amor m'ha condannato.

Solo armommi di lui la destra imbelle,
fin quando alle mammelle io raccogliea
il materno licore e, tenerelle
le membra, in dolci vezzi i dì traea,
né ad altro lume in pueril facelle
rivolsi i rai ch' all'amorosa dea,
né d'altro lume scorsi il ver sentiero
pargoleggiando in sen del cieco arciero.

Non niego già ch'a vari studi ed arte
non rivolgessi con la mente il core,
e che la bella dea posta in disparte,
del suo figlio sdegnassi il cieco ardore,
e che dei scorni miei la maggior parte
non incolpassi il dispietato Amore.
Macché! S'all'opra mia la mente insana
sol di loro seguia l'impresa vana.
. . . .

Godi dunque, importuno,[121] e tu dispiega,
Fama mentita, le svelate piume,
affondi il nome mio ove s'annega
d'ogn' altro nome il risplendente lume.
E con il Fato e col Destino in lega,
abbatti ogni mio vanto, iniquo nume,
ch'io non più curo del tuo dir le strida,
ma solo al Tempo do mia sorte in guida.

La Verità, figlia del Tempo, un giorno
farà chiari i miei sensi e i miei costumi,
e con il volto non di fregi adorno
fia che disveli in me gli ombrati lumi,
e della fama mia tolto ogni scorno,
del ferreo morso in me le onte consumi,
e tal qual è il pensier fia che del core
gli affetti scopra in servitù d'Amore.

Sclama pur, empio e rio, e dì ch'io sia
qual più ti pare, ch'io del tuo dir non curo.
Già il suo passato la mia mente oblia
e attenta attende allo sperar futuro.

---

[121]*importuno*: si riferisce al nume (Fama).

Go right ahead, drown out the facts with lies
to darken each bright aspect of my face.
Despite you, Truth will finally succeed
and make known my life's feelings, loves and deeds.

FROM: SIXTH DRAWER:
ALABASTER, BOHEMIAN CRYSTALS AND IMITATIONS

Woman, Despairing Over Her Lost Beauty, Indicts Women's Frivolity

      Poor me, alas, what's become of my beauty?
Where is the haughty brilliance of my splendor?
Where is my heart's previous cruelty?
Where is the springtime when I was in flower?
Where has it gone, others' pity for me?
Who's dealt my dawn a night before its hour?
Who's looted my treasure from me outright,
to turn my locks of gold to silver's white?
      Where are my ostentations, luxuries?
Where is my way of whimsicality?
Where are the lovely splendors of my eyes?
Where is the lissome stride of mine so comely?
Ah, my bold colors Old Age, impious,
hides under bandages of cruelty,
and Fate, with the evil scalpel of Time,
the beauty of my visage renders dim!
. . . .
      I thus cry out my pain and, in my pain,
of each woman's fierce pain so do I cry.
I decry our love's flight, its curtailed run.
I decry the offenses to our beauty.
I decry the small sphere of our rotation
and the foreshortened thread of our life's joy.

Sommergi pur il ver con la bugia,
rendi ogni chiaro del mio volto oscuro,
ch'alfin la Verità fia che ti scopra
di mia vita gli affetti, i sensi e l'opra.

DAL: Sesto cassettino:
Alabastri, diamanti di Boemia e gioie false

Donna dolendosi della perduta bellezza
accusa le leggerezze delle donne[122]
    Misera, ohimè, e dov'è mia beltade?
Dov'è del mio splendor la luce altera?
Dov'è del petto mio la crudeltade?
Dov'è del mio fiorir la primavera?
Dove, dove n'andò l'altrui pietade?
Chi diede al mio mattin sì tosto sera?
Chi dispogliato m'ha del mio tesoro
togliendo al bianco argento i groppi d'oro?
    Dove sono i miei sfarzi e i miei favori?
Dov'è del mio trattar la bizzarria?
Dove son dei miei lumi i bei splendori?
Dov'è dell'andar mio la leggiadria?
Ahi, ché sol l'empio Veglio[123] i bei colori
nasconde sotto benda iniqua e ria,
e, con l'empio scarpel[124] del Tempo, il Fato
il bel del volto mio rende oscurato!
. . . .
    Sclamo[125] dunque il mio duolo e nel mio duolo
d'ogni altra donna il fiero duolo io sclamo.
Sclamo del nostro amor sì corto il volo,
e la nostra bellezza offesa io chiamo.
Sclamo del nostro giro il picciol polo,
e del nostro gioir lo scorcio stamo.[126]

---

[122]In the first two octaves, the poet makes use of the theme *ubi sunt* [where are] commonly used in the Renaissance and usually associated with the passing of time and the destruction of powerful empires. Margherita applies this theme strictly to women's loss of beauty and youth. See also Introduction, p. 30.

[123]*Veglio*: Vecchio (Il Tempo). Time was depicted as an old man with wings.

[124]*scarpel*: scalpello.

[125]*sclamo*: esclamo.

[126]*stamo*: stame, filo della vita.

Weeping for our misfortune more than once,
the gifts that nature gave me I denounce.
     I weep and, in my weeping, weep another,
for each beauty's beauty already wept.
I weep for my own light in others' splendor,
that to another's light my beauty's slipped.
I weep that others' rays hold my bright star.
I weep for youth my once verdant years kept.
For each prized worth of mine I weep my worth:
I weep as thousands weep upon this earth.
     Ah, no! If woman I was born, just what
of good could I ever hope from my ventures?
Only women a nest of pain create;
only to them fall wicked misadventures.
Who speaks the word 'woman,' just hope of hurt
would offer up with its injurious cares.
Ours is the sex with most unhappiness:
'woman' denotes damage, dolor, distress.
     Woman alone was born for one sole fate,
to struggle, caring for children and home,
ever to worry, so to cultivate,
amid varied concoctions, her own harm.
So to appear loveliness consummate,
she forfeits the stars of her own light's charm,
and with sundry cosmetics, ambergris,
in vain pursuit her loveliness destroys.
     What greater struggle and what greater pain
is there than seeing a woman in love?
To seem more fair than fairest on the scene,
and prettier her pretty life to prove,
she traps herself, with graces, in gold chains;

E piangendo in mille altre mia sventura,
disgrazio i doni che mi diè natura.

    Piango e nel pianto mio d'ogn' altra bella
piango la già d'altrui pianta bellezza.
Piango in altro splendor la mia facella,
e nell'altrui facella mia vaghezza.
Piango nei raggi altrui mia vaga stella.
Piango in più verde età mia giovanezza.
E d'ogni pregio mio piango i miei pregi:
piango il pianto in mill'alme e mille regi.

    Macché! S'io donna nacqui e che di bene[127]
giammai sperar potevo a mie venture?
Sol la donna si fe' nido di pene,
son proprio delle donne empie sventure.
Chi donna disse,[128] sol dannosa spene
proferir volse di dannose cure,
né mai sesso di lor fu più infelice:
donna danno, dolor, doglia predice.

    Nacque la donna sol per sol stentare
tra le cure di casa e dei figliuoli,
e per affannar sempre a coltivare,
tra gli aromati vari, i propri duoli.
Per bella più apparir, vaga sembrare,
perde del proprio lume i propri soli,
e tra vari alberelli[129] ed ambracani,[130]
ridur[131] di sua beltade i pensier vani.

    Qual affanno maggior, qual maggior pena
dar si può che veder donna invaghita,
per più bella apparir tra belle in scena,
e più linda mostrar la linda vita,
trar da mille vaghezze aurea catena,

---

[127]At this point, Margherita bitterly comments on the sad lot of women who are destined only to care for house and children. They find an escape in leading a frivolous existence dedicated to their toiletries and clothes, and envying each other. (See also Introduction, p. 31.) Margherita condemns such a life in a humorous way, but some of her accusations are still valid today, especially if applied to women who are fashion fanatics.

[128]Here Margherita inverts the meaning of the proverb *Chi disse donna, disse danno*.

[129]*alberelli*: matite cosmetiche.

[130]*ambracani*: ambra grigia. Ambergris: substance secreted by sperm whales and found floating in seas or on shorelines, used in the production of perfumes. It was and still is rare and very expensive. Melville describes it in Chapters 91–92 of his *Moby-Dick*. For a scientific explanation, see Kemp.

[131]*ridur*: rendere.

lost mid those arts, her art no more she'll have,
and with thoughts sundry, sundry implements,
with sundry marks and signs, her face she paints.

    To guarantee her locks cascade just so,
with a neat part, upon her painted visage,
and that her white whiteface be seen to glow
a deep vermilion, courtesy of rouge,
and for the gilding of her gilded hairdo,
to make it look partly bound, partly loose,
she uses such art and such cogitation,
more than it takes to build a sovereign nation.

    Lovely Semiramis, when she was told
that she had lost her realm, grasped in her hands,
as enterprise, her aureate locks of gold,
now in this way, now that, plaited some strands
and left others unkempt, to get a hold
on what she saw as her real loss — not lands —
dismissing the downfall with much less care
for a lost realm than for disheveled hair.

    The art woman adopts to form, in spills,
over her ears in an array of tone,
now a plucked feather, now Iberian frills,
now pretty ribbons in the color brown,
or sometimes even rich mines of gold jewels
spread like a lovely flower over curls golden,
is work without compare, an expertise:
thus does her mind all other work erase.

    To don a dress and then in sundry ways
decorate it with threads from white to ruby,
with varied colors, varied appliqués,
to feign appearance of roses or lily,
and styles by thousands so to improvise,
and to invent new fashions constantly,
are efforts that outdo even Columbus
who journeyed to unknown, untraversed seas.

. . . .

e tra mill' arti l'arte aver smarrita,
e con vari pensier, tra vari ordegni,
il volto impennellar di vari segni?
     Per far cader in ciocca con lindura
parte del crin sul pennellato volto,
e sul bianco imbiancato dar pittura
di bel vermiglio dal cinabro tolto,
e del dorato crin l'indoratura
far apparir qual cinto e qual disciolto,
s'usa tanto artificio e tanto ingegno,
che men cura richiede ergere un regno.
     Semiramide bella, allor ch'intese
già perso il regno, tra le man tenea
l'aurati groppi d'oro e 'n varie imprese
or questi, or quelli in treccia raccogliea,
mezzi incolti lasciolli e andare intese
prima a quel che già perso in sé vedea,
stimando meno cura alle ruine
del perso regno ch'allo sconcio crine.
     L'arte poi, che s'adopra in far cadere,
sopra le orecchie, di vario colore
or penna scarnatrina,[132] or gale ibere,[133]
or vago nastro di color di more,
ovver d'aureo monil ricche miniere
spander sull'aure trecce in vago fiore,
è oprar senza pari, è maestria
ond'ogn' altro operar la mente oblia.
     Per vestirsi una veste e 'n varie guise
quella smaltar[134] tra 'l bianco di vermiglio,
e di vari color varie divise
far apparire tra le rose e 'l giglio,
e in mille usanze di fogge improvvise,
ad ognora trovar nuovo consiglio:
è studio tal ch'l vario studio avanza
del genovese[135] in non fermare[136] usanza.

. . . .

---

[132]*scarnatrina*: distaccata (da ornamento).
[133]*gale ibere*: ornamenti spagnoli.
[134]*smaltar*: decorare con ricamo.
[135]*genovese*: Christopher Columbus, born in Genoa.
[136]*non fermare*: andare oltre.

If then in church, the very place where pity
leads hearts to repent of their guilt and sin,
one lovelier, with lovelier finery
and in rich clothing happens to be seen,
in an assault of spite, in such fierce fury
the others bat their wings making a scene,
then go with downcast eyes, with humble stoop,
like clucking hens when forced out of the coop.

. . . .

And then she who does more beauty possess,
in seeing another beauty feels but pain
and such torment, dolor at once so fierce,
that both living and life does she disdain.
No breast exists with heart of such largess,
or soul that holds such pride in its domain,
or spirit bold within a woman's heart,
she'll not wage war with every other skirt.

. . . .

No less than others, I, too, in my place,
unhappy, suffered rancor similar
and, at my pace, unable to surpass
their pace, I kept pace only with mad labor.
Also in me, as in them, wants arose
for shoes bejeweled and for those golden mixtures,
and mid feminine wants my own desires
I turned foolishly to unneeded spheres.

. . . .

Poor me, now with repellent countenance,
(if not repellent, at least taken thus),
I see no mortal eye cast me a glance,
no salute, not one, to my loveliness.
As all good from my beauty's relevance
is lost with the tribute of beauty's goddess,
others regard me only to despise,
despising in me my pomp, brio, ways.
Just this alone is woman's recompense.
This is Fate's prize at last, in disposition.
Our beauty bequeaths but this heritance.
This is, from our acquiring, acquisition.
This is the capture of so much conveyance.

S'in tempio poi, dove pietade i cori
tragge a pianger sue colpe e i propri danni,
altra, più bella e con più bei lavori,
veggono ivi apparir tra ricchi panni,
d'astio l'assal così fieri furori,
che dall'altrui mirar battono i vanni,
e con le luci a terra in atto umile,
paion la chioccia fuori del covile.
. . . .

La pena poi, ch'ogni beltà maggiore
prende nel rimirar altra bellezza,
è tal tormento e sì fiero dolore
ch'il viver con la vita si disprezza.
Né petto così franco ha tanto core,
né seno in seno tien tanta fierezza,
né spirto così ardito è in cor di donna
che guerra non le faccia ogn'altra gonna.
. . . .

Non men delle altre nel mio posto anch'io,
infelice, provai simil rancori,
e non potendo il passo al passo mio
passar, passando fei pazzi lavori.
Anco in me, tra l'altrui, salse il desio
d'ingemmati coturni[137] e misti d'ori,
e tra voglie donnesche il mio volere
folle rivolsi a non dovute sfere.
. . . .

Ed or, misera me, con laido volto,
e se non laido, almen per tal tenuto,
non veggio occhio mortal ver me rivolto,
non scorgo a mia beltà pur un saluto.
E come il bello mio d'ogni ben sciolto,
e della bella dea perso il tributo,
altri sol mi rimira per disprezzo,
sprezzando in me le gale, il sfarzo e 'l vezzo.
Questa sol delle donne è la mercede.
Questo è 'l premio ch'al fin ne porge il fato.
Di questo il nostro bel ne lascia erede.
Questo è del nostro acquisto l'acquistato.
Questo è 'l predato delle tante prede.

---

[137]*coturni*: scarpe.

This is what's left from prior dispossession.
And for such labor, here's the final topper:
more lovely were you, you're now more so pauper.
. . . .
         Leave aside, thus, everything you enjoy,
the bright flower of youth's flowering so pretty,
and to me, wise already, turn an eye
to realize what was, now past, my beauty.
Such that I am now, know that you will be;
neither will Time show towards you greater pity:
but in you, the same weapons will bring night,
your springtime's withering, at your most bright.
. . . .
         I, for my part, surrender — every care
from my cosmetics' pen I've now abandoned;
I'll prove no lovelier for all my bother;
my cheeks no longer shine from sleight of hand.
Though they might shine like gold, I wish no more
to ply the mad pursuit of makeup's blend;
let them reveal, with waters of clear font,
Time's opus in step with age's affront.
. . . .
         Never has there been husbanded with rhyme
gracious beauty, fashionable deportment,
nor have Muses, with but beauty sublime,
been known to play any sage instrument.
Rhyming does rage for fashion overwhelm,
and silver hair, not gold, shines more resplendent;
not just at any age, in any vase,
may one plant rhymes and the fruits of Parnassus.
         In Helicon, the ornate face is censured
more than Love's opus, than Apollo blonde,
nor is a made-up, pretty face admired,
nor powdered chest, nor neck powdered around.
Neither is perfumed shoe prized or desired,
nor a clear gush of liquor that's unsound;
instead, cheeks natural in veil hirsute
Parnassus admires — agèd wisdom's merit.
         For Poetry impoverished, without frill
and bare, is painted on the ancient scrolls,

Questo è l'avanzo del già rifiutato.
E questo è l'opra di tanta fatica:
quanto più bella già, or più mendica.
. . . .

     Lasciate dunque, tutte che godete,
il bel fior del bel fior di vostra etade,
e in me le luci, omai sagge, volgete,
scorgendo qual già fu la mia beltade.
Tal qual io sono ancor voi diverrete,
né il tempo avrà di voi maggior pietade:
ma con le armi medesme in voi fia sera
nel più vago sfiorir di primavera.
. . . .

     Io per me già m'arrendo e d'ogni cura
dispoglio omai l'impennellata mano,
né più bella mi fia per mia fattura,
né più con l'opra mia le gote spiano.
Sian pur di color d'or, ché di mistura
più non vo' esercitar l'officio[138] insano,
ma discopra di lor limpida fonte
l'opra del Tempo e del lor tempo l'onte.
. . . .

     Non fu mai coltivata con le rime
vaga bellezza e lindo portamento,
né mai le Muse con beltà sublime
si videro adoprar saggio strumento.
Ogni lindura il verseggiar opprime,
e più dell'oro splende il crin d'argento,
né in ogni età s'ammette o in ogni vaso
piantar le rime e i frutti di Parnaso.
     Si sprezza in Elicona un volto ornato
più delle opre d'Amor, del biondo Apollo,
né s'ammira un bel volto ben lisciato,
o d'imbiancato petto, un bianco collo.
Non si prezza coturno profumato,
o di vano licor chiaro rampollo,
ma d'una schietta guancia in velo irsuto,
in Parnaso s'ammira un sen canuto.
     La poesia mendica e senza spoglie,
nuda si pinge sull'antiche carte,

---

[138]*officio*: lavoro.

and only tributary leaves of laurel
she proudly enjoys and in part fulfills,
singly conserves her thoughts, works of her soul,
to her desires unfolds the naked sails,
and is not pleased by fair breast, pretty face,
but solely for her work enjoys the praise.
    Good-bye, then, cosmetics and tiny vials,
good-bye vases and cabinets of mixture,
good-bye white paste, rouge, good-bye makeup quills,
good-bye to the gold bleaching of black hair,
good-bye mirrors, tweezers, hairpins for curls,
talc lotions good-bye, good-bye painted flair:
from this time forth, my face goes unembellished
because Parnassus spurns a cheek that's polished.

from: Seventh and Bottom Drawer: Peridots and Hyacinths

The Author, Advised by Benedetto Guerrini to Burn Some of Her Poems, Suffers Desperately

    Let each offspring of mine burn and with each
let my pen burn, every evil to cover.
Let my volumes be scattered, out of reach,
so in me no rhyme be left to discover.
And you who waste your time, your work, your speech,
no more, Muse, no more does your labor serve:
sinister Fortune subjugates your cantos,
disturbs all of your peace in endless guise.
    I torch, yes, Guerrini, I torch and burn,
it's true, my sweat along with my privations.
I torch the works of my thought and concern,
and I torture over their conflagrations.
By just a touch reduced to ash in turn,
my long labors I cede unto the winds.
Ah, I could not hope from them any good
than my bad luck to which I gave no heed.

e sol dal lauro tributarie foglie
altera gode e si ricopre in parte,
solo dei suoi pensier le opre raccoglie
e spiega ai suoi desir le nude sarte,
né d'un bel volto o d'un bel sen si gode,
ma sol dell'opra sua gode la lode.
    Addio dunque ampolline, addio alberelli,
addio vasi, addio stipi di mistura,
addio biacca e cinabri, addio pennelli,
addio del nero crin l'indoratura,
addio mollette, addio vetri e scarpelli,
acque di talco addio, addio pittura:
non più fia ch'il mio volto inorpellate,[139]
ché Parnaso non vuol gote lisciate.

DAL: SETTIMO ED ULTIMO CASSETTINO: CRISOLITI E GIACINTI

L'autrice, consigliata da Benedetto Guerrini di bruciare alcune sue rime, si duole disperatamente[140]

    Ardano i parti miei e coi miei parti
arda la penna ed ogni mal si copra.
Disperdansi i volumi in varie parti,
né più fia mai che rima in me si scopra.
Non più, Musa, non più, non serve oprarti,
tu perdi il tempo e con il tempo l'opra:
sinistro nume[141] i canti tuoi soggiace
e turba in mille guise ogni tua pace.
    Abbrucio, abbrucio, sì, Guerrini, è vero
ch'abbrucio i miei sudori ed i miei stenti.
Abbrucio le opre mie col mio pensiero,
e dalle vampe lor traggo tormenti.
Ridotte in poca polve di leggiero
le mie lunghe fatiche io cedo ai venti.
Ahi, che non altro pro sperar potevo
che le sventure mie che non credevo.

---

[139]*inorpellate*: abbellite.
[140]For comment, see Introduction, p. 31.
[141]*sinistro nume*: il Fato.

My words are burning and in ashes strewn
to dust already falls my scribbled page,
and in its flame, as if lost in the ruin,
my spirit struggles, by anguish besieged.
I weep over the carnage, weep at treason
to youthful thoughts, my own hurt to assuage;
no other hurt is equal to my bane,
as I am a unique palace of pain.

       I torch the pages, yes, and with them then
I spurn each work beckoning yet untried.
To blinded horror, I tilt the bright dawn
of my clear mirror, now of light denied.
No more in this place flourishes my pen,
nor does it produce fruit for Arno's pride —
with its penned pages scattered where you please,
quiet, my pen views Tuscan fields with ease.

       You burn, oh offspring mine, you burn while I
become a block of ice in your cruel fire.
In flames, my every thought you thus destroy
and I, from my concern for you, expire.
Oh numen, forever evil to me!
Oh star, where but ill for good I procure!
Oh rhyme, oh Muses, oh Helicon's font,
do you accept towards my words such affront?

       Guerrini, oh Guerrini, what ensues?
Alas, to such fierce and cruel destiny
must I, my pen subjected thus, peruse?
To so much has my destiny condemned me?
What mind more than mine ever proved more pious?
What soul more than mine lived more trustingly?
Ah, harsh Fate only war with me will have,
and Fame with her, to bury me alive.

       Oh speech, you harbor death! Unto the fire,
unto fire must my offspring be condemned,
nor would they a more welcome end desire!
Condemned to fire? Alas, what have I done?
Halt, unjust flame, hold back a minute more.
Extinguish, friendly gods, these blazes heathen!

Ardono i detti miei e incenerito
già cade a terra il mio vergato foglio,
e nella fiamma sua, quasi smarrito,
si strugge il spirto mio nel mio cordoglio.
Piango la strage sua, piango il tradito
mio pensier giovenil, di me mi doglio,
né 'l mio dolor qual si sia duol pareggia,
poiché son sol di doglia unica reggia.

Abbrucio i fogli, sì, e seco ancora
ogn' opra sprezzo ch'a ciò far m'adduce.
Rivolgo in cieco orror la vaga aurora
del chiaro specchio a cui si niega luce.
Non più la penna mia qui si rinfiora,
né più sull'Arno i frutti suoi produce,
ma in cenere disperde i suoi pennati[142]
e cheta ammira dell'Etruria i prati.

Voi ardete, o miei parti, ardete e io
nel vostro crudo ardor divengo un ghiaccio.
Voi distruggete in fiamme il pensier mio
ed io con il pensier per voi mi sfaccio.
O nume, ai miei desir per sempre rio!
O stella, ove ogni mal per ben procaccio!
O rime, o Muse, e d'Elicona o fonte,
così dei detti miei soffrite le onte?

O Guerrini, Guerrini, ohimè, che fia?
Dunque sotto sì fiero e crudo Fato
soggiacer deo mirar la penna mia?
A tanto il mio destin m'ha condannato?
Qual più di me fu mai di mente pia?
Qual spirto più del mio visse affidato?
Ahi, che solo empia Sorte mi fa guerra
e, viva, con la Fama mi sotterra.

O detto, che m'uccidi! Al fuoco, al fuoco
si denno[143] condannare i parti miei,
né per loro vi fia più grato loco!
Al fuoco condannati? Ohimè, che fei?
Ah, ferma, iniqua fiamma, arresta un poco.
Spegnete le empie vampe, amici dei!

---

[142]*pennati*: fogli su cui è scritto con la penna.
[143]*denno*: devono.

Apollo, don't you see I burn outright
the work of your own work in your plain sight?
        But no! For Heaven never sent me fortune
or made me, with my work, felicitous.
Poor me, in my own town so was I born,
so lived, will live on, with unhappiness.
Prey only was I of ill luck's predation,
phoenix ever renewed to hurtfulness,
thus I must not, oh God, hope or pretend
my precipice will one day meet an end.
· ·
        Cursed be the Muses and cursed be as well
the one who first discovered poetry.
Cursed also be my too-indirect style,
as my misfortunes redouble today.
Cursed be my speech, my sayings, one and all.
Cursed let me be for whimsicality.
And cursed let be the minute and the hour
when I found in Apollo my aurora.
· ·
        My hand must not sully a folio
with others' fraud and overt falsifyings,
but I must cry out only of my woe,
my ruin and disastrous sufferings.
Threshold or river of Parnassus, no,
I must not try to cross with my clipped wings,
but rather than seek out a rhyme for verse,
let my voice thus my misfortunes express.
        Good-bye then, rhymes of mine — Muses, good-bye;
my poems, at your own peril stay behind.
Good-bye pen — the cause of my loss is you;
let someone else adopt you, proudly donned.
Good-bye cruel vase, evil and without mercy,
where infelicitous inks I once contained.
Good-bye my thoughts, good-bye my feeble lyre;
to poet's prize no more will I aspire.

Apollo, ohimè, che fai? Non vedi ch'ardo
l'opra dell'opra tua sotto il tuo sguardo?
  Macché! Se mai ventura il ciel mi diede,
né mai delle opre mie mi fe'[144] felice.
Tal nacqui, ohimè, nella nativa sede,
tal vissi e viverò sempre infelice.
Sol preda fei di sventurate prede,
e fui sempre nel duol nuova fenice,
onde non più sperar mi debbo, o dio,
ch'abbia mai fine il precipizio mio.
. . . .
  Maladette le Muse e maladetto
fia colui che trovò la poesia.
Maladetto il mio stil poco diretto,
ch'oggi rinnova la sventura mia.
Maladetto il mio dir con il mio detto.
Maladetta di me la bizzarria.
E maladetto sia quel punto ed ora
ch'in Apollo scorgei[145] mia vaga aurora.
. . . .
  Non lice al braccio mio macchiare il foglio
delle altrui frodi e troppo chiari inganni,
ma sol sclamar io debbo il mio cordoglio,
le mie ruine e disastrosi affanni.
Né di Parnaso o di Permesso[146] il soglio
io debbo entrar coi miei tarpati vanni,[147]
ma senza andar cercando al verso rima,
le mie sventure la mia voce esprima.
  Addio dunque, mie rime, o Muse, addio,
rimanete miei carmi a danni vostri.
Addio penna, cagion del danno mio,
altro di voi s'adorni e altier si mostri.
Addio vaso crudel, spietato e rio,
ove rattenni gl'infelici inchiostri.
Addio mio debil plettro, addio pensieri,
più poetici onor non fia ch'io speri.

---

[144]*fe'*: fece.
[145]*scorgei*: scorsi.
[146]*Permesso*: Fiume del Monte Parnaso.
[147]*tarpati vanni*: tagliate ali.

I hold my tongue — in silence cruel, lifelong
I'll live, and in another place; and where
Apollo beckons other souls to song,
I'll suffer tacitly eternal care.
Let she who's sought in Helicon belong;
alas, for me, the sky rains ruin there:
from now on, so I'll be more truly tranquil,
my musings burned forever will keep still.

Taccio, e tra rio silenzio la mia vita
qui vivrò sempre e in altro loco, e dove
Apollo l'alme altrui al canto invita,
farò tacendo ancora eterne prove.
Sia pure in Elicona altra gradita,
ch'a me in Parnaso il ciel ruine piove,
ond'ora per goder più vera pace,
l'arso mio motteggiar per sempre tace.

FROM: **THE CYPRESS GROVE (1640)**

Tears of the Alp
    Italy, she of every people queen,
is bound by seas and over earth has rule,
as within her reigns one whose hand divine
locks and unlocks the sphere celestial.
Since Heaven would grave fate against her destine,
shaken she saw her proud majesty fall,
her grandeur levelled by armed forces where
all lay engulfed, buried by others' ire.
      Thus she declared: "Oh, how transient they were,
those honors of mine from eras long past.
How lightly did the trophies disappear
of all my glories, into air so fast!
They arm against me now, Fates even graver.
If mid false gods, I, lucky once, did boast
my triumphs, now with more sinister fortune,
I am of pain the prey, of death the scorn.
. . . .
      "I'm forced to flee, but where I take my flight
depends upon permission from the stars,
for it seems that wherever I set foot,
to glory, virtue, there rebellion brews."
As Destiny against her would ignite,
she journeys forth to meet the storms of Mars,
and towards the Alps to the most remote site
directs her steps with pain, redoubled hurt.
      She looks about — a vista fierce — the Po,
his right horn broken off and bloody, goes.
Anguished he wails, his hair disheveled so,
his urn shattered, his face drained of repose.
The Dora, too, sounds out, one with the Po,
lament uninterrupted and there flows

DA: *LA SELVA DI CIPRESSI* (1640)

Le lagrime dell'Alpe[148]
    L'Italia, chè dei popoli regina,
dai mari è cinta ed alla terra impera,
poich'in lei regna chi con man divina
serra e disserra la celeste sfera.
Come il Ciel contro lei grave destina,
scossa vedea la maestade altera,
e i suoi fasti dalle armi al pian rivolti
inabissar nelle ire altrui sepolti,
    sicché diceva:[149] "Oh, come furon brevi
nella passata età gli onori miei.
Oh, come all'aria momentanei e lievi
delle mie glorie sparvero i trofei.
Or i Fati vèr me s'arman più grevi;
e se già fausta, fra mentiti dei
vantai trionfi, or con sinistra sorte
son preda del dolor, scherno di morte.
. . . .
    Fuggir mè d'uopo,[150] né per dove io prenda
la fuga, or mi concedono le stelle,
ch' ovunque avvien che i passi miei distenda,
miro a gloria e virtude opre rubelle."
Sì dice, e come il rio[151] destin l'accenda,
di Marte ad incontrar va le procelle,
e verso le Alpi in più remoto suolo
i passi drizza e cresce pene al duolo.
    Mira, ed è fiera vista, il Po che rotto
e sanguinoso il destro corno porta:
s'ange con chiome dissipate e sotto
ha franto l'urna ed ha sembianza smorta.
E la Dora con lui non interrotto
spiega lamento e, quasi in lor sia morta

---

[148]In these octaves, Margherita deplores the devastation brought about by the wars between France and Spain fought on Italian soil. Her description is gloomy but powerful. She uses the theme of Italy personified (see Introduction, pp. 32–33) and personifies the rivers Po and Dora as well as the Alp.
[149]*diceva*: parla l'Italia personificata.
[150]*d'uopo*: necessario.
[151]*rio*: cattivo

in them dead hope of honor in waves bitter
with pain, dolor, to form a sea entire.

    But trifling are the surges of their tears,
as more ferocious, grave, war-occupied,
blood-laced become the fields wherein but sorrows
ensanguined fill the bitter countryside.
Every hill rises wailing with death's cries —
Fate is extreme where warriors collide.
The earth, once inn, may but in worth be seen
to be so many men's funeral urn.

    Bemoaning Fate, those waters rigorous
between themselves take painful consolation,
move where the Alp, with horrors grandiose,
her castle keeps on crossroads of the wind.
They travel, spill through vales in choruses
plaintive with sighs, torrents, sore lamentation.
Spurred on again by fear and rush of weapons,
these rivers turn back to the Apennines.

    Through tracks from whence they came, again they plough
to witness once again such baleful carnage —
to native soil and to fatherland go
in order to denounce the martial rage.
Her cruel martyrdom therefore to let flow,
Dora to the Alp queries: "Why this scourge
of Luck in Italy, our seat of favor,
made the austere refuge of massacre?

    "From parts remote, each one to reach these shores
yearns but for glory — that one thought conserves;
against my peace, with mercenary Mars,
and to my ruin, acrid battle moves.
Mid hostile ranks, all my good vanishes;
I'm superb prey of foreign powers' motives.
What's more, within my banks and welcomed home,
I find that I lie buried in my tomb."

    "No less than I — I, too," the Po expounds,
"am greedy prey of their impulsive force.
Mid their assaults I, in fragmented sounds,
run errantly, of my own pomp voracious.
My kingdom, of all others throne of thrones
believed itself to be, where now it lies

la speme degli onori, in onde amare
di pena e di dolor forman un mare.
    Ma lievi son dei pianti loro i flutti,
poiché più grave e più feroce a gara
il sangue occupa i campi e solo lutti
ha sanguinosi la campagna amara.
Gemito e morte son i poggi tutti,
ed è d'estremi Fati ivi ogni gara:
la terra, ch'era albergo, appena vale
esser a tanti corpi urna fatale.
    Dei crudi Fati piangono i rigori
e tra lor si consigliano, dolenti,
girne ove l'Alpe ha maestosi orrori
e reggia inalza sulle vie dei venti.
Vanno e versan tra vie dai flebil cori
di sospiri e di pianti Etne e torrenti.
Dalle armi spinti e dal terror ripresi,
all'Appennin tornâro i fiumi stessi.
    Risolcano quelle orme, onde venîro,
a rimirarne strage sì funesta,
ed alla patria e al padre lor se n' gîro
a detestar la marzial tempesta,
sicché sfogando il crudo suo martiro,
dice all'Alpe la Dora: "E qual infesta
Sorte in Italia ha 'l nostro seggio eletto,
se deve esser di strage aspro ricetto?
    Ognun che giunge da remota parte
e bramoso di glorie il pensier serba,
per mia ruina con straniero Marte
muove alla pace mia battaglia acerba.
Tra schiere ostili ogni mio ben si parte,
e son di sforzi altrui preda superba,
e più, ché dentro le mie rive accolta
entro la tomba mia giaccio sepolta."
    Né meno il Po soggiunge: "Anch'io sono
dei grand'impeti altrui preda rapace.
Tra le percosse lor franto risuono
e di mie proprie pompe erro vorace.
La reggia mia degli altri fiumi il trono
già vantar si credeva ed ora giace

with nymphs abandoned and upon earth strewn,
my waves abounding with war's fluctuation."
    The Alp, unable to withstand their plaint —
her crown of coarse and splintered knotty oak,
her mantle into countless pieces rent,
her snowy tresses plucked out in one stroke —
became perturbed, moaned, loosened the restraint
wholly to all her woe, and thus she spoke.
(The woodland gods, at her lament, were felled.
Water nymphs wept — river on river swelled.)
    "Oh you of adverse stars, my useless Fate,
alas, why did you have me guard so well
Italy's kingdoms, have me with such height
raise up my spine in a mountainous wall,
so that the pass to Italy was shut
against enemy fire and hostile steel;
only to have me here, with my own furor,
between my people and myself wage war.
. . . .
    "The woods resound with nothing but sad omens,
and but cruel death unto us they predict.
The night holds nothing for us but dark signs
that are the horrid escorts of cruel Fate.
The limbs of trees hold naught but birds unclean.
The soil holds naught but luck unfortunate.
Within my breast, the world, a theater cruel
appears, and a lachrymose spectacle.
. . . .
    "The grass returns no more to dress my shores,
nor with its emerald hues colors each hill,
now that these bloody and sorrowful waters
soak the whole place around and overspill.
My woods tumble down to the valley floors;
no pine, no oak, her tresses can extol.
In order to construct machines of war,
to empty fields are cut forests entire.

con le sue ninfe abbandonata a terra,
e sono le onde mie flutti di guerra."
    Più l'Alpe il dire non sostenne e franto
il rozzo serto suo di querce annose,
e lacerato in cento parti il manto,
e svelte in un le chiome sue nevose,[152]
si conturbò, lagnossi e sciolto intanto
il freno al suo dolor così rispose.
(Languîro al suono i boscarecci numi,
piansêr le ninfe e crebber fiumi ai fiumi.)
    "O delle avverse stelle inutil fato,
a che, lassa, voler ch'io prenda cura
dei regni d'Italia ed a me sia dato
col tergo erger a lei sassose mura[153]
ed il varco per me sia riserrato
ad ostil ferro ed a nemica arsura,
e dai propri furori in campo oppressa
fo coi popoli miei guerra a me stessa.
. . . .
    Suon il bosco non ha che tristi auguri[154]
non presagisca a noi di cruda morte.
Non ha la notte se non segni oscuri
che son di crudi Fati orride scorte.
Altro i rami non han che augelli impuri.
Altro il suolo non ha che fiera sorte.
E di spettacol lagrimoso ed atro
il mondo nel mio sen fatto è teatro.
. . . .
    L'erba non più le piagge mie riveste,
né de' smeraldi suoi colora il colle,
poich'ivi d'onde sanguinose e meste,
il tutto intorno è ricoperto e molle.
Cadono al pian recise le foreste,
né più il pino o la quercia i crini estolle,
ché, per comporne macchine guerriere,
campi aperti si fan le selve intiere.

---

[152]Note the poet's effective variation in attributing to the personified *Alpe* a rustic crown of oak branches and snowy hair.

[153]The Alps seen as a natural barrier to keep invading armies from entering Italy.

[154]Nature has become desolate — birds no longer sing, flowers don't grow, trees are cut down to make war machines, entire forests are destroyed — an ecological disaster.

"Sylvan himself has nowhere to reside,
and must defend from sun's rays any shade.
Stripped of their trees, my peaks bare their backsides;
never again will woods see boughs, nor glade.
The nymphs weep for their embattled abode;
the birds for other skies their feathers spread.
Ever against the gods, my harm to cause,
go the cruel Fates in hand with the cruel stars.

· ·

"Alas, it's of no use that I am rock,
my body a stone block from head to toe,
for so cruel is my pain, wicked and toxic,
and so grave are my mournful cries of woe,
that even rock have they the power to break,
move beasts to pity as trophies to show:
and where the hard soil boasts hardest terrain,
it would without doubt soften at my pain.

"If at my mountain slopes I likewise gaze
where you, Italy, chose to place your gates,
or if towards the Ligurian boundaries
I'm granted now and then to set my sights,
or if on Lombardy I fix my eyes,
midst hurt, midst death, where sight necessitates,
on every side I look, that part is crushed;
each work I see is turned to Martial waste.

"Since nothing holds sway over destiny,
and since the world has neither rules nor laws,
hence ever threatening let each ship see
Nereus rise from azure ocean floors.
Let night surge — let daytime vanish away;
with constant lightning flash, let glower the skies!
By misery crushed and broken piece by piece,
let mountains crumble into the abyss.

"Let the spring never smile for me again,
when with bright flowers the fields are color-tossed;
nor let the dawn to the high sphere return,

Più Silvano non ha dov'egli alberghi
e dai raggi del sol le ombre difenda.
Nudi i miei monti han d'alberi i lor terghi,
né fia ch'il bosco i rami ivi riprenda.
Piangon le ninfe gli abbattuti alberghi
onde l'augello altrove il volo stenda.
E fino per mio danno incontro a' dei
son le stelle crudeli e i Fati rei.

. . . .

Ah, che non giova a me che sasso io sia
ed abbia di macigno i membri miei,
ché la mia pena è sì nocente e ria
e son sì gravi i miei dolenti omei[155]
che di franger i sassi hanno balia,
impietosir le belve han per trofei;
e quale ha 'l duro suol più salda cote,[156]
alle mie pene intenerir si puote.

Pur se le falde del mio monte io guardi
ove tu poste, Italia, hai le tue porte,
o verso il confin ligure gli sguardi
girar talora a me sia dato in sorte,
o sull'Insubria[157] gli occhi miei non tardi
fissar d'uopo mi fia, tra duol, tra morte
ogni lato che miro è scossa la parte,
ogni opra che vegg'io strage è di Marte.

Deh, poiché nulla val contro il destino,
e più 'l mondo non ha norma né leggi,
sempre si veggia incontro al cavo pino[158]
Nereo[159] inalzarsi dai cerulei seggi.
Sorga la notte e partasi il mattino,
con perpetui baleni il ciel lampeggi!
E scosso alle miserie e franto al duolo,
ruini il monte e s'inabissi il suolo!

Più non rieda per me la primavera,
che di bei fiori i campi suoi colora;
né più ritorni sull'alta sfera,

---

[155]*omei*: lamenti.
[156]*salda cote*: pietra dura.
[157]*Insubria*: Lombardia.
[158]*cavo pino*: nave.
[159]*Nereo*: divinità marina, padre delle Nereidi.

except to reappear in mournful frost;
let not the sun with its haughty lamp shine;
the moon, moment to moment, her strength lost,
never let rise again, her light withheld.
Over the living, let death now be god!"
. . . .
      To such sad and such dismal invocations
by Mother Alp, the Po, doleful, in tears,
swelled himself up with muddy undulations;
with waves anew, the Dora swamped her shores.
Unmoored, languishing at such agitation,
the rivers turned back to their banks once more;
spilling with heavy, resonating pains,
with tears rather than waves, they filled the sands.
      Italy, too, her face turned towards the Heavens,
in vain wept for her lands to ruin lost;
her cheeks wholly shot through with fragile veins,
her breast brimming with lachrymose hoarfrost.
Immersed in dolor, bitterly she rends
her mantle and attacks her hair unloosed,
shatters her golden crown, imperious,
weeps for the reign of Alp and her demise.

Tirsi Stabbed

      On Arno's banks, in dulcet play sojourned,
Lilla one day held at her bosom, joyous,
two darling children and, unto them turned,
kissing now this, now that one, clasped them close.
And with their gestures, charming ways, entwined,
"Oh glad part of my bosom," she then posed,
"fruit of my womb, where of my good I view
impressed the image fair, myself in you.
      "Of my delightful Sun, the image vivid
are you, embellished semblance of my ardor,
for through you on these shores, oh yes, indeed,
happy I live, in service to Amour.
But why, Tirsi, alas, leave so deprived
my eyes, so wanting of your lovely splendor?
Return to me, return, and in my breast
take, with your children dear, sheltering rest."

se non con brine flebili, l'aurora;
né più splenda del sol la lampa altera,
e la luna mancando ad ora ad ora,
per non risorger più, tolgane il lume,
e sia la morte dei viventi il nume!"
. . . .
A così tristi e sì funesti auguri
dell'Alpe genitrice, il Po col duolo
e col pianto a se flutti accrebbe impuri,
e di nuov' onde empì la Dora il suolo.
Languidi a tanto affanno e mal sicuri
entro le sponde lor tornâro e solo
colmi di gravi e risonanti pene,
di pianti più che d'onde, empîr l'arene.
L'Italia, anch'essa verso il ciel conversa,
pianse in van le sue flebili ruine.
Tutta ha la gota d'egre vene aspersa
e colmo ha il sen di lagrimose brine.
Nel suo dolore amaramente immersa
squarcia il suo manto e lacera il suo crine;
d'or la corona imperiosa frange
e del regno dell'Alpe il danno piange.

Tirsi trafitto[160]

Tra dolci scherzi, in riva all'Arno accolta,
un dì Lilla gioiva e 'n sen tenea
due cari pargoletti, e a lor rivolta,
or questa, or quel baciando a sé stringea.
E nei lor vezzi e nei lor moti involta,
"o lieta del mio sen parte" dicea,
"parti, in cui del mio ben rimiro impressa
la bella imago e scorgo ognor me stessa.
Del mio leggiadro sole imagin vive,
simolacri adorni del mio ardore,
ora sì, che per voi su queste rive
vivo felice in servitù d'Amore.
Ma come, Tirsi, ohimè, mie luci prive
cotanto rendi del tuo bel splendore?
Ritorna a me, ritorna, e nel mio petto
abbi coi cari figli anco ricetto."

---

[160]For comment, see Introduction, p. 33.

When now she seems to hear, feel, to discern
horror's grave voice, messenger of affliction
that 'Lilla, Lilla' cries and, of a sudden,
'Lilla' cries out again, wounded in tone.
Midst hope and fear, delighted yet in pain,
she dares not move to confront her vexation.
She stands, a living marble effigy —
yearning to see, from seeing shies away.

      Now in voice more terrible, in more pain,
Lilla hears herself called, and she conceives
it's Tirsi who calls out; no longer hidden
is the hurt that she feels, yet won't believe.
He staggers towards her, wounded; she, yet stricken,
casts worried gaze, knows not what she perceives.
Tirsi with knife wound in his neck, she grasps,
sees, hears and stares at him and then she gasps.

      Upon bare soil, she leaves her children dear;
no more does care for them at her breast press,
and she abandons them, sad, luckless there,
bereft, prey unto a hope dubious.
No longer do their games with charming gesture
entice her heart in an hour such as this.
As if a sterile trunk of tree, and barren,
with but mute sounds can she complain and moan.

· ·

      Her hands clasped tight, she now fixedly sees
the fair throat, stabbed through and from which now flood
sanguineous drops — the spirit in him flees;
it is his life immersed within the blood.
With hands clutching her breast, she turns her eyes
towards one whose soul is by pain so absorbed.
With mercy's touch, she wants to give him aid
but fails and shrieks, and dares not say a word.

· ·

      "Ah you, unhappy children, whose cruel Fate
would label you at birth with the name 'orphan' —
haughty, she moves against you with Death's threat.
Already do you suffer her grave burden.
You, you, children, lament! — for me make short

Quando le pare udire, e scorge e sente
voce grave d'orror, nunzia di stento,
che "Lilla, Lilla" chiama e di repente,
"Lilla" ripiglia con doglioso accento.
Tra speranza e timor, lieta e dolente,
non osa ella incontrare il suo tormento.
Stassi quasi di marmo effige viva,
brama vedere e di veder è schiva.

Ecco con più terribile e penosa
voce Lilla chiamarsi ode, e s'avvede
che Tirsi è quel che chiama e non più ascosa
è la doglia che sente, e pur non crede:
ferito s'appresta, e in lui dubbiosa
fissa ella i lumi, né sa quel che vede.
Dal ferro nella gola aperto il mira,
lo scorge, il sente, il guata[161] e poi sospira.

Lascia sul nudo suolo i parti amati,
né più di lor la cura il sen le preme,
li abbandona infelici e sventurati.
Restan in preda di dubbiosa speme
né più dei loro scherzi i moti grati
le lusingano il cor sulle ore estreme.
Ma quasi steril tronco e senza prole,
tra muti accenti si querela e duole.

. . . .

Incrocia ambe le mani e fisso mira
la bella gola, che trafitta versa
stille di sangue, in lui lo spirto spira,
ed è la vita sua nel sangue immersa.
Stringe le mani al petto e i lumi gira
vèr chi l'alma nel duol mostra sommersa.
Vuol l'amante aiutar con man pietosa,
e langue, e stride, e di parlar non osa.

. . . .

"Ah voi figli infelici, a cui la sorte,
appena nati, di pupilli[162] il nome
diede, proterva, ed in poter di morte.
Già soffrite di lei le gravi some.
Voi, voi figli, piangete e a me più corte

---

[161]*guata*: guarda.
[162]*pupilli*: orfani.

the hours left to me to pull at my mane.
Plaintive, accelerate for me my death,
for in your pain I forfeit my life's breath.
. . . .
     "Yes, yes, weep, children! Who, upon his breast,
will now rock you to sleep, or hug you close?
Who will be there to heed your cares, not least
to hold my misery in his dear embrace?
Unhappy orphans, with such luck, the cruelest,
who'll lend you aid while I am turned to ice?
No father and no mother — who'll take in
the spoils of you who are so clothed in pain?
     "Ah, you call 'Padre' — he does not respond.
You scream, frustrated — he seems not to hear.
Mixed up, immersed in suffering, is the sound
of your two voices and my fate obscure.
Ah, to your plaint, with feeble waves I'm bound
to spread therein, poor me, my own cruel fever.
And, while unto my plaint you also weep,
we form a fragile brook of human hope.
     "And you, poor girl, more than an innocent
orphan boy, your lot's more exposed to chance.
You, poor girl, deceived, infirm, discontent —
to a worse lot destiny would advance.
Boys lose a father, where sundown portends
to girls, at day's calm close, no sufferance,
but metes you a cruel star that's seen to flare
and circle around you with misadventure.
     "Ah, how much better, with your cringing fate,
not to be born at all amid such strife,
as you rose, wretched, to stars obdurate
a subject, from the prime years of your life.
For you unborn, Heaven's storms did not wait —
within the womb, you met with your first griefs.

le ore rendete a lacerar le chiome.
Flebili accelerate il morir mio,
e al vostro duolo la mia vita oblio.

. . . .

     Sì, sì, figli, piangete! E chi più fia
ch'allettandovi al sen, vi stringa in braccio?[163]
Chi vostre cure e la miseria mia
a curar prenderà nel caro laccio?
Chi, pupilli infelici, in così ria
sorte aita vi dà, mentr'io m'agghiaccio?
Chi senza il padre e senza madre accoglie,
in panni di dolor, le vostre spoglie?
     Ah, voi "padre" chiamate: ei non risponde.
Voi delusi stridete ed ei non cura,
immerso nel dolore il suon confonde
di vostre voci e di mia sorte oscura.
Ah, che nel pianger vostro in flebil onde
spargo, misera me, mia cruda arsura.
E mentre voi piangete al pianto mio,[164]
formiam di mortal speme un fragil rio.
     E tu, misera,[165] più dell'innocente
pupillo, in cui la sorte è più proterva,
te, delusa bambina, egra e dolente,
a peggior sorte il tuo destin conserva.
Al figlio manca il padre, e l'occidente[166]
a te di pace in quel cader riserva
l'iniqua stella, ch'avvampar si mira
a tue venture e contro te s'aggira.
     Ah, quanto meglio per tuo fato imbelle
era non nascer tra cotanti affanni,
se misera sorgesti a crude stelle,
soggetta nel più bel dei tuoi prim' anni.
Non nata, il ciel ti minacciò procelle
e nell'alvo ti scorse ai primi danni.

---

[163]The sad destiny awaiting orphans was already represented by Sophocles, through Tecmessa, in his *Ajax* 92.

[164]*piangete al pianto mio*: variante del verso di Tasso *il pietoso pastor pianse al suo pianto* (*Gerusalemme liberata* VII, 16, v. 8).

[165]The poet rightly observes that, as orphans, girls are in a worse situation than boys.

[166]*occidente*: tramonto.

From mother's bosom, just moments outside,
in swaddling clothes you lie, without a guide.
    "You, of my womb, fruit infelicitous,
to what misfortunes does Heaven condemn you?
The word 'padre' your tongue's yet to produce
when evil dagger strikes him from your view.
Wretched boy are you, your mother no less
but more so wretched, if cruel fate is due
to part your father from you, cold as frost,
remove from me part of myself, the best.
    "But no! Let not my life remain alive,
if my soul from me death would disunite.
The soul disjoined from body will not save,
as soul to body Heaven does unite,
and soul outside of self, one cannot have,
nor soul with soul — one's never seen such sight.
Self cleft from soul breathes not. Ah, bitter fate!
If my soul fails, what serves my life to wait?
    "To die! To die! And you, my children dear
who, with your pain, my own you amplify,
let my death teach you of death's methods clear,
if my tearful plaint prepares you to cry.
Be not miserly in death with your father,
for from him you have your life's lively joy.
Give, to the one who gave you mortal spoils,
your pains of woe along with your death's ills.
    "To die! To die! Babies by love begot,
I cannot see you parted from my pain.
My babes, apart from furies of your Fate,
I ask you share with me my bitter bane.
But, poor me, what's the use? Misfortunate,
sad children! Folly! Ah, I cannot reason!
Their father gone and children in such dolor —
will I, deluded, remain on this shore?

. . . .

Ed ora, appena fuor del sen materno,
resti tra fasce ancor senza governo.[167]
    E te, del grembo mio parto infelice,
a quai sventure già condanna il cielo?
Sciolta la lingua ancor non 'padre' dice,
e del padre ti priva iniquo telo,
misero figlio, è più tua genitrice
miserabil di te, s'in freddo gelo
il padre sorte ria da te diparte
e toglie a me di me la miglior parte.[168]
    Macché! Non viva mai resti mia vita,
se l'anima da me morte disgiunge.
Non può star l'alma al corpo disunita,
se 'l Ciel col corpo l'anima congiunge.
Anima fuor del seno a' spirti unita
non mai si vide, o 'l sen da' spirti lunge
aure spirò vitali. Ah, fato accerbo!
Se l'alma cade, a che la vita io serbo?
    A morire, a morire! E voi, miei cari
figli, ch'al mio dolor doglie accrescete,
voi mia morte di morir impari,[169]
s'al mio pianto di piangere apprendete.
Non siate al genitor di morte avari,
se la vita da lui vivi godete.
Rendete, a chi vi diè le mortal spoglie,
del mal le pene e del morir le doglie.
    A morire, a morire! O parti amati,
parti che dal mio duol partir non veggio,
parti ch'a parte del furor dei Fati
meco nel mio dolor dolente chieggio.
Ma, misera, a che pro? Ah sventurati,
figli infelici! O folle! Ahi, che vaneggio!
Senza il padre! E dei figli intante pene
delusa resterò su queste arene?
. . . .

---

[167]The last four lines of this octave recall Marino's sonnet on human misery, but they are closer to Turini Bufalini's version which alludes to the tomb, *nel sen materno*, of a child before birth, *anzi che nato,* and, once born, to feel the first chains *entro le fasce* (*Autobiographical Poems* 192).

[168]*di me la miglior parte* (Petrarca, XXXVII, 52).

[169]*impari*: insegni.

"Death, why delay? Ah, cruel one, don't deny
my breast, but spread it with your icy horrors.
Please satisfy for me my wish to die,
and be death's builder now, as death I choose.
Life I already scorn and, living, I
douse in my breast the flames of my spent ardors.
Say what? Where am I? In this extreme hour,
the hope of life is turning in our favor."

. . . .

Hapless Elisa
Here the Author, Under the Name Elisa, Describes Part of Her Life
   On Tiber's shore, in the Eternal City,
was born a mortal woman. Fate, her escort
in faith and friendship, shaped her life-to-be,
with Luck and Virtue, handmaids at her birth.
Ceased then were the harsh storms of Destiny.
Horror lay low, as did ferocious Death.
To her, as to a goddess, the whole world
with its great weight and honors' tribute, bowed.

   As on a royal throne, image was she
of goddess Venus, a copy in kind.
Solely in burning for her were they happy —
every unconquered heart, every great mind.
She formed her lines of lovers, and more lovely
in his immortal splendor Cupid turned.
It seemed that she, with an arch of her brow,
could pluck from Jove his fulminating arrow.

   Above the others did her triumphs rise;
never was there a woman more sublime.
All placed hers above others' qualities;
of merit, the prime glory did she claim.
For her, Apollo left the climes of Pindus —
racing from stars, Pallas and Juno came.
She witnessed, obedient to her trophies,
the gods themselves turn to her from their skies.

Morte, ché tardi? Ah cruda, il petto mio,
deh, spargi omai del tuo gelato orrore.
Appaga di morire il mio desio
e sii fabbra di morte a chi si more.
Già la vita disdegno e, viva, oblio
nel sen le fiamme del mio spento ardore.
Ma che dico? Ove son? Sulle ore estreme
di vita nel mio ben torna la speme."

. . . .

Elisa infelice[170]
Qui l'autrice sotto nome di Elisa descrive parte della sua vita
Del Tebro in riva, sotto care stelle,
nacque donna mortal che fide scorte
ebbe di Fato amico e, fatte ancelle,
sorsero al nascer suo Virtude e Sorte.
Cessaron del Destin l'atre procelle:
giacque l'orror, né inferocì la Morte.
Ed a lei, qual a dea, col suo gran pondo,
tributario d'onor, chinossi il mondo.

Quasi in trono real, sì degna imago
fu simulacro della dea d'amore,
e sol d'arder per lei si rese pago
ogni gran spirto ed ogni invitto core.
Formò schiere d'amanti e ognor più vago
si fe' Cupido all'immortal splendore.
E sol parea con un girar di sguardo
toglier a Giove il fulminante dardo.

In trionfi d'onor tra le altre sorse,
né qual essa fu mai donna sublime;
suoi vanti ogni alma a quei gran vanti porse
e dei merti portò le glorie prime.
Pallade, e Giuno, a lei dagli astri accorse,
Febo di Pindo abbandonò le cime,
e vide ubidiente ai suoi trofei
dai lor cieli rivolgersi gli dei.

---

[170]For comment, see Introduction, p. 33. All modesty aside, in the first octaves Margherita describes herself as a very beautiful woman, almost a goddess, who charmed men with her beauty and singing. But then Fortune abandoned her. She was scorned in Rome and had to leave her native city to experience the hardships of exile.

The Graces gifted her with gracefulness
and with all influences beneficial.
The stars donated treasured qualities
to soul so fair, to face so beautiful.
With gilded hook, all men would she entice.
To dulcet sin was every heart in thrall,
each glance of hers a dart which seemed to say:
'I need only my beauty, Love, to slay.'

      To beauty's merit, she would likewise add
musical skill in tune with subtle sounds.
Each man dulcetly unto her she lured
and took joy in those happy, tortured ones.
She was, as if new goddess, all-adored;
the winds would hush to listen to her tones.
The stars had never, from Heavenly spheres,
aligned in one such attributes as hers.

      Oh hopes untrue, beneficence fallacious —
before us you change form so rapidly!
Elisa once enjoyed such tranquil peace,
mistook as lover this same, divine sky.
Whence, in bestowing good, Fortune mendacious
dispenses with her hope. Then gone awry,
each star in Heaven, insolent, with harm
threatens her dulcet joy with its harsh storm.

· ·

      Even the common crowds turn enemy —
they scorn her and her name's dragged through the dirt.
Fame, mocking her, flies at her shamelessly —
abusive, declares war and mounts assault.
There's not a single tongue that doesn't sharply
wag satires of her — each chimes in with hurt
and flaps about to exclaim and complain.
Apollo shuns her — Cynthia shows disdain.

· ·

      From lap of Love, here is Elisa, fallen,
at her most bright, at her most lucky hour.
She wanders back, forth, miserable and in pain,
by Fate and Venus struck with hate and ire.
Growing impatient mid such suffering then
she vowed to take her leave of Tiber's shore.
She hopes, instead of her final demise,

A lei dieder le Grazie i moti loro,
ed ogni influsso amico in lei rivolto,
le stelle diffondean pregio e tesoro
a sì vaga alma, a sì leggiadro volto.
Gli animi possedea con amo d'oro.
Era ogni cor in dolci errori involto,
ogni guardo era strale e parea dire:
"Amor, sol mia beltà valti a ferire."

Al pregio di beltade ella aggiungea
musico vanto di soavi accenti.
Dolcemente ogni spirto a sé traea
e godea fortunati i suoi tormenti.
L'adorava ogni cor qual nuova dea,
s'arrestâro a sue note infin i venti,
né mai sì degni, dall'eccelso giro,
tai pregi, qual in lei, le stelle unîro.

O speranze mentite! O ben fallace,
come tosto fra noi muti sembiante!
Godeva Elisa sì tranquilla pace
e fin lo stesso ciel scorgeva amante.
Quando Fortuna, nel suo ben mendace,
ogni speme dilegua e, fatta errante,
dalle alte sfere ogni proterva stella
minaccia a dolci gioie aspra procella.

. . . .

Fin l'ignorante plebe a lei nemica
mostrasi e 'l nome suo con scherni atterra.
Fama, a scorno di lei, vola impudica,
oltraggiosa l'assale e muove guerra.
Lingua non v'è che contro lei non dica
pungenti carmi; ognun il suon disserra,
ognun freme, ognun sclama, ognun si duole,
la sdegna Cinzia e le s'oppone il Sole.

. . . .

Ecco in sen dell'Amor Lisa cadente,
e nel più bel del suo felice stato,
erra e s'aggira misera e dolente
in odio e in ira a Venere ed al Fato.
Onde fra tanto duolo impaziente
dal Tebro stabilì prender commiato.
E senza aspettar ultime ruine,

to heal on Arno her past injuries.
  Scorning her native land, lost and afflicted
she goes, of gold depleted, full of wounds.
On Arno does she hope to find some aid,
and now despises the Tiberian sands.
That Tiber's good be shunned by one so mocked,
Fury desires and thus justly commands.
In the end, she departs for a place where
Destiny pelts her with crueler affair.

. . . .

  If hapless she once lived, more painfully so
a beggar-star assails her, to gain rule.
If languid she departed Tiber, now
on Arno all her hopes would she dispel.
To weeping she returns — a fallen shadow,
she endures life as her last hours toll.
In torture's lap, with such words of complaint,
over her destiny does she lament.
  "Oh Tiber fortunate, when will it be
that, in your lap, I'll arise from such horror?
When will it be I'll see my plight unlucky
lifted from misadventure on your shore?
Within your arms, when will it pass that she,
cruel Luck, can work her harm on me no more?
Within your riverbed, from Arno flown,
will I to my paternal roof return?

. . . .

  "To me in swaddling clothes, did Fortune grant,
in adverse turns, a state pitiable.
I felt, yet in my cradle, languid want;
Fate sentenced me to plaint continual.
My voice and breath I formed out of lament;
in weeping will my heart dissolve, distill.
Mid tears and pain, and thrust beyond my bosom,
my spirit ever finds a hostile home.
  "Though I changed sky, ah, the effect is nil,
for Fate does ever against me advance.

sull'Arno ai danni suoi spera dar fine.
    Sprezzando il patrio albergo, egra e smarrita,
vanne povera d'or, colma di pene.
Spera sull'Arno ritrovare aita
ed odia omai le tiberine arene.
Vuole il giusto furor ch'ella, schernita,
abborrisca del Tebro ogni altro bene.
E parte alfin e si traporta[171] dove
più rie sventure il fier Destin le piove.
. . . .

    S'infelice già visse, or più dolente
mendica stella la combatte e preme.
E se dal Tebro se n' partì languente,
ora sull'Arno perde ogni sua speme.
Ritorna al pianto e, fatta ombra cadente,
soffre del viver suo le ore più estreme.
E 'n seno del martir con tai parole
del suo destino si querela e duole.

    "O Tebro fortunato, e quando fia
ch'io nel tuo sen da tanto orror risorga?
Quando sarà che la sventura mia
sulle tue arene sollevarsi io scorga?
Quando avverrà, nel braccio tuo, che ria
non più la Sorte a me suoi danni porga?
E dall'Arno disgiunta, entro il tuo letto,
ritorni a rivedere il patrio tetto?
. . . .

    Fin dalle fasce, con nemici giri,
mi diè Fortuna lagrimevol tempre.
Provai fin nella cuna egri desiri
e condannommi il Fato a pianger sempre.[172]
Di lamento formai voce e respiri
onde sol fia ch'in pianti il cor distempre.
E tra lagrime e duol, lo spirto ognora
abbia fuor del mio seno aspra dimora.

    Ah, che cangiar di ciel nulla mi giova
e sempre il Fato contro a me s'avanza.

---

[171]*traporta*: trasferisce.

[172]These lines recall Turini Bufalini's autobiographical verses in which she defined herself as *per pianger nata*, destined *alle lagrime, al dolore* and forced to suffer *fin da la cuna* (*Autobiographical Poems* 54 and 68).

If lightning strike of Love proves to me vile,
let Jove's thunderbolt take predominance.
In me, Harm works to reinforce his skill;
aside from death, I've no deliverance.
Since Love breaks faith with me, let broken lie
every elemental fidelity."
　　　At such a plea, Heaven all-powerful
appoints Aminta Elisa's companion.
He, too, under the turns of wrathful wheel,
against cruel Fates, had struck misfortune down.
The stars, at such a union, stood in thrall;
both destinies were intertwined in one.
Despite treacherous Fate, here in one breast,
two souls inhabited a single nest.
　　　The same will, same desires, possess the two;
both of their bosoms nurture yearnings equal.
Loving but one another, they know joy;
their hearts brim with affection mutual.
From them does pain depart — languishment also,
and each cloud clears way to a sky that's tranquil.
To others, the winged Archer's rash and flighty;
to them alone, most faithful does he stay.

· ·

　　　Now tender poems of love does she compose,
and strums her lyre with fine jokes' liveliness.
To sounds of battle, brave minds does she rouse,
and in Athena's hand places the lance.
And now the Fates, harder than marble statues,
she teases gently from their rigid stance.
Tuscan kings' prizes now her verses name —
with them, she would immortalize her fame.
　　　She's mad to hope — for she who lies oppressed
by Fortune's wrath has Destiny's disdain.

· ·

To mock her poems, the Heavens with disgrace,
with vile esteem and crazy honors rain.

S'ha 'l fulmine d'Amor per me vil prova,
sovra me quel di Giove abbia possanza.
Il Danno ogni suo sforzo in me rinnova,
né, fuor che di morire, altro m'avanza.
E poich' Amor per me la fede oblia,
rotta ogni fé tra gli elementi sia."
     Quando a tal suono il Ciel, che tutto puote,
ad Elisa compagno elegge Aminta,
ch'in ira anch' egli dell'eccelse rote
avea tra Fati rei sua sorte vinta.
Restar le stelle a tale innesto immote[173]
e fu d'ambi la sorte in un'avvinta,
e sì contro l'oprar del Fato infido
fecer due alme in un sol petto il nido.

     Hanno pari il voler, pari il desire,
di brame eguali si nutrisce il seno.
Sol l'un nell'altra sa d'amore gioire,
ed è di pari affetto il cor ripieno.
Parte da loro il duol, manca il languire,
ed ogni nube cangiasi in sereno.
E per altri volubile e leggiero,
solo è fido per lor l'alato arciero.

. . . .

     Ora scioglie d'amor teneri carmi[174]
e la sua lira con bei scherzi avviva.
Desta or nobili spirti al suon delle armi
e l'asta impugna alla Palladia diva.
Ora i Fati, più rigidi dei marmi,
del lor rigor soavemente priva.
Or narra dei re toschi i pregi in canti
e con lor pensa d'eternar suoi vanti.

     Ma folle spera. Chi di Sorte in ira
soggiace oppressa è del Destino a sdegno.

. . . .

In scherno dei suoi carmi il ciel le piove
onte di folle onor, di vil stime,

---

[173]The eight lines that follow are a variation of Sarrocchi's octave: *Natura avvince, con tenace nodo / d'amor, di carità, sovente un core, / ma con più saldo e più soave modo / fa di santa amistà possente amore: / due anime che lontan d'inganno e frodo, / seguan chiara virtù, verace onore, / simili di costume e pari d'anni, / conformi nelle gioie e negli affani* (*La Scanderbeide* [1606], IX, 97).

[174]Here the poet describes her written work.

It seems Apollo himself, on Permessus,
disparages the merits of her verse.
      Given her pen's worth even less than nil,
and that she, with weak hand, marks her page badly,
(as prized far more are all others' inks feeble,
and Fortune gives out gifts unequally),
she loses her desire to lift the quill,
casts off her thought to reach the starry sky.
She reins in yearnings and in agitation
turns to Aminta with a declaration:
      "Aminta, of my heart the lucky bait,
look at the vain result of your advice.
Thus rendered to me is more hapless yet
my distant hope of possibilities.
Ah, I'm just left, alas, to hesitate
at Fate's mad plan for my hostile demise.
Apollo's of no use against my torments,
and sad Helicon hosts ill-starred events.
      "With loss of wealth, I've likewise lost the flower
of my intellect and my mind with you.
To me, no good turn would Fortune allow;
instead, out of great prospects, we've got zero.
Your star's to blame, or my Fate's adverse power;
I'm left afflicted, while you beg and borrow.
With ink and paper, and unlucky cards,
perished is the best part of us, in shards.

. . . .

      "I'm leaving you, Aminta, for a sky
more foreign than this. Do not hope or pray
for my return, and further do not try,
or give much thought, my bad luck to allay.
Once I'm far from the Arno, it may be
Heaven's less mean to me, Fortune less fey.
As Tiber's brother, Arno, casts me scorn,
he teaches me to flee greater disdain."

e par che sprezzi, dentr' il bel Permesso,
i pregi dei suoi canti Apollo stesso.
    Visto che nulla la sua penna vale
e che mal verga debil man le carte,
ché più si pregia ogn'altro inchiostro frale,
e Sorte i doni inegualmente parte,
cangia pensiero e non più d'erger l'ale
ella ha desir sulla stellata parte.
Frena le brame e con diversi affetti
contrari snoda verso Aminta i detti.
    "Aminta, del mio core esca felice,
ecco l'oprar delle tue voci invano.
Tal si rende vèr me vie più infelice
di mie fortune lo sperar lontano.
Ah, che sol peritar, lassa, mi lice,
l'infesto fine del mio fato insano.
Apollo nulla vale ai miei tormenti
e 'l flebile Elicona ha infausti eventi.
    Col dispendio dell'or teco ho disperso
il fior dell'intelletto e della mente.
Non ha Sorte il suo giro in me converso,
anzi, dal molto s'è ritratto un niente.
O sia tua stella, o sia mio Fato avverso,
tu mendico ne resti ed io dolente.
E sugl'inchiostri e sull'infauste carte
s'è perduta di noi la maggior parte.[175]
. . . .
    Ti lascio, Aminta, e vado a ciel straniero
più ch'a me questo fusse. E non più fia
che speri rivedermi, o col pensiero
sollevar tenti la sventura mia.
Forse lunge dall'Arno men severo
il Ciel sarammi e sorte avrò men ria.
Poiché fratel del Tebro anch' ei mi sdegna,
e tra scherni maggior fuggir m'insegna."

---

[175]*Non sum qui fueram: periit pars maxima nostri.* This verse by Maximianus (*Elegia* I, 5), will become famous with Ugo Foscolo's hendecasyllable *Non son chi fui; però di noi gran parte*.

Florence's walls, once loved, she leaves behind —
Elisa suffering and lachrymose —
and, with the hills of Tuscany abandoned,
in pain directs her journey towards Parnassus.
Accompanied by murmurs of the wind
are her complaints. She goes on without pause.
Her work voluminous — her enemy —
at the feet of Apollo she would lay.

Her best poetic works she bears with her,
those that she wrote while on Lazio's sands
and those that she composed, with rhymes more rare,
on Arno's shore, beneath Tuscan expanse.
In letters and in prose, the bitter ire
of Fate she grieves, and most harsh are her pains.
She walks on until finally arriving
where Muses' waters surge from their pure spring.

Atop the mountain peak, one can discern
Apollo's regal seat against gold stars.
His palace is not wrought of polished stone,
nor are its walls hung with fine tapestries,
nor do Indian gems, greed's booty taken,
light up the space with their noble torchères:
in epitaphs and learnèd wit, all around,
the walls are with the written word adorned.

Therein, the doorways, windows and the joists,
the thresholds, doorposts and the vaulted domes,
all have with poems been most lovingly chased,
where to their marvels Virtue offers welcome.
Even the spot where Phoebus' throne is raised,
beautiful, sculpted reliefs line the room
with poets' likenesses. Thus every hall
does genius and arts' excellence extol.

About the court goes wandering old Dante,
heavy with years and with his works — here Petrarch,
Bembo, Guidaccioni, Casa up front
forming a crown around the shining monarch.

Lascia d'Arno le mura, un tempo amate,
Elisa lagrimevole e dogliosa,
e, le piagge d'Etruria abbandonate,
vèr Parnaso il cammin drizza penosa.
Dal mormorar delle aure accompagnate
son le querele sue. Gira e non posa,
e vuol dei suoi volumi, a sé nemica,
deporre a piè d'Apollo ogni fatica.

Seco ha dei carmi suoi le opre più chiare
e quanto scrisse mai nel Lazio suolo
e quante fabbricò rime più rare
all'Arno in riva sotto etrusco polo.
Prose e lettere vi mesce e, le ire amare
dei Fati sospirando, aspro ha 'l suo duolo.
E tanto stende il piè ch'alfin arriva
ove 'l castalio umor[176] pura ha la riva.

Del monte in cima sollevar si vede
la gran reggia d'Apollo alle auree stelle.
E non di pietre lucide ha la sede,
o d'arazzi sul muro opre novelle,
o le gemme dell'India, avare prede,
vi spandon le lor nobil facelle,
ma dotte arguzie ed epitafi intorno
rendono di lor note il muro adorno.[177]

Vi sono le porte e le finestre anch' esse,
e le soglie e gli stipiti e le volte,
tutte di carmi vagamente impresse,
ov' ha virtù sue meraviglie accolte.
E sin nel loco dov' il soglio eresse
Febo, con belle immagini son scolte[178]
poetiche figure; ed ogni parete
pregio è d'ingegni ed eccellenza d'arte.

Per la corte s'aggira il vecchio Dante,
d'anni e d'opre gravoso; avvi il Petrarca,
il Bembo, il Guidaccioni e 'l Casa inante,
che fan corona al lucido monarca.[179]

---

[176]*castalio umor*: fonte castalio (delle Muse).
[177]Apollo's palace is modest, not like the palaces described in chivalric poems. It is embellished only with poems chiseled onto the walls and ceilings. Note that Margherita singles out eight poets at Apollo's court – five men and three women.
[178]*scolte*: sculpite.
[179]*lucido monarca*: Apollo.

Sarocchi's there; noble in countenance,
Colonna. And with scorn, Fate to dispatch,
does Gambara advance. The weaker sex,
immortally its virtuous rays reflects.
  Surprised is every soul to see so pained
one who on Tuscany had turned her heels.
Each poetess reveals a concerned mind,
commiserates and shares personal ills.
Each lauds Elisa's beauty and commends
her brilliant talent. With friendly goodwill,
all lead unto their god for presentation
the one struggling with Fate in lamentation.

· ·

  "Apollo, I am she whose stars sublime
would make subject to lamentable fate.
I'm that Elisa whom, in ceaseless storm,
outrageous Death does ever toss about.
Never on me did Heaven's lustrous beam
turn bright; instead only as adverse escorts
to me were the sky's unlucky rotations —
at my pains ever unmoved in their motion.
  "After cruel Fortune's lengthy mockery,
did I begin to trace your steps, alas!
A darker purview did blind Luck decree,
while my good works Destiny would abase.
Fate gathers up more damages to harm me,
while wicked Envy leaves me nearly breathless;
and with the stars, united within me
conspire Nature, Fortune and Destiny.

· ·

"From studies' cares, reproof is all I have —
but harm and ruin to me is my rhyme.
To ignorance, poor me, my skills I give
as offerings. Lachrymose frost I am,
my Helicon; nor do I, from your merit,
perceive, other than plaint, a benefit.

· ·

V'è la Sarrocchi e in nobile sembiante,
la Colonnese,[180] e a scorno della Parca
la Gambara s'avanza, e 'l sesso frale
nei suoi rai di virtù splende immortale.
    Stupisce ogn'alma in rimira dolente
lei che dal tosco regno il piè discioglie.
Ciascuna mostra torbida la mente
e comuni con lei fa le sue doglie.
Loda quelle vaghezze e rilucente
l'ingegno anco vi scorge, onde le voglie
mostrale amiche ed a lor dio presenta
chi del destin si lagna e si tormenta.
. . . .

    "Apollo, io son colei, cui le alte stelle
fêron[181] soggetta a lagrimevol sorte.
Io quella Elisa son che tra procelle
m'agita ognora l'oltraggiosa Morte.
Lucide a me del cielo le facelle
mai non girâro, anzi contrarie scorte
mi fûr sempre di lui gl'infelici moti,
nel giro loro alle mie pene immoti.
    Dopo lungo schernir d'empia Fortuna,
a seguir le orme tue mi diedi, ahi lassa,
ma più 'l mio stato cieca Sorte imbruna
ed il Destin le mie grandezze abbassa.
Contro me 'l Fato maggior danni aduna,
né l'empia Invidia respirar mi lassa[182]
e con le stelle unito in me congiura
il Destino, la Sorte e la Natura.
. . . .

Dalle cure de' studi il biasimo prendo
e son le rime in me danni e rovine,
all'ignoranza, ahi, lassa, i voti appendo
di mia virtude. Lagrimose brine
son, l'Elicona mio, né dai tuoi vanti
altra mercè prov'io che dei miei pianti.
. . . .

---

[180]*Colonnese*: Vittoria Colonna.
[181]*fêron*: fecero.
[182]*lassa*: lascia.

"I thought, as woman — oh insanity —
that all hearts would rejoice at my frail lyre
and that, equal to my poems' quality,
would be the pleasure that all would acquire.
But I see that each mind, cruel and in envy,
would shoot at me darts of enemy fire;
that I beat wave on wave, plough but the dust;
that by the air my verses are dispersed.

. . . .

"Why is it — when as well as anyone,
I render a page writ in my ink pure —
I'm nonetheless cheated at your great throne
and pecked upon by crude beaks bent to injure?
The purple cloak of fame, let others don!
My words I'll scatter to the winds no more.
I'll keep still. As my song's no longer heard,
Time need not fear from me illustrious fraud."

. . . .

"Becalm yourself — for even I, Apollo,
had to herd sheep on earth, subject to judgment.
For Daphne I felt pain bitter and foul;
my dolor has the very winds lament.
Elisa, to the times in which we dwell,
to disregard, must you ascribe your torment.
To Phoebus, it's not Arno that proves fell:
to Virtue, Heaven's star itself is rebel.
"The laurel branches that verdantly crown
brows Apollonian have bitter leaves.
Waters from Helicon's font crystalline
instruct one not to poke fun but to grieve."
He spoke — at those words exalted, divine,
her tears Elisa stems, her pain relieves.
Her bad luck's like a god's. Though Fate be cruel,
Elisa lets the parity console.

Già credei, come donna, o mia follia,[183]
ch'ogni alto core del mio plettro frale
gioir dovesse e che dell'opra mia
godimento traesse al merto eguale.
Ma scorgo ch'ogni mente, invida e ria,
colpi in me scocca di nemico strale,
e che le onde percoto e solco in polve,
e al vento i fiati miei l'aura disssolve.

. . . .
 Perché debb'io, s'a par d'ogni altro il foglio
vergato rendo dei miei puri inchiostri,
defraudata restar nel tuo gran soglio,
punta da crudi ingiuriosi rostri?
Più al vento i detti miei spander non voglio,
di favolosa fama altri s'inostri.
Io taccio e già ch'il mio cantar non s'ode
da me 'l Tempo non tema illustre frode."

. . . .
 "Rattempra l'alma, ché soggetto anch'io
già fui nel mondo a pascolar armenti.[184]
Duol soffersi per Dafne,[185] acerbo e rio,
ed anco del mio duol lagnansi i venti.
E non men all'etade ed all'oblio,
Elisa, ascriver devi i tuoi tormenti,
ché non dell'Arno, ma del cielo è stella
ch'a Febo è infesta ed a virtù rubella.
 Il verdeggiante allor, che cinge i crini
ai seguaci d'Apollo, ha foglia amara.
E l'onda dei lor fonti cristallini
più ch'a scherzare a lagrimare impara."
Sì dice, ed agli accenti alti e divini,
Elisa i pianti affrena e 'l duol rischiara.
E si consola ché, se 'l Fato è rio,
ha le sventure sue pari ad un dio.

---

[183]Margherita complains that her poetic work, a woman's contribution, found no appreciation.
[184]Parla Apollo che fu condannato da Giove a pascolare gli armenti di Ammeto, perché aveva ucciso i ciclopi.
[185]*Dafne*: Daphne, a chaste nymph pursued by Apollo, was, at her own entreaty, changed into a bay tree.

FROM: *THE MARTYR CECILIA* (1644)

FROM: CANTO I: THE BATH

Oh Muse, who in vain over Tuscan rivers
sang of light jests and of ardors insane,
henceforward turn your gaze unto the stars,
reveal to me the wealth of Heaven's reign.
Refine my instrument, display your feathers
for sacred praise unto Cecilia virgin;
with voice more grateful, more melodious,
honor my lyre with more beautiful verse.

No more of mortal glory in accent frail
will I expound to fickle breezes errant.
With us, scant peace is found in serene mortal
mid worldly want and covetings inconstant.
To greatness does misery prove the equal.
Lover of its own fall is vile contentment.
And for hope, falsifying and so fleeting,
the heart contrives eternal suffering.

Phoebus's sacred throne, how much in vain
did you, obtuse, crowd with earthly affections,
declaiming to deaf breezes of your pain;
and with the love-god's objects and distractions
your folio, ill-written, you did stain.
You hoped, from out of shadows, clear solutions
and, foolish, thought to lift to noble good,
effortlessly, your songs misunderstood.

Of more than this must be Helicon's sphere
where I from baseness may rise to the height;
let not my lips touch the Castalian water,
but to the stars let my wings reach in flight.
I turn my verse to Heaven, my one desire
to turn to happy joy my hurtful plight.
Risen from shadows of my lethargy,
I sing about the trophies of God's glory.

DA: *CECILIA MARTIRE*[186] (1644)

DAL: CANTO I: IL BAGNO

Musa, ch'invano sovra 'l tosco fiume[187]
lievi scherzi cantasti e folli ardori,
invèr[188] le stelle omai rivolgi il lume,
e dei regni del Ciel m'apri i tesori.
Tempra il mio plettro e spandi le tue piume
della vergin Cecilia ai sacri onori,
e, con voce più grata e più canora,
di più bei carmi la mia cetra onora.

Non più di mortal gloria accento frale
sarà ch'i' spieghi a mobil aura errante.
Vana pace ha tra noi seren mortale,
ha mondano desire brama incostante.
Alla grandezza è la miseria uguale.
Il rio contento è dei suoi danni amante.
E per caduca mentitrice spene,
a sé fabbrica il core eterne pene.

Quanto invano di Febo il sacro soglio,
stolta, calcasti con terreni affetti,
dicesti alle sorde aure il tuo cordoglio
e del dio degli ardori[189] i lievi oggetti
macchiasti indarno il mal vergato foglio.
E dalle ombre sperasti i chiari effetti
e, folle, ti credesti ai nobil vanti
lieta innalzar tuoi mal intesi canti.

D'uopo è d'altro Elicona, onde poss'io
dai bassi campi sollevarmi al polo,
né 'l labbro immerga nel castalio rio,
ma le ali impenni tra le stelle a volo.
Volgo al Cielo i miei carmi e sol desio
in dolce gioia mutar l'aspro duolo.
Sorta dalle ombre dei letarghi miei
delle glorie di Dio canto i trofei.

---

[186]For comment, see Introduction, p. 34.
[187]*tosco fiume*: Arno.
[188]*invèr*: verso.
[189]*dio degli ardori*: Amore.

But with what tones will I loosen the sound
and with what pen discern to write the verse?
Do I, in mortal spoil, sinner unarmed,
dare postulate upon eternal greatness?
Do I, in whom low thought, weak wants, abound
name the One who does earth and Heaven bless?
Of soul languishing and of body frail,
do I, with Heaven's works, venture to deal?
     Ah, the call to my low star is unjust,
for Fate does not hand so much to my sort,
after the prolonged reeling of cruel tempest,
that I glorify the supernal court.
In high light, air celestial, one's not placed
who now lies halfway between life and death.
To struggle up from earth's to no avail
for one whose heart with earthly fault is full.
     Obtuse, what am I saying? Why such fright?
The Lord of Life gathers to Him each soul
who, hurt and penitent, and with words sweet
requests His pardon for desires vile.
With open arms does He penitence greet,
our Lord so great, who donned a mortal spoil
and, full of ardent zeal, full of His mercy,
points us Heavenward when from sin we flee.
     Cecilia, you who would to harmony
of resonant instruments musical
upon the airy ways hold in delay
the very winds, their plumage stunned, immobile —
and sweet in Heaven now, with melody,
cloisters of ardent spheres you strive to fill —
as I ready to sing of you with pride,
refine my song and my bold venture guide.
· ·
     Cecilia drew from the fine Roman seed
the glories of her blood. Although in pain,
of fierce tyrant's contempt she took no heed
but felt, mid injuries, breezes serene.
Like rock unconquered by waves at high tide
and driving back sea's ire to the shoreline,

Ma con quai voci fia che 'l suono i' scioglia
e la penna vergar carmi si scerna?
Io, peccatrice inerme in mortal spoglia,
oso parlar della grandezza eterna?
Io, ch' ho basso il pensier, debil la voglia,
tento nomar chi 'l mondo e 'l Ciel governa?
E con alma languente e fragil velo
ardisco di trattar le opre del Cielo?

    Ah, che non lece alla mia bassa stella,
tanto avanzarsi a me non dà la sorte,
dopo lungo rotar di ria procella,
le glorie espor della superna corte.
Non scorge aura celeste, alta facella,
chi già se n' giace semivivo a morte.
Ergersi dal terreno non ha valore
chi di colpe terrene ha colmo il core.

    Ma, deh, stolta, che dico e che pavento?
Ah, ch' il Padre di vita ogni alma accoglie
che dolente e pentita in dolce accento
perdón gli chiede dell'erranti voglie.
Tiene aperte le braccia al pentimento
il gran Dio, che vestì mortali spoglie
e, colmo di pietà, d'ardente zelo,
a chi fugge le colpe addita il Cielo.

    Tu, Cecilia, che spesso all'armonia
di risonanti musici strumenti
ritardar festi sull'aerea via
con attonite penne immoti i venti,
e dolce, anco sul Ciel, di melodia
riempi i chiostri delle sfere ardenti,
mentre cantar di te mi prendo a vanto,
reggi l'ardire mio, tempra il mio canto.

. . . .

    Traea Cecilia da roman germoglio
del suo sangue le glorie. E, bench' in pene,
del fier tiranno[190] non temea l'orgoglio,
e sentia tra l'offese aure serene.
Qual suole in mezzo alle onde invitto scoglio,
che rispinge del mar le ire alle arene,

---

[190]*fier tiranno*: Tuscio Almachio, prefetto di Roma, nel poema.

her forceful soul, amid hate's waves forborne,
broke through the hurt and at death threw back scorn.
    The great renown of those called Caecili,
(by Latins a name prized for years) culled fame;
each brow of theirs, during both peace and war,
of honor unconquered wore the acclaim,
and on the Appian Way, a sepulchre
does pompously their memory proclaim.
Cecilia then, from such a seed descending,
vowed her pure heart unto supreme love's King.

· ·

    Shocked is the air, and in sounds sown with dread
rages more fierce by hour mid portent sights;
at Phoebus' lightning, thunder breaks to spread
and hurl down on Cecilia cruel frights.
Thick is the fog and there amid the cloud
bright rays are scattered from the God of Light.
The sky's in gloom, shrouded over in horror,
glittered with gelid flame and ice afire.
    The air scintillates tempestuously,
and between fiery blazes takes in breath.
Sparks of all kinds cascade down from the sky
that shakes with thunderbolts and breathes out wrath.
The earth now sways with fear, in agony,
and everywhere one looks — the look of death.
With lightning, arrows, the whole sky in warning
announces, amid storms, eternal mourning.
    The scorching water heaves — its irate back
stretching up to the level of the skies:
now out from the restraining bank it breaks
and now, to cause its wrack, in high surge rises.
Fervid, with bellows merciless, it shrieks;

tal nei flutti degli odi anima forte
spezzava i mali ed ischernia la morte.
     Dei Cecili il gran nome, infra latini
pregio nei lustri andati, ebbe famoso,
ed in pace ed in guerra a loro i crini
ornò d'invitto onor cinto fastoso,
ed han dell'Appia via dentro i confini
sepolcro memorabile e pomposo.[191]
Scesa da germe tal, Cecilia il core
puro consacra al re del sommo amore.[192]

. . . .

     L'aria, ch' è scossa, in spaventoso suono
più fiera ognor tempesta, e tra portenti,
di Febo ai lampi scatenato il tuono
avventa sopra lei crudi spaventi.[193]
Grave è la nebbia e tra le nubi sono
spersi del dio del lume i rai lucenti.
È coperto d'orror, è tetro il cielo,
ha fuoco algente ed infocato gelo.
     Di tempestoso umor l'aria sfavilla
e tra vampe di foco ha i suoi respiri.
Cader sembra dal ciel ogni scintilla,
e che fulmini scota[194] e danni spiri.
La terra s'ange[195] e di timor vacilla,
e aspetto è di morte ove si miri.
Di lampi e di saette il ciel tutto
annunzia fra tempeste eterno lutto.
     S'alza l'acqua cocente e 'l dorso irato
invèr le stelle sollevar si scorge:
or esce fuori del ristretto lato,
ed or, per ruinare, in alto sorge.
Fervida stride e, con muggir spietato,

---

[191]Poetic license. Margherita claims that Cecilia descended from the Roman family of Quintus Caecilius Metellus, conqueror of Crete, and alludes to the tomb of his daughter, Caecilia Metella, still standing on Via Appia Antica in Rome.

[192]*re del sommo amore*: Dio.

[193]The poet describes the horror — flames, hot water, waves, steam, lightning, thunder, loud roaring of ferocious animals, and hissing of snakes — created by the devil in Cecilia's bath, where she was supposed to die, but did not. It is a Baroque display of the poet's ability to create descriptive variations.

[194]*scota*: agiti.

[195]*ange*: s'affligge.

with floods billowing past the shore it flies,
spraying and spreading, midst the drops afire,
its flames and fumes and sparks and ice and terror.
    The house of Saint Cecilia starts to shake,
(the earthquake stirring it to spread its wings),
and trembles even more than trees now struck
down from the sky's fulminant darts of lightning.
To his brimstone most burnt all seems alike,
and is, Hell's chasm where Pluto is king.
A room no more resembling, it's the realm
of earthquakes, blazing in frenzy aflame.
    On her by hundreds, thousands, you discern
thunderbolts thrust, each with an ardent torch
of flames, of arrows and of sparks that burn.
The large house is no longer large enough.
The very walls scintillate sparks in turn,
their marbled bosoms blistering at the touch.
The whole place steams from out the Stygian doors,
as Hades' king vents his enflamed desires.
    The house, as ship exposed to wind's ire fierce,
is pounded by the impact of the waves.
The Roman virgin simply turns her eyes
and mid pains, as if bound by joy behaves.
The wild tide shrieks and then breathes out with fires,
batters its wrath against the shore and raves,
with sparks and burning vapors once again
thunders against her its scorching disdain.
    Cecilia catches no flame from that ardor.
At the fire's flickering, her breast congeals:
to her, it seems warm lymph, not scalding water,
compared to her own scorching, pious zeal.
Despite the boiling foam, terrible roar,
she's glad, this beauty meant with God to dwell.
In martyrdom, more constant by the hour,
she proves the more to be Christ's enflamed lover.
    Of those monsters' cruel arms she has no fright,
nor of the hydra-headed waters' poison;

fuor dell'usata sponda i flutti porge,
e spruzza e spande, fra l'ardenti stille,
fiamme, fumo, terror, gelo e faville.

Dell'alma Diva[196] la magion si scote
e 'l terremoto in lei v'agita l'ale,
né sì tremanti gli alberi percote,
tratto dal cielo, fulminante strale.
Sembra di Pluto[197] la più ardente cote,
ed è di lui il baratro[198] infernale.
Stanza più non somiglia e fatta è reggia
di terremoti ov'il furor fiammeggia.

Veggonsi contro lei a cento, a mille,
i folgori rotar l'ardente face
di fiamme, di saette e di faville.
Non è l'ampia magione omai capace.
Le mura stesse versano scintille
ed il marmo ha d'ardori il sen mordace.
E tutte sfoga, dalle stigie soglie,
il re delle ombre, l'infiammate voglie.

Tal legno[199] suol, dei fieri venti all'ira,
tutti gl'impeti in sé provar dell'onda.
La vergine romana i lumi gira
e tra le pene di dolcezza abbonda.
Stride il flutto agitato e fuoco spira,
e batte le ire nella forte sponda,
e di faville e di vapori ardenti
fulmina contro lei sdegni cocenti.

Non s'infiamma Cecilia a quell'ardore,
e tra flutti di fuoco ha sen di gelo:
le par tepida linfa il caldo umore,
in paragon del suo cocente zelo.
Dalle bollenti spume al rio fragore
gode la bella riserbata al Cielo,
e fatta nel martirio ognor costante,
più si mostra di Cristo accesa amante.

Non teme di quei mostri il crudo artiglio,
né delle idre paventa il fier veneno,

---

[196]*alma Diva*: Cecilia.
[197]*Pluto*: qui per il diavolo.
[198]*baratro*: abisso.
[199]*legno*: nave.

mid tortures, her brow grows but calm and bright,
as she arms her soft breast with resolution.
With tender tint of rose, with lily's white,
amid the flames her face is most serene.
Her whole self, well-prepared for Heaven's prize,
cedes not to fire, nor to dark compromise.

      Of the Stygian king's torch, she has no fear,
nor does her heart, racked to its core, feel pain.
Her hardy spirit locks against the ogre,
remains unharmed by the fiery terrain.
Locked within her, by grace of Heaven's stars,
is a rare constancy. By God sustained,
she finds but dulcet bed, delightful game.
The wave terrifies not — she scorns the flame.

      The virgin beautiful, who feels the heat,
grieves not the hurt from punishments severe
for, in Hell's blazing lake, to give her comfort,
there softly blows a breeze of genteel air.
Through the afflictions, her composure's sweet;
of Heaven's love, her face is a proof clear.
Amid those sparks, amid that gelid Hell,
she flames the more for God with ardent zeal.

      Just so, the oak disdains, as if deflector,
the blows of ire from winter's rebellions.
Just so, amid high waves, the rock as vector
throws back wicked attacks of icy winds
and, holding fast, is of each assault victor
over formidable, atrocious storms;
thereby does virtue disdain every harm
and does, against all violence, stand firm.

      And so, the virgin to whom Rome gave birth —
she, of the strong, ancient progenitress
destined to virtue's glory unto death;
she who, mid hurt, evinced but friendliness;
born to the martyr's palm and laurel wreath —
thus scorns the ire of Pluto nemesis,

ma rasserena tra le pene il ciglio
ed arma di fermezza il molle seno.
E con rosa gentil, con bianco giglio,
tra le fiamme il suo volto ha ben sereno.
E tutta delle stelle ai premi accinta,
non cede al fuoco, né dall'ombra è vinta.

    Del re stigio la face non l'atterra,
né, dal suolo agitata, al core ha pena.
Anima forte contro l'orco serra,
e non le noce l'infocata vena.
La grazia delle stelle in lei riserra
insolita costanza e, di Dio piena,
v'ha dolce letto e dilettevol gioco.
Non teme l'onda e schernisce lo fuoco.

    Sente la bella vergine gli ardori,
né pur si duole delle crude offese,
ché tra vampe d'averno,[200] ai suoi ristori,
spira soavemente aura cortese.
Dolce prova gli affanni e degli amori
del Cielo il volto è testimon palese.
E tra quelle faville, tra quel gelo,
più s'infiamma per Dio d'ardente zelo.

    Così quercia disprezza il fiero scontro
delle crude del verno ire rubelle.
Così scoglio nelle acque ai venti incontro
respinge d'Aquilon[201] le scosse felle
e vince, in sé costante, ogni riscontro
delle atre, formidabili procelle,
poiché virtude ogni contrario sprezza
e nelle violenze ha la fermezza.

    La vergine, a cui diè[202] Roma il natale,
che fu dei forti genitrice antica
e di virtù la gloria a lei fatale
del lauro trionfal fu sempre amica,
a palme[203] nata fra 'l nocente male,
schernisce di Pluton l'ira nemica,

---

[200]*averno*: inferno.
[201]*Aquilon*: vento gelido.
[202]*diè*: diede.
[203]*palme*: simbolo di martirio.

and vigorous mid harms does she rejoice
as her mind meditates on hymns of praise.
      She then says: "Flames, to me welcome and dear —
vapors, who set afire my soul, to claim —
and torches of the sun more calm and clear
that show, through all the hurt, the way sublime —
ah, let my heart immersed in these waves bitter
feel every sweetness. Through this turbid clime,
let it be that He'll part the starry veil
to open to me Heaven's promised trail.
      "Yes, yes, you drops, yes, yes, blazes, grow higher!
Burn up my bosom; I burn more with love!
Inflame my soul, put my breast to the pyre!
To such a heart, the flames but lightness prove.
With greater blaze, you'll not set me afire;
I blaze with fire from my own Lord above.
Although I'm youthful yet, tender of age,
I meet the hurt. I do not flee the outrage.
      "Let jump at me fierce lions on the prowl
with bloody lips intent upon my death!
Let coil and spring to harm me dragons foul
and let virulent poison arm their teeth!
Let harpies, manticores and serpents shrill
mete out their frights and let them stir up wrath!
In vain appear phantoms of subterfuge
wherever virginity finds a refuge.
      "Go right ahead, monsters — your ire mordacious
against my breast, yes, yes, accelerate;
with freezing venom, with torches atrocious,
your fierce desire to harm me, satiate!
I hold within me firm spirits vivacious.
I fear nothing; to God I'm consecrated.
In vain you battle Him with your disdain:
unto the King of Light cedes the dark reign.
. . . .
      "Catch fire, oh my heart; in happiness burn,
and may you find, in this blazing terrain,
spirit alive with life. Let be reborn
that phoenix in the ardor of your pain.
And if such fortune you may come to earn,

anzi, tra danni vigorosa gode
e medita la mente inni di lode.
     Poi dice: "O fiamme a me gradite e care,
vapori, ch' accendete l'alma mia,
faci del sol più serene e chiare
che mostrate fra 'l mal l'eccelsa via,
deh, provi il core tra queste onde amare
ogni dolcezza ed a me dato sia
ch'in torbid' acque lo stellante velo
m'apra colui che mi promette il Cielo.
     Sì, sì, stille, sì, sì, vampe, crescete!
Abbruciatemi il seno, ardo d'amore!
Infiammatemi l'alma, il petto ardete!
Sono lievi le fiamme a tanto core.
Voi con fuoco maggior non m'accendete
di quello, onde m'accese il mio Signore.[204]
E bench'in età molle, in tener anni,
non fuggo dagli oltraggi e scontro i danni.
     Sorgano contro me fieri i leoni
con sanguinose labbra a morte intenti!
S'aggirin a mio danno aspri dragoni
e di venen funesto armino i denti!
Arpie, scille, procustri e gerioni
déstin ire e ritrovino spaventi!
Di larve mentitrici è van l'aspetto
ov' ha verginitade il suo ricetto.
     Sì, sì, mostri, sì, sì, le ire mordaci
accelerate contro il petto mio,
e con freddo venen, con atre faci,
contro me saziate il fier desio!
Ho di fermezza in me spirti vivaci
e nulla temo, consacrata a Dio.
Invano s'arma contro lui lo sdegno:
cede al Re della luce il fosco regno.
. . . .
     Raccenditi, o mio core, ardi felice,
e sia per te quest'infocata vena
vivo spirto di vita. E qual fenice
rinasci nell'ardor della tua pena.
E se provar tal sorte a te pur lice,

---

[204]*mio Signore*: Cristo.

of your whole life, it's the breeze most serene.
Mansion on high of Love celestial,
all of your lightning bolts on me let fall."

. . . .

FROM: CANTO II: THE MARTYRDOM

Eastward, above a caravan of rose,
the Dawn, who transforms ice to tiny pearls,
her lustrous hair entwined with gemstones precious,
chased off the clouds, silvered the sky in whorls.
Limpid, amid splendor diaphanous,
with sapphires bright, the Air colored her veil:
to morning's goddess moved, with ostentation,
the Hours delightful and breezes serene.
Nature herself painted her face with rays.
The earth in competition sprouted flowers.
In forests, nightingales unloosed their lays;
the greyhound coursed with ease through green of bowers.
When, in bosom of sleep, Almachius
feels his heart stir with unusual ardors,
with venomous ghosts raging in his nightmare,
feels his soul start to shake, his breast to flare.

. . . .

"And now, just a mere girl, of that sex vile,
young in age, a soft bud, will overthrow,
break down and overthrow in reckless style,
the house invincible of great Augusto?
Ah, such a pride I find detestable!
Thus, with her life, all female pride let go
extinct!" So speaking, he at his heart's core
becomes all hate, all anger and all horror.
Then from his room, like Pluto from dark pathway,
burning with fury goes the evil one.
More than an asp filled with ferocity,

è l'aura di tua vita a pien amena.
L'alta magione degli amor celesti
tutti i fulmini suoi su me tempesti."
. . . .

DAL: CANTO II: IL MARTIRIO

Sovra carro di rose in oriente,
l'Alba, che cangia in fine perle il gelo,
cinta di ricche gemme il crin lucente,
scacciava le ombre e inargentava il cielo.
Limpida l'aria, allo splendor ridente,
di bei zaffiri coloriva il velo,
e fean[205] pompa alla diva dell'albore[206]
amene le aure e dilettose le Ore.
Di rai natura il volto suo pingea.
La terra a gara germogliava i fiori.
Tra boschi i canti l'usignol sciogliea
e il veltro scorrea fra verdi orrori.
Quand'Almachio, ch'al sonno in sen giacea,
prova nel petto non usati ardori,
e con larve di furie e di veneno,
sente scotersi l'alma, arder il seno.[207]
. . . .
"Ed ora una donzella, un sesso vile,
ch' ha nella fresca età, molle germoglio,
abbatterà, con temerario stile,
del forte imperator l'invitto soglio?
Ah, 'l suo vanto per me si prenda a vile,
e con la vita il femminile orgoglio
estinto manchi!" E a questo dir[208] nel core
è tutt'odio, tutt'ira, e tutto orrore.
Esce, qual Pluto dall'oscura foce,
della camera il reo, di furie ardendo.
E fatto più d'un aspide feroce,

---

[205]*fean*: facevano.
[206]*diva dell'albore*: Aurora.
[207]Note the contrast between the serene beauty of dawn and the villain's (Almachio's) violent rage.
[208]È Almachio che parla a se stesso.

he slithers everywhere to spread his poison.
He hails his henchman, and pitilessly
orders the blow horrific to be done
to virgin Cecilia; by anger fed,
orders her body be cleaved from her head.
     "Now see," he says, "and put to test, vile girl,
whether your dead god will your life defend,
whether your serving Christ's of much avail
against my hand that head from body rends.
See if your virtue's firm against the steel.
And as, over your life, my power extends,
go, boast about His works; with your words vain
defend yourself from my hands if you can.
     "On, on, my trusty man, take sword of steel
and let your hand be armed with fearless ardor!
Strike hard the blow against that wicked girl.
The veins of Urban's handmaiden go sever.
Anoint the bath with her spilt blood as well
and stain the step of that sick spirit's door.
To her frail bust execute the deathblow,
as to victim sacrificed to Augusto!"
. . . .
     In varied timbers, high harmonic currents
he hears resound mid play of lyres' strings,
as invisible voices with sweet accents
of Heaven's grandeur to Cecilia sing.
Mixed with that sound, a refined instrument
now forms (as if with other sounds competing)
musical melody in tone so sweet
that it restrains and melts the tyrant's heart.
     The girl divine, on organ resonant,
(its hollow woods a work industrious),
lets fly her fingers as with God's intent;
inspires the spirit of virtuousness
that, in the face of doom, can wax triumphant,

va d'ogni intorno il suo venen spargendo.
Il carnefice chiama e ad alta voce
della vergin Cecilia il colpo orrendo
comanda al fiero, e con irato volto
vuole il capo di lei da lei disciolto.[209]
E dice: "Or vedi, vil donzella, e prova
se 'l tuo dio morto il viver tuo difende,
e se 'l servir a Cristo ora ti giova
contro la mano che 'l tuo capo offende,
se contr' il ferro in te virtù si trova.
E s'a tua morte il mio poter si stende,
va', le opre vanta, e coi tuoi detti vani
difenditi, se puoi, dalle mie mani.
Su, su, fido ministro,[210] il ferro cingi,
ed intrepido ardir t'armi la mano.
Contro l'empia donzella il colpo stringi.
Svena l'ancella dell'iniquo Urbano.[211]
Aspergi il bagno e del suo sangue tingi
il suolo che calcò lo spirto insano.
E dài colpo di morte in fragil busto,
qual vittima consacrata al forte Augusto."[212]
. . . .
Sente di varie tempre alto concento
e cetre armoniose ode sonare,
ed invisibil voci in dolce accento
le superne grandezze a lei cantare.
E talor, misto al suon dotto strumento,
quasi a gara tra lor in un formare
musica melodia con ton sì dolce
ch'il cor tiranno gli raffrena e molce.[213]
La Diva allor su risonanti legni,
ch' han di concave canne ordini industri,[214]
con le dita trascorre e, del Ciel degni,
v'infonde spirti di virtude illustri,
che vincer ponno dell'oblio gli sdegni,

---

[209]Almachio orders the *carnefice* [the henchman] to decapitate Cecilia, because she survived the torture in her bath.
[210]*fido ministro*: il carnefice.
[211]*Urbano*: il papa ai tempi di Cecilia, secondo Margherita.
[212]*Augusto*: l'imperatore romano.
[213]The henchman, upon entering Cecilia's house, is at first enchanted by the divine music.
[214]Description of a small organ.

can mock the impetus of Time pretentious,
beat back against the ire of adverse fate,
incinerate the lightning bolts of death.
. . . .
     Upon her neck, the henchman, fierce with anger,
once, twice, struck her and three strikes realized.
The Roman girl does not to death surrender;
her inner splendor cannot be excised.
Shut fast are death's doors so she cannot enter.
Not by fate is this beauty compromised.
Infused entirely with celestial grace,
immortal breast has she, eternal place.

. . . .

from: Canto III: The Temple

     The Lord on high there prevails over all —
He, of eternal progeny, the Godhead —
and at his feet, within luminous circle,
He sees the sun, flaring with rays of gold,
bring autumn, spring, in turns continual,
winter and summer to the immense world;
and through dark air, with her ivory bow aimed,
darting at shadows, the Moon, silver-clad.
. . . .
     At the Lord's throne, spirits with wings abound,
infinite rows of pure intelligence
who, with eternal and delightful sound,
laud the Great King of every element.
Of these, the blessèd, many can be found
mantled in glory rich and in rays ardent.
And at their melodies, worthy of praise,
echoing go the realms of the vast skies.
     God lives on high, Sovereign Divinity,
who diffuses His being everywhere.
He grants the day its luminosity;
Oblivion flees condemned to the dark sphere;

prender a scherno gl'impeti dei lustri,
ribatter le ire dell'avversa sorte
e incenerire i fulmini di morte.

. . . .

    D'Almachio il servo, sovra 'l capo, forte
tre volte il colpo ripercosse irato,
né pur soggiace la romana a morte,[215]
né lo splendor di lei resta eclissato.
Son chiuse del morire a lei le porte.
Non è la bella sottoposta al fato,
ma di grazie celesti infusa a pieno
eterne ha le ore ed immortale il seno.

. . . .

DAL: CANTO III: IL TEMPIO

    Sta Dio là sovra donde al tutto impera,
Padre increato dell'eterna prole,
e sott'i piè, nella lucente sfera,
vede avvampar con raggi d'oro il sole,
e ricondurre autunno e primavera,
verno ed estate alla terrena mole,
e, con l'arco d'avorio all'aria bruna,
saettar le ombre l'argentata luna.

. . . .

    Al trono del gran Dio splendon accanto
schiere infinite di pennute menti,[216]
e con eterno dilettevol canto,
lodano il sommo Re degli elementi.
E dei beati v'è gran stuol, ch' ha manto
ricco di gloria e di bei raggi ardenti.
E ai concenti lor, di lode degni,
son eco appena dei gran cieli i regni.
    Dio siede in alto ed è sovrano nume,
che diffonde se stesso in ogni lato.
Il dì vago ha da lui ridente lume,
l'Oblio se n' fugge a tenebre dannato,

---

[215]Cecilia survived the three strikes permitted by Roman law in beheadings, but only for a few days.
[216]*pennute menti*: gli angeli.

Time spreads its odious feathers far away;
Fate, too, serves Him, obedient to His order.
Whoever rules on earth is, through His zeal,
controlled and governed by celestial rule.
　　　He, the Prime Cause, does forever create
how much we may receive of earth's abundance.
With His own sight He blesses others' sight
and reignites all with His own resplendence.
He's sweet prize of good souls — of uncontrite,
unvanquished Foe who metes out righteous penance.
Those boastful of superior might in war
He, powerful, triumphant, rends asunder.

. . . .

FROM: **CANTO IV: THE TOMB**

. . . .
　　　Each soul lists sweetly while her praise is sung.
Throughout the cavern, one hears cantos boom,
and with highest applause does the air throng.
Sainted, Cecilia's placed in sacred tomb,
in the clear resonance of divine song.
Chased from the cave is any shadow's gloom.
The saints return to dwell in Paradise;
on earth, to honor her, Urban gives voice.

spiega il Tempo lontan l'odiose piume
e serve a cenni ubbidiente il Fato.
E chi regge la terra è dal suo zelo
e regolato e governato in Cielo.
        Egli è prima cagion che sempre crea
quanto il mondo fra noi fertil produce.
Con la sua vista l'altrui vista bea
e a tutti risplendente in sé riluce.
Dei buoni è dolce premio e all'alma rea
giuste pene comparte e, invitto duce,
chi vanta forza più superba in guerra,
potente scote e trionfante atterra.

. . . .

DAL: CANTO IV: IL SEPOLCRO

. . . .
        Dolce ogni spirto a tali accenti gode
e l'aria ai sommi applausi intorno è scossa.
Lo speco rimbombar ai canti s'ode.
E ripongon la Diva in sacra fossa
al chiaro suon della divina lode:
è dall'antro ogni tenebra rimossa.
Tornan i numi in Cielo a far dimora
ed Urbano Cecilia in terra onora.[217]

---

[217]This is the concluding octave of the poem. Cecilia is buried after being eulogized by her husband Valerius who, together with his brother, Tiberius, descended from Heaven in the company of angels. Note the poet's insistence on music [*canti*] and on light [*luce*], symbol of God, which expels all darkness from the catacomb [*antro*]. Cecilia became the patron saint of music. Music is repeatedly described by Margherita as a powerful force of jubilation that has a calming effect on the human psyche.

FROM: *DIANA'S WOODS* (1647)

The Alps: To the Royal Lady of Savoy
      Christina, humbly to you comes the one
who lived, to your great merits, always handmaid,
and who, beneath the wrath of gods divine,
suffered from her cruel star hard life indeed.
On course perpetual, from her fierce Fortune,
unhappy, she her evil days received.
Distilled with pain in turbid waters' churn,
to sorrow's sea was Margherita born.
      With studies long and work industrious
I tried to write virtue into my page,
so with Helicon's throng illustrious,
I'd be part of Apollo's entourage,
to scatter with my pen the years that race —
to conquer with my skill nature's style savage —
so that my name, amid those limpid crystals,
I'd hear resounding go throughout the vales.
      Nothing, alas, can launch my pen for flight,
nor can my weak hand produce much of worth.
I find myself by harsh blows gravely hit;
by destiny I'm thrown down to the earth.
Your grace alone can lift me to the height
and from this evil beating lead me forth.
Let bitter Fate oppress me at her will —
sweet is my fall, if you support me still.

. . . .

DA: *LA SELVA DI DIANA* (1647)

L'Alpi: A Madama Reale di Savoia[218]
 Cristina, a te se n' viene umil colei
che sempre visse ai tuoi gran merti ancella,
ed ebbe in ira dei superni dei
fiero il tenor della sua cruda stella.
E con perpetuo corso i giorni rei
trasse, infelice, da fortuna fella,
stillossi di dolor in torbid' acque,
e Margherita a mar di pene nacque.

 Con lunghi studi e con fatiche industri
tentai vergar della virtù le carte,
e anch'io tra i spirti d'Elicona illustri
là, nel tempio d'Apollo esser a parte,
scuoter con la mia penna i mobil lustri,
di natura lo stil vincer con l'arte,
e fare tra quei limpidi cristalli
della mia fama risuonar le valli.

 Ma nulla può della mia penna il volo,
né tanto val della mia man la possa.
Sono respinta dalla sorte al suolo
e gravemente in me medesma scossa.
Sol puote la tua grazia aprirmi il polo
e sollevarmi dalla ria percossa.
Fato acerbo a sua voglia or mi sommerga,
dolce mi fia il cader, purché tu m'erga.

. . . .

---

[218]For comment, see Introduction, p. 35.

from: The Author, Under the Name Artigemma, Called to Albano by Lavinia Buratti to Sing in the Presence of a Number of Ladies, Praises Each

To Lavinia Buratti

      In the fair realm of Lazio, just when
the god Apollo shines with twice his light,
and crowned with grapes beneath rays of the sun,
to joy awakens lovers fortunate,
Lavinia resides, and with that fun,
musical harmonies would cultivate.
She gathers to her nymphs in rich attire —
all Tiber's Alban beauties there appear.
      She summons Artigemma — in sweet comments
asks her to choose the notes and lead the rest
mid bacchanalian games, high entertainments,
despite the drink (old age's nemesis).
To the soft sounds of those beautiful accents,
all applaud her, friend of the Bacchic feast,
wherefore, rejoicing, towards the crowd she faces
and in heavenly voice then improvises.
      The first Lavinia, from Quirinal's dome,
displayed the arms of Troy, raised up with splendor
the Campidoglio for imperial Rome.
She was a rock of faith and firmness sure.
In Alba, with her mastery supreme,
she laid foundation for the throne and there

DA: L'AUTRICE SOTTO NOME DI ARTIGEMMA CHIAMATA IN ALBANO DA LAVINIA BURATTI A CANTARE ALLA PRESENZA DI NUMEROSE DAME COSÌ LODA OGNUNA DI LORO[219]

A Lavinia Buratti[220]
    Nel bel regno del Lazio, allora che suole
lo dio d'Anfriso[221] raddoppiar suoi vanti
e, coronato d'uva ai rai del sole,
desta alle gioie fortunati amanti,
stassi Lavinia, ed a quei scherzi vuole
aggiunger d'armonia musici canti,
stuolo di ninfe adduna e, in fogge rare,[222]
quanto ha il Tebro vaghezze in Alba[223] appare.
    Artigemma a sé chiama e in dolci accenti
vuol che note disciòglia[224] e lor predica,
tra baccanari giochi, alti contenti
ad onta del liquor d'età nemica.
Al soave spirar dei bei concenti
applaude ogn'alma alla baccante amica,
ond'ella festeggiante in lor s'affisa
e con voci di ciel così improvvisa.
    Lavinia[225] già sul Quirinale[226] altero
vantò l'armi troiane e il Campidoglio[227]
fastosa eresse al tiberino impero,
e fu di fede e di fermezza un scoglio.
In Alba, con sovrano magistero,
i fondamenti porse, ch'l regio soglio

---

[219]For comment, see Introduction, p. 35.
[220]*Lavinia Buratti*: moglie di un figlio di Giulio Buratti. Un ramo della famiglia toscana dei Buratti si stabilì a Roma nel Cinquecento. Giulio è ricordato nel 1641 fra i conservatori di Roma (Rendina 164).
[221]*dio d'Anfriso*: Apollo (dal nome del fiume in Tessaglia dove Apollo pascolava il gregge di Ammeto.
[222]*ninfe . . . in fogge rare*: dame vestite in modo ricercato.
[223]*Alba Longa*: nome originale romano di Albano, località vicino a Roma.
[224]*che note disciòglia*: che canti.
[225]*Lavinia*: Secondo la legenda elaborata da Virgilio, Lavinia, figlia di Latino, re di Lazio, insieme al marito Enea, stabilì la base di quello che diventerà poi l'impero romano. Si noti che Margherita attribuisce tutta la gloria a Lavinia.
[226]*Quirinale*: una delle colline di Roma su cui sorgeva il Tempio di Quirino (Marte dei sabini).
[227]*Campidoglio*: centro religioso e politico di Roma antica.

reigned queen, and pledged, in hand with nuptial dowry,
a realm — token of faithful matrimony.
　　　You, new Lavinia, raise high the glories
of virtue, beauty, and to studies boast
you're friend. To make eternal memories,
the words of my rough song you would request.
Let that be one of your great victories.
To you, let Tiber equal joy attest,
for in the lap of peace, joyful you rule;
with virtue's strings you secure every soul.
　　　That first queen built Campidoglio with honors —
to studies, you, new Campidoglio build.
With arms she quelled ferocity of others —
you subjugate others with your acts bold.
Her dowry was a realm — a heart is yours,
enriched with realms, adornments thousandfold.
Fame, with your deeds bedecked, as signifier
your glory spreads, your merits to admire.
　　　Let nobles honor you as a new queen,
for you rule Lazio. With greater trophies
let Quirinal applaud you, lovely Latin,
child of the gods, image of faithfulness.
To you, let cede the first Lavinia.
Before you here kneels Tarpeo's hill joyous,
as virtue, Alban goddess, you sustain.
You are, more than chaste Muses, worthy Sun.

To Porzia Mazzarino

　　　Porzia, in your pomp, oh, ancient heroes
I recognize — in your pride, their aplomb.
To you, my words I joyfully unloose —
you can immortalize my name, my poems.
Meanwhile, by its three lilies stemmed, your rose
that you encrusted with diamonds and gems,

calcò reina,[228] ed in tributo diede
un regno d'immeneo pegno di fede.[229]
      Tu, novella Lavinia, ergi le glorie
di virtù, di beltade, ed alzi vanto
di studi amica e, ad eternar memorie,
chiedi le voci del mio rozzo canto.
Sian di quella le tue maggior vittorie
ed il Tebro di te god' altretanto,
ch'in grembo della pace il regno godi
e ad aure di virtude ogn'alma annodi.
      Quella d'un Campidoglio eresse l'onore,
e tu di studi un campidoglio eregi.
Con le armi ella abbattè l'altrui furore,
e tu soggioghi altrui con atti egregi.
Ella un regno ebbe in dote, e tu d'un core
ricca ch' ha mille regni e mille fregi.
La Fama, adorna dei tuoi fatti, spira
le glorie tue ed i tuoi pregi ammira.
      T'onori il nobil stuol nuova reina
ch'al Lazio imperi, e con maggior trofei
t'applauda il Quirinale, vaga latina,
simulacro di fé, parto de' dei.
Ceda l'altra ai tuoi pregi. Ecco t'inchina
il Tarpeo[230] festeggiante e in Alba sei
nume, ch'alla virtù porge sostegno
e delle Caste Suore[231] un sol più degno.

A Porzia Mazzarino[232]

      Porzia, dal fasto tuo, deh, i prischi eroi,
le glorie riconosco entro i tuoi vanti.
Fastosa i detti snodo a te, che puoi
eterni far con il mio nome i canti,
mentre tua rosa, con i tre gigli suoi,[233]
tempestasti di gemme e di diamanti,

---

[228]*reina*: regina.
[229]*un regno d'immeneo pegno di fede*: Lavinia portò in dote il regno d'Alba.
[230]*Tarpeo*: Rupe Tarpea, precipizio della collina del Campidoglio, sta per Campidoglio o Roma.
[231]*Caste Suore*: le Muse.
[232]*Porzia Mazzarino*: seconda moglie del padre del cardinale Giulio Mazzarino.
[233]An allusion to the coat of arms of the Mazzarino family, received from the king of France through Cardinal Mazarin.

demonstrates that the king, numen of France,
is, to your splendors, Sun and radiance.
      You've forehead silvery white — of pure gold's spun
your hair, that in fair ringlets spreads to fall.
Your eyes are two suns to a destined one
whose gaze is led to fix thereon in thrall.
Your lips to rubies are like twin companions.
Pearls are your teeth. Distinguished overall,
at your fair breast, your diamonds animate,
enjoy, highly serene, their every merit.
. . . .
      Upon you, Porzia, the lucent spheres
the name 'mother' to noble son bestow,
and from the Seine, rich jewels to you he bears,
triumphant father of great Giulio,
in glory. Those proud men disdain the force
of the feared Turkish squads, knowingly so.
At their commands, with spheres subservient,
stars of the Heavens spin, obedient.

To Prudenza Buratti de' Massimi, for the Crystal Star She Wears in Her Hair While Pregnant

      Amid your golden ringlets artfully shines
the image of a lovely star, Prudenza,
that in sun's rays lights up with happiness
to herald in your womb grand pregnancy.

mostra ch'il re, che della Gallia è nume,
è fatto ai tuoi splendori e sole e lume.
    Hai d'argento la fronte e d'or più fino
è il crin che spande in vaghe anella avvinto.
Son le luci due soli onde a destino
lume ch'ad affissarvi il guardo è spinto.
Le labbra in te rassembrano il rubino.
Sono di perle i denti ed, in distinto,
godono i pregi lor nel vago seno
d'animato diamante, alto sereno.

. . . .

    Porzia, a te danno le lucenti sfere
d'alto parto snodar voce di madre,[234]
e dalla Senna a te vaste miniere
porta glorioso il trionfante padre
del gran Giulio: al saper le anime altere
sprezzan del trace[235] le temute squadre
ed ai suoi[236] cenni, con le sfere ancelle,
ubbidienti in ciel giran le stelle.

A Prudenza Buratti de' Massimi[237] per la stella di cristallo che porta fra i capelli essendo gravida[238]

    Tra groppi d'oro con bell'arte splende,
Prudenza, in te, di vaga stella imago,
ed ai raggi del sol lieta s'accende
ad annunziar, nel tuo bel seno, il tago.[239]

---

[234]Having married the father of the cardinal, Porzia became "madre" to Giulio, although she was younger than he.

[235]*trace*: i turchi (padre e figlio non temono i turchi).

[236]*suoi*: loro.

[237]In 1645, Prudenza Buratti married Angelo de' Massimi (1625–1683), the oldest son from the branch of the Massimi family called d'Aracoeli. She is remembered by her sister-in-law, the poet Petronilla Paolini Massimi (1663–1727), as a kind but unfortunate woman — she lost an eye in a carnival accident and, shortly after, an illness kept her bedridden for nineteen years till her death in 1682 (see Costa-Zalessow, 2001, 29–30.) Prudenza's pregnancy must have gone wrong. According to family records she had no children and when Angelo died his inheritance passed to Petronilla's sons.

[238]The star, *stella di cristallo*, seems to have been a symbol of maternity. In Christianity *stella maris* is associated with the Virgin, but it had its roots in the cult of Isis, who was mother of the pagan virgin mothers. Isis was depicted as standing on the crescent moon and surrounded by twelve stars. See Baily 1:232–33.

[239]*tago*: forse da tagós = supremo, cioè, un parto maggiore (di gemelli).

From Castor and Pollux to you descends,
by way of Eastern star, a childbirth prescient.
Bound to Lavinia by noble ties,
awaited are new Romulus and Remus.
       Cheeks soft as flowers have you — milky-white hands.
More beautiful than true gold is your hair.
You've eyes coal-black. Your breast of snow portends
the noble twins that in your womb you bear.
In you, ivory with ebony contends.
From your brow's arch, with arrows even finer
does Cupid strike the heart of one whose place
resides at the throne of your faith and grace.
       Of Giuli, Massimi, you weave a crown
with your progeny strong and vigorous,
fair Latin. Fame already makes it known.
And Destiny, before their deeds, surrenders.
Your fertile womb delights the glad Pomona.
To treasures, he throws wide for you his doors,
wingèd Amour, god of lovers' fruition —
while Zeus himself applauds your parturition.

To the Widow Giulia Errera

       Amid black veils, I perceive a new sun,
Giulia, in your fair face, wrapped in pose proud,
eclipsing dark globes of oblivion.
And Cupid, I see, boasts amid the cloud,
or rather, hid in clouds, a lofty passion
wakens to view, of your rule's certitude,
your glories that, veiled over with dark terrors,
retain, in sky nocturnal, ardent stars.

Di Castore e Polluce[240] in te discende,
per la stella oriental, parto presago.
E di Lavinia in nobil fé ristretta,
Romulo e Remulo il Campidoglio aspetta.
    Hai le gote di fior, la man di latte,
e son dell'or più belli i tuoi capelli.
Di carbonchio hai le luci e nevi intatte
porti nel vago sen d'alti gemelli.
L'ebano con l'avorio in te combatte,
e dall'arco del ciglio i strai[241] piú belli
avventa Amor nel cor di lui che siede
al trono di tue grazie e di tua fede.
    Tessi dei Giuli[242] e Massimi corona
nella tua prole vigorosa e forte,
vaga latina, e già la Fama suona.
Cede alle opre lor vinta la Sorte.
Gode, al tuo fertil sen, lieta Pomona.
Ed apre a te dei suoi tesor le porte,
lo dio pennato di contenti amanti,
ed applaude ai tuoi parti il gran tonante.

A Giulia Errera vedova[243]

    Tra negre bende[244] un nuovo sol vegg'io,
Giulia, nel tuo bel volto in atto altero
starsi tra globi d'eclissato oblio.
E vanta tra nubi il vago arciero,
anzi, ascoso tra nembi alto desio
desta a mirar del tuo sovrano impero
le glorie che velate di terrore[245]
hanno in notturno ciel stelle d'ardore.

---

[240]The twin brothers, Castor and Pollux, known as Dioscuri, stood for bravery and dexterity in fight.

[241]*strai*: strali.

[242]*Giuli*: Il padre di Prudenza si chiamava Giulio (v. nota 220) e il fratello di lei (di cui non conosciamo il nome), era marito di Lavinia. Le due donne erano perciò cognate. Usando *Giuli* e *Massimi* permette alla poetessa di alludere alle famiglie di Roma antica.

[243]Perhaps a relative of Nicolò and Francesco Herrera, who served the papal court from 1623 to 1642 (*DBI* 61: 702–03). Note the poet's repeated contrasting of the black color of the widow's dress with the whiteness of her skin.

[244]*bende nere*: vestiti neri da vedova.

[245]*di terrore*: di nero.

That sun's eclipsed but not wholly obscure,
however draped in black robes it may be.
Death's messenger covers your silver pure
and keeps light from your beauty jealously,
a gloomy lover — with desire impure,
tramples your snows and, to cruel destiny,
condemns your candid breast with veils to hide
the greatest beauty that the skies provide.

　　　Your rays, Errera, cannot err to miss
the true path and direction of your splendors,
but daring suitors of your candid breast
know how to reign among sin's wayward ardors.
Surest homage unto your faithfulness
are these, your veils, that to others seem horrors.
A clever shade allows no light to fall
on your breast's ivory — jealous, holds it still.

　　　Mid snows, let someone your black ink admire —
a soul who's pleased to gaze on beauty's sight.
Let that soul draw, to your shade, sighs afire.
Sun amid clouds, you diffuse lovely light.
Far from you, let Death turn in fickle gyre,
she who would presage harm in cloak of night,
and let the god of deathless laurel's crown
boast that, mid cloud, your splendors shine again.

To Girolama Malvezzi

　　　The grass hugging the ground puts on a dress
of sapphires bright. To lovely buds gives color,
the goddess who brings day so luminous
within bosom of Flora, mid joys dear.
Thus for you, noble damsel, they're in place,
while Tiber gilds the fields here in your honor.
At your fair semblance, this laurel of mine
fells the affront of foul oblivion.

　　　The rose offers to you a lovely ruby —
the lily, necklaces of diamond.
Viola offers dulcet destiny —

Eclissato è quel sol, ma non oscuro,
benché d'oscuro ricoperto sia.
Copre nunzio di morte argento puro
ed invido al tuo bel la luce oblia
tetro amatore, con desire impuro
calca le nevi tue e a sorte ria
danna il candor del petto, e copre un velo
quanto ha di bello e di vaghezza il cielo.
    Errera, non errar ponno i tuoi raggi
il diritto camin dei tuoi splendori,
ma del candido petto arditi ostaggi
imperar sanno tra nocenti ardori.
Sono della tua fé sicuri omaggi
questi ch'agli occhi altrui sembran orrori,
ed asconde alla luce, ombra sagace,
l'avorio del tuo sen, che invida tace.
    Tra le nevi gl'inchiostri intenta ammiri
alma che di mirar beltà s'appaga
e tragga alle ombre tue caldi sospiri.
Sole, che tra le nubi hai luce vaga.
Roti lungi da te volubil giri
colei[246] ch'è in manto ner di duol presaga,
e, tra le nubi rinnovar splendori,
vanti lo dio dell'immortali allori.

A Girolama Malvezzi[247]

    L'erba che preme il suol vestesi intorno
di bei zaffiri, e i vaghi fior colora
la dea ch'apporta luminoso il giorno
tra care gioie nel bel sen di Flora,
e teco, alta donzella, hanno soggiorno,
mentr'a tue pompe il Tebro i campi indora,
ed al tuo bel sembiante il lauro mio
abbatte le onte del nocente oblio.
    Ha la rosa per te vago il rubino,
il giglio di diamanti ha vezzi cari,
la viola ha per te dolce il destino

---

[246]*colei*: la Morte.
[247]Daughter of Marquise Giulia Malvezzi, praised by Costa in a preceding poem (not included here). Giulia Campeggi was wife to Marquis Francesco Pirro Malvezzi of Bologna (Dolfi 508).

she revels, though her scent is not renowned.
Jasmine treasures from Dawn her finery,
and the sweet violet's refuge can be found
between your tresses' ringlets of gold curls —
she wears not frost, but fragrant drops of pearls.
      Like virgin rose, on your maternal stem
you spread your petals to disclose your beauties,
and from your splendors, air gathers a flame
of purest ardor to oppose harsh ice.
To unspoiled thoughts, chaste longings you lay claim,
wherefore you're off on trails across the skies.
You raise the name Maria Girolama,
to weave with laurel your immortal mane.
      Let descend to you, from Castalian spheres,
a marriage fortunate, and to your worth
let august heroes with noble desires
ignite for you and yearn for nuptial faith.
Let's see Love's torch shimmer with golden fires.
Let Quirinal its prized merits bequeath
unto your fame. Everything held as grand
is, in your tribute, spread across the land.

To Baby Lalla, Daughter of Lavinia Buratti

      You, lucky baby girl, I now address,
for honored name of 'Buratti' you hold
to grow its fame. My words I thus release
to you, with your innocent locks of gold.
You, daughter of the one who's my protectress —
you dominate the stars with luck that's bold,
and at your nod, though framed in a child's face,
you witness every heart fall for your grace.
      Lalla, although yet bound in swaddling clothes,
you clearly are the image of true wit,
and though you're lured to milk in early years,
with your wise ways you satisfy each heart.
You've hair of gold, and Cupid shoots his arrows
through your bright eyes. Each heart knows, in a shot,
that from your gaze it draws a bitter fate
and, from the flame that's born, with death will meet.

e gode ad onta dei fragori avari.[248]
Dall'Alba ha i suoi tesori il gelsomino,
ed ha la mammoletta i suoi ripari
dai groppi d'oro del tuo nobil crine,
e con spirti d'odor perle ha per brine.

      Qual suol vergine rosa, apri le foglie
di tua beltade, nel materno stelo,
ed ai splendori tuoi l'aura raccoglie
vampa di puro ardor contr'aspro gelo.
Hai d'intatto pensier, pudiche voglie,
onde campeggi per le vie del cielo,
e di Maria Girolama ergi il nome
per intrecciar d'allor l'immortal chiome.

      Discenda a te, da li castali giri,
imeneo fortunato e ai merti tuoi
s'accenda di magnanimi desiri
brama di regal fé d'augusti eroi.
La face d'or per te scoter si miri
e vanti alla tua fama i pregi suoi
il Quirinale e, quanto ha in sé di grande,
tutto il tributo ai tuoi gran fasti spande.

A Lalla bambina figlia di Lavinia Buratti

      Fortunata bambina, a te mi volgo
ché dei Buratti hai l'onorato nome,
la fama accreschi, e i detti miei disciolgo
a te, ch' hai d'oro l'innocenti chiome.
Tu, figlia di colei ond'io m'avvolgo,
con fortunato ardir le stelle hai dome,
ed ai tuoi cenni, in pueril sembiante,
scorgi ogni cor di tua bellezza amante.

      Lalla, che tra le fasce ancor ristretta,
porti di spirto fortunata imago
e, mentr' al latte ancor l'età t'alletta,
fai d'accorte maniere ogni cor pago.
Hai d'oro il crine e il vago arcier saetta
con i tuoi bei lumi e d'ogni cor presago
è di trar dai tuoi sguardi acerba sorte,
e da fiamma che nasce ha la sua morte.

---

[248] *fragori avari*: fragranza non forte.

Lovely and charming, you have still to learn
to form the word for mother, yet you shoot
darts of fierce passion, with passion make burn
in gentle fire, just through your eyes, each heart.
Release your darts — so each heart, soul in turn
will, through your eyes, spill over with Love's draught,
and at your lips, blazing as ruby's gem,
will turn nocent fire to innocent flame.
　　　Most lovely little girl, within you Nature
has gathered all her arts, one with Amour
who placed your beauty at war with each creature.
For learning, Pallas filled you with desire.
The goddess who administers her ardor
to each breast, and who gave you beauty's honor,
(Venus the amorous), vaunts your face fair
to Lazio and Tiber's ruling shore.

FROM: **SONNETS**

To a Lover Departing the City in Pouring Rain

　　　The Heavens are gone dark, devoid of light.
Day shows itself through stormy nimbus cloud.
Aurora starts her course in fashion squalid,
while Phoebus shrouds his face in purple blight.
　　　Vacillating, the earth within our sight
produces for us only flowers pallid —
in place of dawn, a night monstrous with dread.
Elsewhere does splendor's god illuminate.
　　　The air with tearful plaint, this plaint of mine
gravely accompanies — upon my tempests,
bolt upon bolt the thunder god Jove casts.
　　　Sky weeps, sun weeps, tears from the stars pour down
over my rack. To press for pain acute
amid my plaints, Love strikes with torches lit.

Vezzosetta, leggiadra, ancor non sai
ben proferir nome di madre e scocchi
dardi di fiero ardor e arder fai
in incendio soave i cor con gli occhi.
Avventa i strali sì, ch'ai tuoi bei rai
fia ch'ogn' alma, ogni cor d'amor trabocchi
e dai tuoi labbri di rubino ardente
tragga nocente ardor fiamma innocente.
    Pargoletta vezzosa, ove natura
ogn'arte ha collocata, e il bello Amore
ha posto a gara della sua fattura,
e Palla[249] ha dato ogni studioso umore.
La dea, ch'ai petti somministra arsura,[250]
ha reso a te d'ogni beltà l'onore,
e vanta il tuo bel volto, al Tebro in riva
ch'a Lazio impera, l'amorosa diva.

DAI: SONETTI

Ad amante che parte dalla città mentre piove[251]
    Il cielo è fatto oscuro e senza luce.
Il dì tra nembi di terror si mostra.
Febo d'impure macchie il volto inostra
e squalida l'Aurora il corso adduce.
    Vacillante la terra a noi produce
pallidi fiori ed alla luce nostra
fà d'atra notte formidabil mostra,
ché il dio dello splendore altrove luce.
    E l'aria col suo pianto il pianto mio
grave accompagna ed alle mie procelle
fulmini scote il fulminante dio.
    Piange il ciel, piange il sole, piangon le stelle
ai miei martiri e, per mio duol più rio
tra i pianti, il dio d'amore vibra facelle.

---

[249]*Palla*: Pallade
[250]*La dea ch'ai petti somministra arsura*: Venere.
[251]For comment, see Introduction, p. 36.

FROM: AMOROUS PASSION FOR THE DAYS OF THE WEEK

Monday

    Cynthia, I, once of your followers,
now scorn your ways, and the day to your name
made sacred I abhor, regard as sham
the scorch of that bow and arrow of yours.

    Oh day to me so dreadful, therein lies,
taken from me, mid shades, the adorned flame
of my bright Sun — and there, one in the same,
the god of peace, mid wrath, to my demise.

    Principal day, announcing deeds impious —
augury grave of my cruel haplessness —
transporter to me of my miseries.

    For, if my soul was stoked, ah, by such ardor,
far better that, oh wicked and cruel star,
she'd frozen me alive, the coldest goddess.

To Those in Doubt about Her Compositions

    It's not irrational to be uncertain
on whether a woman of our times has such skill,
where all, it seems, in laziness now dwell
and vice in every soul enjoys its reign.

    Oh stars, this age of ours, vulgar and common,
does skill and virtue far from us repel —
and ignorance, instead, is held ideal,
where high pomp clearly goes to noblemen.

    But no! The one who would ignorance foster,
must judge my pen, as Ignorance has deemed,
but frail, and to my fame do homicide.

    Margherita loves Phoebus — and it's destined
that he with virtue's rays shall be my guide,
while every other mortal lies obscure.

Beautiful Woman to Her Heart

    My heart, what use is it for you to grieve?
This earth holds deadly ravines, dark chimeras,

DA: PASSIONE AMOROSA PER I GIORNI DELLA SETTIMANA[252]

Lunedì

Cinzia, s'io fui delle orme tue seguace
or quelle sdegno ed al tuo nume il giorno
consacrato aborrisco e prend' a scorno,
del dardo tuo, dell'arco tuo la face.

O dì, per me funesto, in cui se n' giace,
a me tolto, fra le ombre il lume adorno
del mio bel sole, ed in cui fa soggiorno
tra le ire, a danno mio, lo dio di pace.

Principio, che m'annunzia opre non pie,
augurio grave di mia sorte rea,
apportator delle miserie mie.

Ah, ché, s'un tanto ardor l'anima ardea,
ben era d'uopo, inique stelle e rie,
che m'agghiacciasse la più fredda dea.

A chi dubita delle sue composizioni[253]

Non è fôr[254] di ragione il titubare,
ch'in donna sia vertude ai tempi d'oggi
ove in ogn'alma par che l'ozio alloggi
e il vizio in ogni sen goda imperare.

O stelle, questo secolo vulgare
fa che lunge da noi virtù se n' poggi
e l'ignoranza in vece sua s'appoggi,
ove gran nobiltà pompe ha più chiare.

Ma non però, chi l'ignoranz' annida,
deve qual lei stimar mia penna frale
e della fama mia farsi omicida.

Margherita ama Febo ed è fatale
che con rai di virtude ei mi sia guida,
mentre fra le ombre giace ogni mortale.

Bella donna al cuore[255]

Mio cor, di che ti lagni? Ha questa mole
precipizi funesti, atre chimere,

---

[252]For comment, see Introduction, p. 35.
[253]For comment, see Introduction, p. 36.
[254]fôr: fuori.
[255]With this sonnet, Margherita offers her variation on the Baroque theme of the futility of passion.

unhappy days and evenings ominous;
the sun's rays move to damage all who live.

    Though in joy's lap, the soul suffers hereof;
the breast despairs and mid visions fallacious,
with flames of black, the light obscurely shows.
What's most unwanted, mortals surely have.

    Fleeting is joy, while pain is everlasting;
grandeur is false and likewise vain are thoughts;
from us, every good vanishes on wing.

    Unhappy one, who to senses insane
cedes without sense, and from the sovereign heights,
deceives, blind as a mole, the distant brain.

Accusing Her Lover of Ingratitude

    You're off for distant parts, yet you don't say:
"I go. Wait here in hope, sufferance and peace."
You deny me, with your soul proud and fierce,
what you'd, cruel one, grant any enemy.

    Oh fortunate time, joyful memory,
when day or evening equally I'd pass,
without suffering Love's futile chimeras,
without the martyrdom of hours unhappy.

    Tyrant, what more harm can you do? Why state
you're not tormenting me when, at the close,
you'd fell the one you stood to elevate?

    Soul even colder than the Alpine snows,
you hid a rigid goal in a face pious.
Ruins are what remain after Love's flight.

On Jealousy

    With wings of black, hair full of snakes entwined,
with hands of ice, she wrings my heart — a monster —
and with a shivering frost, my precious ardor
she spatters until bloody and fear-stained.

    My mind's wrapped up in dolor, and constrained;
soul in my breast's reborn to die once more,
and my face, smeared over with deathly pallor,
appears, next to the living, of life drained.

    Perfidious man! Ah, how can you enjoy
another's breast, deprive me of love's mercy?
Why lace my joy with a venomous brew?

giorni infelici, portentose sere
e gira a danni altrui suoi raggi il sole.
    Qui, nel sen del gioir, l'alma si duole,
il petto s'ange e, tra vision non vere,
ha la luce facelle oscure e nere.
Ed ha sempre il mortal quel che non vuole.
    Momentaneo è il gioire, eterno il duolo,
fallaci le grandezze, i pensier vani,
ed ogni bene se ne fugge a volo.
    Infelice colui ch'ai sensi insani
cede insensato e dal sovrano polo,
talpa, raggira i suoi pensier lontani.

Rimprovero d'ingratitudine all'amante

    Lungi te n' vai, crudele, e pur non dici:
"Mi parto, resta in pace e soffri e spera."
E nieghi a me con alma iniqua e fiera
quello che non si suole anco ai nemici.
    O tempo fortunato, o dì felici,
in cui il giorno mi fu quanto la sera,
e, senza aver d'Amor vana chimera,
non trassi fra i martir le ore infelici.
    Tiranno, e che più puoi, perché dicesti
di non straziarmi, se volevi alfine
ridur colei che sollevar potesti?
    Alma più cruda delle nevi alpine,
sotto sembiante pio, rigido avesti
meta, al volo d'Amor son le ruine.

Di gelosia

    Con ali nere e crin di serpi avvinto,
mostro, ch' ha man di gel, mi stringe il core,
e con tremanti brine il caro ardore
sparge di sangue e di timore tinto.
    Resta lo spirto nel dolor convinto,
l'anima dentro il sen rinasce e more,
e, sparso il volto di mortal pallore,
sembra tra vivi già di vita estinto.
    Ah perfido, e perché d'altra nel seno
godi e mercé d'amor a me non dai
e spargi il mio gioir d'atro veneno?

You've sworn to me you don't know how to lie,
and yet gone dark is my serenity:
one who could trick must never have loved true.

FROM: **THE OTTAVE**

For the Honors Received in Paris from the Queen of France
You, who with honor nourish in your hearts
serious opera, airier refrains —
who thread clear notes between musical knots,
and plait your hair with consecrated fronds —
flee now the centuries' ignorant thoughts
and towards the Seine, its gilded shores and sands,
steer joyfully to landfall with your song,
if for fame, riches and honor you long.
. . . .
Anne . . .
I see already you've subdued and conquered
forces of envy, and to your noblesse
falls victim thus my subjugated heart
while I accept from you honored award.
Loosen, Francesca, the tones of your voice
and with respect before Anne's name bow down.
Let sound out strong the honors of her glories —
invited was your song by royal queen.
. . . .
Through Anne's great fame, it's been permitted us
to unbind our notes for her reverently
and, between breaths of song melodious,
unravel, joyful, lovely harmony.
A soul with scepter, regal cloak, nourishes
with honor, pleasures of high quality.
To pair work's virtue with a value equal
is but accomplished by a royal soul.

The Author's Departure from Rome in 1647
Wretched — to which city shall I now flee
where I might find a refuge for my nest,

Tu mi dicesti che mentir non sai,
e pur è volto in ombra il mio sereno,
ma chi potè ingannar non amò mai.

DALLE: **OTTAVE**

Per gli onori ricevuti a Parigi dalla Regina di Francia[256]
Voi, che nel sen a pro d'onor, nutrite
di studiose fatiche aure seconde
e tra musici groppi accenti ordite
e il crin trecciate di sacrate fronde,
secol d'ignoranza omai fuggite,
e della Senna alle dorate sponde
approdate fastosi il vostro canto,
se desiate onor, ricchezza e vanto.
. . . .
Anna,[257] . . .
per te vegg'io già rintuzzate e dome
dell'invidia le forze e a tua bontade
vittima è fatto il mio soggetto core,
mentre tragge da te premio d'onore.
Onde, Francesca,[258] le tue voci snoda
e d'Anna il nome riverente inchina,
ed alle glorie sue gli onori s'oda,
che permise al tuo canto alta regina.
. . . .
Permise a noi, della grand'Anna il vanto
di riverente a lei discior gli accenti,
e tra respiri d'armonioso canto
fastose dispiegar i bei concenti.
Alma che tratta scettro e regio ha il manto,
nutrisce a pro d'onore alti contenti.
E ad opra di virtude il merto equale,
solo sa compartire alma reale.

Partenza da Roma dell'autrice nel 1647
Misera, e qual città per lo mio scampo
in cui ritrovi a ricovrarmi il nido?

---

[256]For comment, see Introduction, p. 36.
[257]*Anna*: Anna d'Austria, regina di Francia, vedova di Luigi XIII e madre di Luigi XIV.
[258]*Francesca*: sorella di Margherita.

camp with my losses — in which wave of Lethe,
submerge what's said about me, the unrest?
Where shall I find light for my destiny,
a friendly shore offered me in this tempest?
And under what sky now will it be given
that on my ruins Fate will shine serene?

      Ever with scorn and miseries involved —
dupe of the goddess who vanquishes thrones —
shadow among the living, of joy deprived —
alive to Fortune's wheel of adverse turns —
exposed to evil, from all good removed —
born only to weave threads of hope's unknowns —
I'm granted to fly to the spheres and soar,
only to crash down to the earth once more.

      Fatherland, why? Like mother, I adored you,
and far from you wept over my migrations,
and while I paused my wanderings at the Arno,
the thought of you drew forth my lamentations.
I christened you the site of all my joy,
the place of my content and aspirations.
My heart, when distanced from you, deemed no higher
the world's vast empire than a vain desire.

      Tiber, a thousand times did I attune
my voice, afflicted, to your murmurings.
Through air, the winds carried to you, in turn,
accents harsh with sounds of my sufferings.
My joys I labeled but pensive privation
and I drew from delights but tortured things.
Far from your womb and all that's fortunate,
I felt the portent of sinister death.

      Yet, proud one, you disdain me, give me chase,
deprive me of what you'd not dare deprive
a foreign beauty. Ruthless, you embrace
those born on murky shores, new to arrive.
You freeze me, your own daughter, in the ice
of your waves, envious, and you'll not give
a poor room for my nest on native sands —
cruel smithy of my torments and my pains.

In qual onda di Lete i danni accampo
e sommergo di me l'infausto grido?
Ove di mia fortuna io scorgo il lampo
che appresti a mie tempeste amico lido?
Ed in qual cielo omai scorger mi è dato
rasserenarsi a mie ruine il Fato?
          Sempre tra scherni e tra miserie involta,
bersaglio della dea che reggi scote,[259]
ombra tra vivi ed al gioir sepolta,
sol viva al sostener d'avverse rote.
Al male esposta, ad ogni ben ritolta,
nata per intrecciar speranze ignote,
cui solo è dato sormontare il volo
sovra le sfere per cader nel suolo.
          Patria, a che pro? Qual madre io t'adorai
e lontana da te piansi i miei giri,
e mentre sopra l'Arno il piè fermai,
sempre trassi per te pianti e sospiri.
Albergo di mie gioie io ti chiamai,
stanza dei miei contenti e di desiri.
Stimò il mio cuor, ch'era da te lontano,
l'alto impero del mondo un desir vano.
          Tebro, che mille volte i miei concenti
accordavo dolente ai tuoi fragori
e portarono a te, per l'aria i venti,
accenti infausti al suon dei miei dolori.
Chiamai le gioie mie pensosi stenti
e trassi dai diletti aspri martori.
Lunge dall'alvo tuo e d'alta sorte
stimai portento di sinistra morte.
          E pur fiero mi sdegni e mi discacci,
e nieghi a me quel che negar non osi
a straniera vaghezza ed empio abbracci
parto, che vien a te dai lidi algosi,
e me, che te son figlia, invido agghiacci
nelle onde tue, e nieghi ai miei riposi
povera stanza sulle patrie arene,
fabbro nocente di tormenti e pene.

---

[259]*dea che reggi scote*: Fortuna.

   Profit from me, oh mortal, turn your mind
and ponder carefully, affix your gaze
upon my damage — in that evil find
the fragile heights and the rule based on lies.
And while your past mistakes you've time to mend,
armor your breast against the noxious arrows
of adverse Fate with cruel Fortune allied:
to helmsman wise, the way is open wide.
   Flee the harsh turns of hostile revolutions,
the fickle commoners and their grim eyes.
Submerged are honors in horrors' solutions:
from nascent destiny does peril rise.

· ·

   Empires are bound to fall — to ruin thus
go human splendors. What on earth has breath,
by hope is anguished, disturbed of repose,
while one's soul wends a labyrinthine path.
Serpents in wait lie hidden under flowers,
and mother of our happiness is Wrath.
Down here, nothing that's true seems to remain,
if not for what is futile or insane.
   Let my fate harsh example to you serve.
Do recognize, within my own, your errors,
for I, only to err again, now live
and move around with the revolving hours.
No trace of applause to me I conserve.
Enfeebled, I go begging after honors.
Where I had cradle once on native soil,
I find a hostile sky and Fortune cruel.
   I live bereft of gold, move to the plan
of blind Fate, who once raised me to the stars.
Instead of claiming highest approbation,
storm upon storm my labor now procures.
Phoebus's light has from me long passed on.
From font of honor, only flames and arrows
they hurl at me, Muses of Helicon,
and I net for my hair no laurel crown.

A mio costo, o mortali, in me volgete
cauti la mente, ed affissate il guardo
nel danno mio, e nel mal scorgete
frali l'altezze e l'imperar bugiardo.
E mentre a tempo a ravvedervi sete,
armate il sen contro nocente dardo
di Fato avverso e di Fortuna ria:
a sagace nocchiero il tutto è via.

    Fuggite aspro rotar dei giri avversi
e dell'errante volgo il torvo ciglio.
Sono gli onori entro gli orror sommersi,
e da sorte che nasce, erge il periglio.

. . . .

    Son cadenti gl'imperi e ruinosi
i fasti umani e ciò ch'in terra spira,
angue è di speme per turbar riposi,
mentre tra laberinti un'alma aggira.
Stanno le serpi sotto i fiori ascosi[260]
e del contento genitrice è l'Ira.
Né v'è cosa qua giù che vera sia,
se non quanto è di vano e di follia.

    Serva d'esempio a voi mio fato acerbo
ed in me ravvisate il vostro errore,
ché solo per errar viva mi serbo
e mi raggiro col rotar dell'ore;
né degli applausi miei altro riserbo
che gir cadente mendicando onore.
E nel paterno suolo, ond'ebbi cuna,
provo nemico il cielo, empia Fortuna.

    Vado non ricca d'oro, ma quasi al piano
della cieca,[261] che già m'erse alle stelle,
e invece di vantar pregio sovrano,
i miei sudor mi muovono procelle.
Febo fatto è per me di luce vano.
Dal fonte dell'onor dardi e facelle
m'avventano le Suore d'Elicona
e invan d'allor al crin tesso corona.

---

[260]*Stanno le serpi sotto i fiori ascosi*: variante di c*he 'l serpente tra' fiori e l'erba giace*
(Petrarca XL, 6).
[261]*la cieca*: Fortuna.

Robbed of all good, I, defenseless and nude
of hope, alas, far from my native walls
go wandering, and in season most crude,
I do not fear misfortune's angry squalls.
But, like Angelica upon Ebuda,
I bear the wicked turn of Fortune's wheels.
From children parted, I, to foreign sky,
with parted soul, am willed by destiny.

My foot, but not my heart, departs. I pause,
part without parting. Adieu, Quirinal!
To home in foreign land, I set my pace
to follow Phoebus, lose my native soil.
Tiber, I part. This parting ruinous
my soul deplores. Under destiny cruel,
I'm forced to leave you — I've no more in me
the heart to withstand your severity.

Oh hopes fallacious, oh foolish and mad
bosom that nourishes unstable thought —
thought that would place upon the shrine of pride
a vow to empire vain, regency short.
For Fortune wavers — the strong are destroyed.
She loves her rule with inconstancy fraught;
whence down upon me, from her fickle mane,
she casts her blows and lets the ruins rain.
. . . .

Was it not enough for you, wicked one,
I lived for years far from paternal shore,
that towards me you then, goddess inhumane,
condemned my sacred fronds to Lethe's water?
My hope for any good you rendered vain,
even though I partook of the waves clear
from Parnassus's font while near my Arno;
you took from me the light of god Apollo.

Once more you chase me from maternal sands —
heartless, you're pleased to strike me with affront,
cruel one. And further, upon foreign lands,
you'd have me settle at the sacred font.
In Heaven, with heart just, faithful shrine stands.

Povera d'ogni bene, inerme e nuda
di speme, ahi, lassa, dalle patrie mura
me n' vado errante, ed in stagion più cruda
non pavento del tempo alta sventura.
E, qual la bella all'Isola di Ebuda,[262]
porto l'empio girar di sorte dura.
Vado al cielo straniero e dai miei parti
vuole il destin che l'anima diparti.

      Parte il piè, non il cor, parto e m'arresto.
Parto senza partir, Quirino addio.
In altro suolo ad annidar m'appresto
e perdo in seguir Febo il suol natio.
Tebro, mi parto e nel partir infesto
l'alma si duole, e sotto destin rio
ti lascio a forza, ché non ho più core
che basti a sopportare il tuo rigore.

      O speranze fallaci, o folle ed empio
seno che nutre instabile pensiero,
pensier ch'appende di superbia al tempio
voto per breve regno e vano impero.
Varia è Fortuna e, dei più forti scempio,
gode il suo regno instabile e leggiero,
onde tutte su me, dal mobil crine,
scote l'offese e piove le ruine.

. . . .

      Non ti bastava, iniqua, che lontana
più lustri io vissi dalle patrie sponde
e che, fatta ver me diva inumana,
dannasti a Lete le sacrate fronde?
E resa d'ogni ben mia speme vana,
benché cibata delle limpid' onde
del fonte d'Aganippe[263] all'Arno mio,
negasti l'aura del lucente dio.

      Che pur di novo dal materno lido,
empia, mi scacci e fulminarmi d'onte,
cruda, ti piace, ed in straniero nido
vuoi che m'approdi alla sacrata fonte.
Nel Ciel, ch' ha giusto core, è tempio fido,

---

[262]*la bella all'Isola di Ebuda*: Angelica, in *Orlando Furioso* di Ariosto (Canto VIII, 51–67 e X, 92–115).
[263]*Aganippe*: Parnaso.

With hope, I lift my face gravely intent.
And since my faithfulness you have forgot,
let all my faith in you now be as naught.

· ·

    To brighter sky I go, and if I'm due
to change clime, then to change my luck as well
do the stars promise me, and Fate will show
a rich shore, one from which sands of gold spill.
As much as Phoebus here for me shone low,
there he'll shine clear. Let Cynthia assemble
together for my works, in my last days,
the light of pure faith and of honors' praise.

· ·

    A garden full of flowers of hope, alas
poor me, I tended on paternal soil.
And in me, misery mirrored the goddess
who would within her breast all good conceal.
I begged but for what most had in excess
and was of labored pain living example.
Of great Apollo fruitless follower,
I drew from laurel only what is sour.
    And to the many fertile plants of mine,
I saw the slopes turn sterile on Parnassus —
and on my fecund songs, saw bitter turn
the limpid waters of divine Permessus.
To my words humble, proud turned everyone,
even those most endowed with humbleness.
And every eye envious of my glories
stirred my recall of Fortune's injuries.
    Wherefore I leave you, Rome — the vulgar crowd
I leave to wage its war on other persons.
Far do I go — towards new sky I move forward
to weave from laurel leaves the highest crowns.
So trample on my laurel, Rome so proud!
I part, with mockery my recompense:
the tenor of my Fate would have it so.
Adieu Rome, Phoebus, Quirinal! Adieu!

spero e vèr lui alzo la grave fronte.
E giacché la mia fé per te s'oblia,
rotta ogni fede alla tua fede sia.
. . . .

    Vado al cielo migliore e, se mi è dato
di cangiar clima, di mutar fortuna
mi promettono le stelle e scopre il Fato
ricco lido, che d'or le arene adduna.
Quanto Febo per me qui fu turbato,
ivi per me fia chiaro, e si raguna
da Cinzia alle opre mie, sulle ultime ore,
luce di pura fé, vanto d'onore.
. . . .

    Un giardino di fiori di speranza,
lassa, nutrii sulle paterne arene.
E la miseria in me prese sembianza
della dea che nel sen chiude ogni bene.
Fui mendica di quel che ad altri avanza
e vissi esempio di stentose pene.
E, invan seguace del gran dio di Claro,[264]
trassi dal lauro mio sempre l'amaro.

    Ai fertil parti miei insterilire
vidi le piagge di Parnaso istesso,
ed ai fecondi carmi amari uscire
i liquidi cristalli di Permesso,
agli umili miei detti insuperbire
ogni spirto più umile e dimesso.
Ed ogni invido ciglio alle mie glorie
alzò di ria Fortuna empie memorie.

    Onde, Roma, ti lascio, e il volgo rio
lascio ch'ad altri muova aspra tenzone.
Lunge me n' vado e a nuovo cielo m'invio
ad intrecciare d'alloro alte corone.
Calpesta pur, superba, il lauro mio,
ch'io parto e porto scherno in guiderdone:
così vuol il tenor del mio destino.
Addio Roma, addio Febo, addio Quirino.

---

[264]*dio di Claro*: Apollo.

FROM: *THE TRUMPET OF PARNASSUS* (1647)

To the Queen of France

Muse, you who till now from the lap of shade
beheld my poems, henceforth lift up my gaze
to Heaven's light serene, without a cloud;
lustrous let shine my song, my mournful eyes.
Pour joyous notes through pleasing sky and laud
that which immortalizes you — the lilies —
to manifest the deeds of the great Anne.
Render tranquil the air, sweet the paean.
. . . .
The lily is, of all peace, symbol clear.
The lily feeds the air's serenity.
The lily holds, for all lives, essence dear.
The lily's stars emanate every mercy.
The lily crowns the god Apollo fair.
The lily is font of fecundity.
The lily is the frond of light supernal.
The lily is the flower of God eternal.

To Cardinal Mazzarino for Having Her Works Published

Though Daphne once — with fair brow, golden hair
plucked up — fired at a god an arrow shot,
she would have been oblivion's prey, forgot,
if not protected by the wingèd Archer.
Palms won't produce their fruit, they will not bear
when once deprived of soil from native plot.
Therefore, if I have help, I've yet the thought
to bear palm and to claim my laurels' share.

DA: *LA TROMBA DI PARNASO* (1647)

Alla regina di Francia[265]

Musa, tu, che i miei carmi all'ombra in seno
fin qui mirasti, alza i miei lumi omai
di sovrumana luce a bel sereno,
e illustra[266] in un col canto i mesti rai.[267]
Versa note di gioia al cielo ameno
e loda i gigli[268] onde immortal te n' vai
della grand'Anna[269] palesando i vanti.
Rendi placide l'aure e dolci i canti.
. . . .
Il giglio è segno d'ogni pace chiaro.
Il giglio in sé nutrisce aure serene.
Il giglio ha spirto all'altrui vita caro.
Il giglio ha stelle onde ogni grazia viene.
Il giglio è serto al biondo re di Claro.[270]
Il giglio ha fonte di fecondo bene.
Il giglio è fronda del superno lume.
Il giglio è fiore dell'eterno nume.[271]

Al cardinale Mazzarino nel farle stampare le sue opere

Benché Dafne il bel ciglio e il bel crin d'oro
vibrasse un tempo e saettasse un dio,
preda era alfin di smemorato oblio,
se non la proteggea l'arcier canoro.[272]
Non producon le palme i frutti loro,
se prive son d'alto favor natio,
quindi, se aita avrò, spero ancor io
di fruttar palma e d'eternarmi alloro.

---

[265]For comment, see Introduction, p. 37.
[266]*illustra*: rendi chiaro.
[267]*rai*: raggi/ occhi.
[268]*i gigli*: dello stemma reale francese.
[269]*Anna*: regina di Francia.
[270]*re di Claro*: Apollo.
[271]A Baroque glorification of the French heraldic fleur-de-lis.
[272]*canoro*: dolce; *arcier canoro*: Cupido.

For who can say where Helen's to be found?
Dust she's become, dispersed upon the wind
her every prize, or else barely recalled.

    Follow, great Giulio, what you intend —
say that I, Costa, on Aonian sand,
trade transient silver for eternal gold.

To Cardinal Francesco Barberini

. . . .

    A woman of my clan, in chaste enclosure
you kept safe, rescued from the world's blind snares.
You had her spread her wings with desires pure
to turn her mind aloft unto the stars.
While other girls — in whose youthful desire
we see hopes common to their tender years —
with all-competent hand you likewise steer
to save them from the plunder of Amour.

    And I, who far from my paternal nest
nourished imprudently my wayward thought,
ever did bear, buried deep in my breast,
dolor and care as my tormented lot.
Now through your grace, my delight's manifest,
lighter than lightest zephyr in its weight.
And I am glad it's granted me to see
my native land, wrought by your clemency.

    The stately Quirinal I view again,
with majesty extending its great girth;
there, in festivity, the Vatican
so like the sun sparkling above the earth;
the skyline, gravid with its population
of sacred sites; Tarpeo that gives forth
to immortality trophies of martyrs,
where pagan gods and Caesars take no prize.

    I see and kneel at Her Esquiline temple.
She was Christ's temple — this now bears Her name;
She of sublime modesty sole example,

Deh, chi sa dirmi ov'or si miri Elena?
Ah, ch'ella è polve ed è disperso al vento
ogni suo pregio o si ricorda appena.[273]
    Segui dunque, o gran Giulio, il bell'intento,
e dì, s'io, Costa,[274] in quest'aonia[275] arena
compro oro eterno e do caduco argento.

Al cardinale Francesco Barberini[276]

. . . .

Altra del germe mio tra caste celle
hai ritolta del mondo ai ciechi inganni,
e fai che con la mente, in vèr le stelle,
spieghi dei puri desideri i vanni.
Ad altre, in cui l'età mostrar novelle
le speranze vegghiam dei teneri anni,
per torle dell'Amore alla rapina
la man che tutto può, tutto destina.
    Ed io, che lunge dal paterno tetto
nutrìa, mal cauta, altrove i miei pensieri,
e m'eran sempre, nell'interno petto,
le cure ed i dolor tormenti fieri.
Ora per tua mercede il mio diletto
e più lieve de' zefiri leggieri.
E godo che conoscer mi si dia,
nella clemenza tua, la patria mia.
    Per te riveggio il Quirinal pomposo,
ch'auguste moli a meraviglia stende,
e 'l Vaticano, che di sé fastoso
sovra la terra a par del sol risplende,
il cielo, che 'l suo tergo erge gravoso
di sacri tempii, e 'l gran Tarpeo, che rende
più dell'onor dei cesari e de' dei,
immortali dei martiri i trofei.
    Veggio ed inchino sulle Esquilie il tempio[277]
di Lei che tempio fu del sommo nume
e d'eccelsa modestia unico esempio

---

[273]Only events recorded by writers survive.
[274]Note the insertion of the poet's last name.
[275]*aonia*: delle Muse.
[276]For comment, see Introduction, p. 38.
[277]*sulle Esquilie il tempio*: la chiesa di Santa Maria Maggiore.

and of virginity celestial flame.
To cancel each of my sins harsh and fell,
I lift my soul that, upon agile plume,
becomes all zeal, all faith and all desire
to reach, rest in God's grace and therein shelter.

    Although it's true I've not shorn to the root
my hair unruly in luxuriance,
and above my sad face may seem to flirt,
in roaming gold, my mane in its abundance —
yet severed not from Heaven is my heart,
and not adverse to God do I advance:
in motion innocent, the Heavens, too,
have gold and rubies scattered through their blue.

    These shall not be evidence of my errors —
they are reminders rather that years fly,
and Time himself, towards our declining honors,
rages and roars, victorious enemy.
In useless gold languish all of our splendors;
sooner than hair does beauty fall away:
what gifted beauty's possibilities,
Age will oppress and swift Time will erase.

. . . .

    My brother's idle ways alone could make
my circumstances and my days less glad,
but you, on battlefield against bad luck,
a proud leader of armies, are my aid;
and hope that had, alas, in me gone slack,
you'd steel against the arrows' fusillade
from Fortune cruel, who in both war and peace,
attacks the good, lays low her enemies.

    Our sole male offspring, the sole hope of ours,
has sworn his faith to you — my only brother.
My heart no longer fears sinister blows,
but finds stability through answered prayer.
Of our best hopes, the single flower he was,

fu di virginità superno[278] lume.
E a cancellar ogni aspro fallo ed empio,
l'alma rivolgo che, sovr'agil piume
sol per poggiare delle grazie al Dio,
tutta è zel, tutta è fé, tutta è desio.
    Bene è ver che non anco ai piè reciso
dispergo il fasto del mio crine errante,
e scherza ancora sovra 'l mesto viso
il vano della chioma,[279] oro vagante.
Pure il mio cor non è dal ciel diviso,
né avverse al sommo ben volgo le piante,
ch'anco il ciel puro, ch'innocente ha i giri,
ha d'oro e di rubin sparsi i zaffiri.[280]
    Queste non fian a me pompe d'errori,
ma ben memorie che l'età sen fugge,
e 'l Tempo contro li cadenti onori
nemico freme e vincitore rugge.
Languisce il fasto negl'inutil ori
e più lieve del crine il bel si strugge,
e ciò ch'aperse a vil beltà la via,
l'età opprime e il ratto Veglio oblia.

. . . .

    Sol del germano[281] mio l'ozio potea
render men fortunati i giorni miei,
ma tu,[282] ch'in campo contro sorte rea
sei d'armi altero duce, aita sei,
e la speme che, lassa, in me giacea,
rinforzar puoi contro gli strali rei
della crudel,[283] che sempre, in pace o in guerra,
i cari offende ed i nemici atterra.
    Di rampollo virile unica speme,
il mio fratello a te la fede ha dato.
Non più colpi sinistri il mio cor teme,
ma stabile ai suoi voti ottiene il fato.
Ei n'era il fior delle speranze estreme,

---

[278]*superno*: celeste.

[279]*il vano della chioma*: il volume dei capelli.

[280]In answer to those who doubted her repentance, the poet states that she is a penitent even if she has not cut off her hair.

[281]*germano*: fratello.

[282]*tu*: il cardinale.

[283]*crudel*: Fortuna.

but to your arms we'll offer him with pleasure:
for only on the wings of your Bees' stem
can victory to the world's summit climb.
    "Go then, oh brother — enjoy honors granted
from a hand with honors so prodigal.
Deem it as praise to follow his command,
for with firm bit does he vast arms control.
Why do you linger? Don't you hear the sound
that Mars shakes up, the clash throughout the vale?
Ah, what? I remain here and you go hence;
you, robbed of peace — I, placed again in plaints.
    "It's so — your glory gives my only torment;
your battles represent but war to me.
If you should meet your end as a combatant,
all of my good with you in death will lie.
What is it I have said, ah, so imprudent?
My words dispersed be to the winds — away!
Where wings of Barberini Bees take flight,
future felicity is requisite.
    "Yes, yes, fight happily and seize the merit
worthy of you and that great prince in war.
For you, Paolo, for me, unlock both spirit
at once with valor, in heroic air.
May my preoccupations and their weight
be routed from my heart so locked in winter.
Castor and Pollux then, and nothing less
can light from Barberini be to us."
. . . .

FROM: **ARROWS AGAINST THE VOLUBILITY OF THE VULGAR
       CROWD ON THE DEATH OF URBAN VIII**

Second Arrow
    Oh infinite distress, as one can see
instantly vanish, from each breast humane,
affection falsified, sentiments vain;
changed is desire, shifted fidelity!

ma d'offrirlo a vostr'armi a noi fia grato,
ché solo può delle Api[284] tue sul volo
la vittoria del mondo ergersi al polo.

    "Vanne, o germano, e chiari onori godi
da chi d'onori ha prodiga la mano.
A quei cenni ubbidir, stima tue lodi,
che reggono delle armi il fren sovrano.
Su, che pensi? Che fai? Forse non odi
scosso da Marte risonar il piano?
Ah, che dico? Tu parti e io resto intanto,
tu ritolto alla pace, io posta in pianto.

    Deh, che la gloria tua mi dà tormento
e le battaglie tue son guerra mia.
S'avverrà che tu resti in pugna spento,
ogni mio ben con te morto fia.
Ah mal cauta, che dissi? Il suono al vento
disperso vada sull'aerea via,
ch'ove Api Barberine han volto l'ale,
dee la felicitade esser fatale.

    Sì, sì, lieto combatti e acquista palma[285]
di sì gran prence e di te degna in guerra,
a te, Paolo, ed a me, valore ed alma,
l'aura d'eroe sì grande in un disserra.
Sia delle cure mie la grave salma
lunge dal cor che 'l verno in sé riserra.
Non puote se non Castore e Polluce
esser a noi la barberina luce."

. . . .

DALLE: **Saette contro la volubilità del basso volgo
nella morte di Urbano VIII**[286]

Saetta seconda
    O miseria infinita, e pur si vede
in un punto mancar nei petti umani
l'affetto menzoniero, i sensi vani
cangiar le brame e tramutar la fede!

---

[284]*Api*: api dello stemma dei Barberini.
[285]*palma*: vittoria.
[286]For comment, see Introduction, p. 38.

While Fortune smiles, seated is there on high
a soul so great, and with applause insane,
homage is paid him by the crowd mundane;
yet reverence unto destiny gives way.

His kingdom lost, he is therefore become
cruel Fortune's mark. Everyone changes tune —
faithless, exchanges faith for lunacy.

While Urban ruled, to be subject to him
vowed every heart — yet now, through mortal folly,
faith is but blind, love does but traitor turn.

Third Arrow

Oh traitors, how can you expect great mercy
if, in mercy to others, you so fail?
I'll never be like you! As ever faithful
was I, vendetta towards you I now pray.

To put faith into speculative play —
today this, next day that one to cajole;
to change allegiance, know not who has rule —
calls down an arrow shot from hand on high.

Shocked Heaven, oh, what can you have in mind?
Why hold back your cruel turns against all those
who turn on their allegiance glancingly?

It's gold that makes our mortal sight go blind.
The eye will hold the just within its gaze
if God is its sole, lasting solvency.

Fifth Arrow

Rome, Rome, what are you doing? So abjured
the Holy Shepherd is — this you accept,
evil one, and you let his sacred step
be trampled underfoot by your false crowd?

Shepherd so just, the one who was your guide,
who led with pious hand your wayward sheep,
and to high faith away from sin would keep
assembled, your nearly lost multitude.

Ah, let at least upon the unworthy horde,
from strong and righteous arm, a just wrath fall;
Heaven disdains offense to pious soul.

Mentre Fortuna arride e in alta sede
poggia grand'alma, con applausi insani
mostran ossegui a lei gli atti mondani,
ma con la sorte riverenza cede.

Caduto il regno, è di Fortuna ria
fatto bersaglio: ognun cangia tenore
e, infido, la sua fé volge in follia.

Mentr' Urbano regnò, servo ogni core
a lui mostrossi: or per mortal pazzia
cieca è la fede e traditor l'amore.

Saetta terza

O traditori, qual a voi s'aspetta
alta mercede nel mancar altrui?
Io, qual voi, non fia mai: qual sempre fui,
fida, contro di voi prego vendetta.

Far della fede sua pubblica incetta,[287]
oggi questo sedur, domani colui,
cangiar gli affetti e non saper per cui
chiaman, da man divina, alta saetta.

Stupido,[288] o Ciel, che fai? A che più tardi
gl'infesti giri tuoi contro costoro,
che girano gli affetti a par dei guardi?

Le viste dei mortali accieca l'oro
e sol fia che l'occhio il giusto guardi,
se Dio gli è sole d'immortal tesoro.

Saetta quinta

Roma, Roma, che fai? Così schernito
il Pastor sacrosanto a te davante
comporti, iniqua, e le sacrate piante
calpestar fai dal popol tuo mentito?

Così giusto Pastor che custodito
ha con man di pietà le greggi errante,
e dai lor falli all'alta fé costante
raccolto ha 'l popol tuo quasi smarrito.

Ah, lascia omai sovra la plebe indegna
giusta l'ira cader del braccio forte,
il Ciel contr'alma pia l'offese sdegna.

---

[287]*incetta*: raccolta speculativa.
[288]*stupido* : stupito, attonito.

Let Destiny by such daring be conquered.
The wicked well deserve Astrea's trial;
she metes out death with her uplifted sword.

Sixth Arrow

You'd do far better if, oh idle ones,
aside from sonnets or lampoons, instead
you pray God that He, from the stars overhead,
send forceful Shepherd against Fate's cruel turns.

And as for votives, you who've lost your minds,
does chasing wealth and taxes do you good?
Oh, let Heaven decree that greater flood
this sea not suffer from Eurus's winds.

How did he wrong you, Shepherd Barberini,
that you protest so much, exclaim and dis?
Too much good, too much faith and too much honor.

As you are false, pray unto Heaven rather,
that is so just, you're not damned for your sin —
your slander not impugned by wrath of Dis.

To Luigi Rossi for His Orfeo

Fecund embraces of Eurydice
in melic chords does new Euterpe intone,
impressing dulcet song upon the Seine
to soar to Heaven with glory ablaze.

With notes he fashions pleasing harmonies
that, so sublime, drive others' worth to ruin;
wherefore above, in realms Pierian,
his sun will have eclipsed all others' rays.

Look at Luigi, now in Helicon —
among Aonian choir, look, he is called!
Apollo fits him with aureate crown.

Perda a cotanto ardir vinta la Sorte:
contro gli empi è d'Astrea[289] prova ben degna,
vibrar il ferro e fulminar la morte.

Saetta sesta
Quanto fareste meglio, o scioperati,
invece di sonetti e di novelle,[290]
Iddio pregar che, dalle eccelse stelle,
ne dia forte Pastor contr' empi fati.

Invece di scior voti, o forsennati,
ché gite a ricercar monti e gabelle?[291]
Oh, piaccia al Cielo che maggior procelle
non provi questo mar sott' Euri[292] irati.

E che vi fece il barberin Pastore
che cotanto esclamate e tanto dite?
Troppo ben, troppa fede e troppo onore.

Pregate il Ciel, che, come voi mentite,
così giusto ei, non danni il vostro errore,
e sia pena al mal dire ira di Dite.

A Luigi Rossi per il suo Orfeo[293]
Fecondi amplessi entro canori accenti
dell' Euridice un'Euterpe[294] esprime,
e sulla Senna i dolci canti imprime,
che della gloria al ciel se n' vanno ardenti.

Forma di note armonici concenti,
sublimi sì ch'ogni valore opprime,
ond'è che sovra alle pierie cime[295]
sien dal suo sole i raggi altrui già spenti.

Mira Luigi sceso in Elicona
e fra l'aonio coro, ecco, lo chiama
Liceo,[296] ch'omai gli appresta aurea corona.

---

[289]*Astrea*: dea della giustizia.
[290]*sonetti e novelle*: pasquinate in versi e in prosa.
[291]*monti e gabelle*: monti di pietà e uffici di dazi.
[292]*Euri*: venti del sud (scirocco).
[293]For comment, see Introduction, p. 37.
[294]*Euterpe*: Musa della lirica corale.
[295]*pierie cime*: cime di Pieria, sede delle Muse.
[296]*Liceo*: Apollo Liceo (dal tempio che aveva in Liceo).

To render up his virtue does Earth yearn,
because Eternity must surely herald
his lofty name. Fame trumpets his renown.

To Marcantonio Pasqualini

Antonio, I'd venture
to say you are, for us,
an angel in our choir.
In conquering hearts, so far as
your merits to appraise —
not to angels or honors
are you second in worth:
while they may move the sky, you move the earth.

To Buti for His Orfeo

Buti, I, too, for laurel run the course;
at times, the wingèd steed do I spur on.
But scant to me did he his graces don —
Apollo, learnèd king of brilliant splendors.

You give such spirit to melodious zephyrs
with lovely harmony in dulcet tone,
and she applauds you from her starry throne —
the wise Athena of Palladian honors.

Where Muses nest above us, there in Pindus,
you, blessèd swan, breathe airs felicitous,
aside the shore murmuring of your glory.

Climbs such as these, only new Orpheus
could ever have resound with noble cry
of true and miserable Eurydice.

Di sua virtude impoverire, ah, brama
la terra, ch'al suo nome eccelso dona
suono l'Eternità, tromba la Fama.

A Marcantonio Pasqualini[297]

Antonio, io ti direi
ch'al canto qui tra noi,
un angelo tu sei;
ma nel rapire i cori,
ai vari pregi tuoi,
né a loro, né agli onori,
tu ti mostri secondo,
ch'essi movono il ciel, tu giri il mondo.

Al Buti per il suo Orfeo[298]

Buti, anch'io cerco i riveriti allori
e 'l volante destier[299] talora sprono,
ma scarso a me delle sue grazie il dono
fe' il dotto re dei lucidi splendori.

Tu ben dài spirto a zefiri canori
con la vaga armonia del dolce suono,
e applaude a te, dallo stellante trono,
la saggia diva dei palladii onori.[300]

E ben in Pindo, ove han le Muse il nido,
godi, cigno beato, aura felice,
pioché le glorie tue mormora il lido.

Nemmen che un novo Orfeo questa pendice
potea far risonar con nobil grido
della fedele e misera Euridice.

---

[297]For comment, see Introduction, p. 37.
[298]For comment, see Introduction, p. 37.
[299]*volante destier*: Pegaso, simbolo dell'ispirazione poetica.
[300]*diva dei palladii onori*: Pallade Atena.

ABOUT THE EDITOR

Natalia Costa-Zalessow holds a PhD in Romance Languages and Literatures, with emphasis in Italian, from the University of California at Berkeley. She taught Italian for thirty years in the Department of Foreign Languages and Literatures at San Francisco State University until her retirement in 1998, and also offered a special annual course, *Rome: Biography of a City*, for the Department of Humanities. She has published numerous articles in literary journals (*Italica, Forum Italicum, Ausonia, Italian Quarterly, Italiana, Rivista di Studi Italiani, Esperienze Letterarie*, and *Australian Slavonic and East European Studies*) as well as entry essays for the literary dictionaries *Critical Survey of Long Fiction, Critical Survey of Short Fiction, Critical Survey of Drama*, and *Dictionary of Literary Biography* (Vols. 114, 128, 177, and 339). Her groundbreaking anthology, *Scrittrici italiane dal XIII al XX Secolo: Testi e critica*, published in 1982, called attention to Italian women authors — both poets and prose writers — and served as a source for many subsequent researchers. She was responsible for the thirteen Italian women writers included in *Longman Anthology of World Literature by Women* (1875–1975), published in 1989. She is translator of Amelia Pincherle Rosselli's drama, *L'anima — Her Soul*, for *Modern Drama by Women 1880s–1930s: An International Anthology* (1996), and editor of the play's Italian edition for Salerno in 1997. In 2009, Bordighera Press published her monograph on Francesca Turini Bufalini, *Autobiographical Poems*, a bilingual edition translated by Joan E. Borrelli, which focuses attention on this neglected but very original female poet of the early seventeenth century.

ABOUT THE TRANSLATOR

Joan E. Borrelli, a member of the American Literary Translators Association, holds an MA in English Literature/Creative Writing and a second MA in Italian Language and Literature, both from San Francisco State University. She is translator of *Autobiographical Poems* by Francesca Turini Bufalini (Bordighera Press, 2009). Her subsequent translations from Turini Bufalini's works include sonnet and madrigal selections and an excerpt from the narrative poem, *Il Florio*, for *Journal of Italian Translation*. Her translations of the poetry and prose of other Italian authors — Vittoria Colonna, Ciro di Pers, Virginia Bazzani Cavazzoni, Vittoria Aganoor Pompilj, Luisa Giaconi, Matilde Serao, and Anna Banti — appear in a number of scholarly journals and in anthologies by Longman and Routledge. She has published essays of literary criticism in *Critical Companion to J. D. Salinger* (Facts On File, 2011) as well as short fiction in *VIA: Voices in Italian Americana*.

VIA Folios

A refereed book series dedicated to the culture of Italians and Italian Americans.

MARIO MIGNONE, *The Story of My People: From Rural Southern Italy to Mainstream America,* Vol. 111, Italian American Memoir, $17

Vol. 110, in production

JOEY NICOLETTI, *Reverse Graffiti,* Vol. 109, Poetry, $12

Vol. 108, in production

LEWIS TURCO, *The Hero Enkidu,* Vol. 107, Poetry, $14

ALBERT TACCONELLI, *Perhaps Fly,* Vol. 106, Poetry, $14

RACHEL GUIDO DEVRIES, *A Woman Unknown in Her Bones,* Vol. 105, Poetry, $11

BERNARD J. BRUNO, *A Tear and a Tear in My Heart,* Vol. 104, Non-Fiction/Memoir, $20

FELIX STEFANILE, *Songs of the Sparrow,* Vol. 103, Poetry, $30

FRANK POLIZZI, *A New Life with Bianca,* Vol. 102, Poetry, $10

GIL FAGIANI, *Stone Walls,* Vol. 101, Poetry, $14

LOUISE DESALVO, *Casting Off,* Vol. 100, Fiction, $22

MARY JO BONA, *I Stop Waiting for You,* Vol. 99, Italian/American Poetry, $12

RACHEL GUIDO DEVRIES, *Stati Zitta, Josie,* Vol. 98, Children's Literature, $8

GRACE CAVALIERI, *The Mandate of Heaven,* Vol. 97, Italian American Poetry, $11

MARISA FRASCA, *Via Incanto: Poems from the Darkroom,* Vol. 96, Italian American Poetry, $12

DOUGLAS GLADSTONE, *Carving a Niche for Himself: The Untold Story of Luigi Del Bianco and Mount Rushmore,* Vol. 95, Italian American History, $12

MARIA TERRONE, *Eye to Eye,* Vol. 94, Poetry, $15

CONSTANCE SANCETTA, *Here in Cerchio: Letters to an Italian Immigrant,* Vol. 93, Italian/American Studies, $15

MARIA MAZZIOTTI GILLAN, *Ancestors' Song,* Vol. 92, Poetry, $14

MICHAEL PARENTI, *Waiting for Yesterday: Pages from a Street Kid's Life,* Vol. 90, Memoir, $15

ANNIE RACHELE LANZILLOTTO, *Schistsong,* Vol. 89, Poetry/Gay Studies/Women Authors, $15

EMANUEL DI PASQUALE, *Love Lines,* Vol. 88, Poetry and Italian American Studies, $10

JOSEPH ANTHONY LOGIUDICE AND MICHAEL CAROSONE, *Our Naked Lives: Essays from Gay Italian American Men,* Vol. 87, Gay Studies and Italian American Studies, $15

JAMES J. PERICONI, *Strangers in a Strange Land: A Survey of Italian-language American Books (1830–1945),* Vol. 86, Italian American Studies, $24

DANIELA GIOSEFFI, *Pioneering Italian American Culture: Escaping La Vita Cucina,* Vol. 85, Cultural Studies/ Women's Studies/Literary Arts, $22

MARIA FAMÀ, *Mystics in the Family,* Vol. 84, Poetry, $10

ROSSANA DEL ZIO, *From Bread and Tomatoes to Zuppa di Pesce "Ciambotto,"* Vol. 83, Italian American Studies, $15

LORENZO DELBOCA, *Polentoni,* Vol. 82, Italian Studies, $20

SAMUEL GHELLI, *A Reference Grammar,* Vol. 81, Italian American Studies, $20

ROSS TALARICO, *Sled Run,* Vol. 80, Fiction, $15

FRED MISURELLA, *Only Sons,* Vol. 79, Fiction, $17

FRANK LENTRICCHIA, *The Portable Lentricchia,* Vol. 78, Fiction, $17

RICHARD VETERE, *The Other Colors in a Snow Storm,* Vol. 77, Poetry, $10

GARIBALDI LAPOLLA, *Fire in the Flesh,* Vol. 76, Fiction, $25

GEORGE GUIDA, *The Pope Stories,* Vol. 75, Fiction, $15

ROBERT VISCUSI, *Ellis Island,* Vol. 74, Poetry, $28

ELENA GIANINI BELOTI, *The Bitter Taste of Strangers Bread,* Vol. 73, Fiction, $24

PINO APRILE, *Terroni,* Vol. 72, Italian American Studies, $20

EMANUEL DI PASQUALE, *Harvest,* Vol. 71, Poetry, $10
ROBERT ZWEIG, *Return to Naples,* Vol. 70, Memoir, $16
AIROS & CAPPELLI, *Guido,* Vol. 69, Italian American Studies, $12
FRED GARDAPHÉ, *Moustache Pete is Dead! Long Live Moustache Pete!,* Vol. 67, Literature/Oral History, $12
PAOLO RUFFILLI, *Dark Room/Camera oscura,* Vol. 66, Poetry, $11
HELEN BAROLINI, *Crossing the Alps,* Vol. 65, Fiction, $14
COSMO FERRARA, *Profiles of Italian Americans,* Vol. 64, Italian American, $16
GIL FAGIANI, *Chianti in Connecticut,* Vol. 63, Poetry, $10
BASSETTI & D'ACQUINO, *Italic Lessons,* Vol. 62, Italian American Studies, $10
CAVALIERI & PASCARELLI, eds., *The Poet's Cookbook,* Vol. 61, Poetry/Recipes, $12
EMANUEL DI PASQUALE, *Siciliana,* Vol. 60, Poetry, $8
NATALIA COSTA-ZALESSOW, ed., JOAN E. BORRELLI, translator., *Autobiographical Poems of Francesca Turini Bufalini,* Vol. 59, Poetry, $18
RICHARD VETERE, *Baroque,* Vol. 58, Fiction
LEWIS TURCO, *La Famiglia/The Family,* Vol. 57, Memoir, $15
NICK JAMES MILETI, *The Unscrupulous,* Vol. 56, Humanities, $20
BASSETTI, ACCOLLA, D'AQUINO, *Italici: An Encounter with Piero Bassetti,* Vol. 55, Italian Studies, $8
GIOSE RIMANELLI, *The Three-legged One,* Vol. 54, Fiction, $15
CHARLES KLOPP, *Bele Antiche Stòrie,* Vol. 53, Criticism, $25
JOSEPH RICAPITO, *Second Wave,* Vol. 52, Poetry, $12
GARY MORMINO, *Italians in Florida,* Vol. 51, History, $15
GIANFRANCO ANGELUCCI, *Federico F.,* Vol. 50, Fiction, $15
ANTHONY VALERIO, *The Little Sailor,* Vol. 49, Memoir, $9
ROSS TALARICO, *The Reptilian Interludes,* Vol. 48, Poetry, $15
RACHEL GUIDO DE VRIES, *Teeny Tiny Tino's Fishing Story,* Vol. 47, Children's Lit, $6
EMANUEL DI PASQUALE, *Writing Anew,* Vol. 46, Poetry, $15
MARIA FAMÀ, *Looking For Cover,* Vol. 45, Poetry, $12
ANTHONY VALERIO, *Toni Cade Bambara's One Sicilian Night,* Vol. 44, Poetry, $10
EMANUEL CARNEVALI, Dennis Barone, ed., *Furnished Rooms,* Vol. 43, Poetry, $14
BRENT ADKINS, et al., ed., *Shifting Borders, Negotiating Places,* Vol. 42, Proceedings, $18
GEORGE GUIDA, *Low Italian,* Vol. 41, Poetry, $11
GARDAPHÈ, GIORDANO, TAMBURRI, *Introducing Italian Americana,* Vol. 40, Italian American Studies, $10
DANIELA GIOSEFFI, *Blood Autumn/Autunno di sangue,* Vol. 39, Poetry, $15/$25
FRED MISURELLA, *Lies to Live by,* Vol. 38, Stories, $15
STEVEN BELLUSCIO, *Constructing a Bibliography,* Vol. 37, Italian Americana, $15
ANTHONY J. TAMBURRI, ed., *Italian Cultural Studies 2002,* Vol. 36, Essays, $18
BEA TUSIANI, *con amore,* Vol. 35, Memoir, $19
FLAVIA BRIZIO-SKOV, ed., *Reconstructing Societies in the Aftermath of War,* Vol. 34, History, $30
TAMBURRI, et al., eds., *Italian Cultural Studies 2001,* Vol. 33, Essays, $18
ELIZABETH G. MESSINA, ed., *In Our Own Voices,* Vol. 32, Italian American Studies, $25
STANISLAO G. PUGLIESE, *Desperate Inscriptions,* Vol. 31, History, $12
HOSTERT & TAMBURRI, eds., *Screening Ethnicity,* Vol. 30, Italian American Culture, $25
G. PARATI & B. LAWTON, eds., *Italian Cultural Studies,* Vol. 29, Essays, $18
HELEN BAROLINI, *More Italian Hours,* Vol. 28, Fiction, $16
FRANCO NASI, ed., *Intorno alla Via Emilia,* Vol. 27, Culture, $16
ARTHUR L. CLEMENTS, *The Book of Madness & Love,* Vol. 26, Poetry, $10

VIA Folios

A refereed book series dedicated to the culture of Italians and Italian Americans.

JOHN CASEY, et al., *Imagining Humanity,* Vol. 25, Interdisciplinary Studies, $18
ROBERT LIMA, *Sardinia/Sardegna,* Vol. 24, Poetry, $10
DANIELA GIOSEFFI, *Going On,* Vol. 23, Poetry, $10
ROSS TALARICO, *The Journey Home,* Vol. 22, Poetry, $12
EMANUEL DI PASQUALE, *The Silver Lake Love Poems,* Vol. 21, Poetry, $7
JOSEPH TUSIANI, *Ethnicity,* Vol. 20, Poetry, $12
JENNIFER LAGIER, *Second Class Citizen,* Vol. 19, Poetry, $8
FELIX STEFANILE, *The Country of Absence,* Vol. 18, Poetry, $9
PHILIP CANNISTRARO, *Blackshirts,* Vol. 17, History, $12
LUIGI RUSTICHELLI, ed., *Seminario sul racconto,* Vol. 16, Narrative, $10
LEWIS TURCO, *Shaking the Family Tree,* Vol. 15, Memoirs, $9
LUIGI RUSTICHELLI, ed., *Seminario sulla drammaturgia,* Vol. 14, Theater/Essays, $10
FRED GARDAPHÈ, *Moustache Pete is Dead! Long Live Moustache Pete!,* Vol. 13, Oral Literature, $10
JONE GAILLARD CORSI, *Il libretto d'autore, 1860–1930,* Vol. 12, Criticism, $17
HELEN BAROLINI, *Chiaroscuro: Essays of Identity,* Vol. 11, Essays, $15
PICARAZZI & FEINSTEIN, eds., *An African Harlequin in Milan,* Vol. 10, Theater/Essays, $15
JOSEPH RICAPITO, *Florentine Streets & Other Poems,* Vol. 9, Poetry, $9
FRED MISURELLA, *Short Time,* Vol. 8, Novella, $7
NED CONDINI, *Quartettsatz,* Vol. 7, Poetry, $7
ANTHONY TAMBURRI, ed., *Fuori: Essays by Italian/American Lesbians and Gays,* Vol. 6, Essays, $10
ANTONIO GRAMSCI, P. Verdicchio, Trans. & Intro., *The Southern Question,* Vol. 5, Social Criticism, $5
DANIELA GIOSEFFI, *Word Wounds & Water Flowers,* Vol. 4, Poetry, $8
WILEY FEINSTEIN, *Humility's Deceit: Calvino Reading Ariosto Reading Calvino,* Vol. 3, Criticism, $10
PAOLO GIORDANO, ed., *Joseph Tusiani: Poet, Translator, Humanist,* Vol. 2, Criticism, $25
ROBERT VISCUSI, *Oration Upon the Most Recent Death of Christopher Columbus,* Vol. 1, Poetry, $3

Published by Bordighera, Inc., an independently owned, not-for-profit, scholarly organization that has no legal affiliation with the University of Central Florida and the John D. Calandra Italian American Institute, Queens College/CUNY.